Stephen Cartmell is a former university lecturer, travel writer, racing enthusiast and dedicated golfer. He is the author of the highly entertaining *From Aintree to York: Racing Around Britain*, which was published by Bantam in 2006. A Lancastrian by birth, Stephen is now 'exiled' in Hertfordshire.

D1342437

Also by Stephen Cartmell

FROM AINTREE TO YORK

and published by Bantam Books

GOLF ON THE EDGE

Stephen Cartmell

BANTAM BOOKS

LONDON · TORONTO · SYDNEY · AUCKLAND · JOHANNESBURG

TRANSWORLD PUBLISHERS
61–63 Uxbridge Road, London W5 5SA
A Random House Group Company
www.rbooks.co.uk

GOLF ON THE EDGE
A BANTAM BOOK: 9780553818086

First publication in Great Britain
Bantam edition published 2008

Addresses for Random House Group Ltd companies outside the UK
can be found at: www.randomhouse.co.uk
The Random House Group Ltd Reg. No. 954009

The Random House Group Limited supports The Forest Stewardship Council (FSC),
the leading international forest certification organization. All our titles that are
printed on Greenpeace approved FSC certified paper carry the FSC logo.
Our paper procurement policy can be found at
www.rbooks.co.uk/environment

Typeset in 12/13½pt Granjon by
Kestrel Data, Exeter, Devon.
Printed in the UK by
CPI Cox & Wyman, Reading, RG1 8EX.

2 4 6 8 10 9 7 5 3 1

To all golfing masochists who share
my love of traditional seaside links

ACKNOWLEDGEMENTS

There have been times during my journey around the coast of Britain, when I have stood on the 1st tee of these magnificent links golf courses and quivered with a strange emotional recipe of joyous anticipation and trembling fear. I would like to thank all those members, PGA professionals, club secretaries, presidents, captains, greenkeepers and general golfing hoi polloi who joined me in a round of golf and didn't even raise an eyebrow when I played like a dog. Fortunately, this wasn't a frequent occurrence, and I therefore also owe a debt to those volunteer members who made little protest when this self-confessed 'hacker' managed to play to single figures. What all these people shared was a universal courtesy and a generous sense of humour. Without their good company, their myriad tales and their obvious love of links golf on the watery edge of Britain, this book could not have been written.

CONTENTS

Selected courses are listed in order of the author's itinerary and do not reflect any element of preference.

Brora
Royal Dornoch
Nairn
Cruden Bay

Kingsbarns
North Berwick
Dunbar
Western Gailes
Seahouses
Shiskine
Turnberry
Southerness
Ardglass
Castletown
Brancaster
Nefyn
Pennard
St Enodoc
Trevose

INTRODUCTION

For those who know me, any claim I might make to having lived 'life on the edge' would be met with contemptuous laughter. I am proud, however, of once having eaten four cream crackers without drinking a glass of water and, on another occasion (with disastrous results), having volunteered to play the role of a somnolent sheep in a school nativity play. But these two examples constitute the sum total of my contribution to heroic living. What cannot be denied, however, is my claim to having been born on the coastal edge of Britain: I spent my formative years on the brink of the western seaboard and began my far from illustrious golfing career on the shoreline of the Irish Sea.

Ever since a particularly unfortunate experience, I have resisted the temptation to divulge that I was 'raised' on a links course. Some years ago, whilst being interviewed for membership of my present club, I made the mistake of announcing this innocent but seemingly tragic history. A rumour soon spread that I had once been a homeless child brought up in a greenkeeper's shed. There followed many months of embarrassment when letters of sympathy flooded through my post box and anonymous cash donations became a common event. Naturally, I did nothing to contradict this speculation until the charitable windfall provided enough capital for a brand-new set of clubs and a winter break in Antigua.

On reflection, I suppose it is always possible that, if not raised, I may well have been spawned on a links course (a not uncommon event in my home town). But, in truth, I was conceived and nurtured in a fine house overlooking the sea and, if I leaned far enough out of the attic window, could just catch sight of the fluttering flag on the infamous 8th hole.

Whatever the case, the often rugged British coastline has stayed in my blood. Though, over time, I have been fortunate enough to enjoy, amongst others, the inland manicured pleasures of courses such as Wentworth, Gleneagles, Sunningdale and Ferndown, I have usually completed my round with a gnawing sensation of being underwhelmed. There was always a feeling that something was missing, that my golfing soul was crying out for more than had been delivered. Like a child denied his favourite sweets, I longed for the instinctive pleasures of a windswept links, bordered by a truculent sea.

Just as there has been a timeless debate regarding the primacy of the chicken or the egg in the evolutionary pecking order (it *was* the chicken), there has been a longstanding dispute over the origins of the links course species. No doubt some fusty old academic could provide evidence that an early and crude form of golf was played on a desolate Icelandic beach when mammoth stew was considered to be haute cuisine. Sporting historians might also take great delight in informing us that Mary, Queen of Scots may well have played on a links course as far back as 1567. As she's now been dead for more than four hundred years and played off a handicap of thirty-six, I find this of little interest. What is far more certain is that golf was being played on Musselburgh Links, Edinburgh, in 1672 and was, perhaps, a result of an earlier chance meeting between two landowners, taking the air on a chilling January morning. To satisfy the modern appetite for cliché, they will be referred to as Hamish and Gordon. Their conversation may well have developed as follows:

A Chilled January Morning on the Coastline of the Firth of Forth, Scotland

Hamish: 'It's a chilled January morning on the Firth of Forth, Scotland, Gordon.'
Gordon: 'Aye. So it is, Hamish.'
H: 'It's a poor bit of land you have here, Gordon.'
G (*a man of few words*): 'Aye.'
H: 'You've tried growing wheat?'
G: 'Aye. Too much salt in the air.'
H: 'Oats? Barley?'
G: 'Aye. Too much sand in the soil.'
H: 'Cattle? Sheep?'
G: 'Aye. Too little grass.'

They walk on in silence. Gordon, out of character, suddenly shouts out.

G: 'Mind that wee hole, Hamish!'
H (*looking down*): 'You mean this wee round hole that appears to be exactly four and a quarter inches in diameter and has an old stick lying beside it?'
G: 'The very one.'

Hamish moves to one side and trips over a round pebble. In anger, he kicks the stone out of the way and it rolls into the hole.

G: 'I bet you couldn't have done that using the old stick that's lying next to that four-and-a-quarter-inch round hole.'
H: 'A small wager, sir?'
G: 'My daughter's hand, sir!'
H: 'So be it.'

Hamish retrieves the pebble, takes up the gnarled stick and from six feet away knocks the stone into the hole. In the far distance and from a high window of a large house overlooking the scene, a plaintive female voice cries out in despair.

G: 'So. You have ma daughter, Hamish. And I have an idea.'
H: 'An idea?'
G: 'Aye. For this old piece of land.'
H: 'And your idea, sir?'
G: 'A "Knocking a Pebble into a Hole" Club, Hamish. Clubhouse, annual fee, eating tavern, one or two members, a few basic rules, dress code and a terrifying secretary. That should do it.'

The rest is history and the golfing devil is in the detail of Hamish and Gordon's brief exchange. Golf generally, and links courses in particular, came into existence because no other use could be found for the barren terrain. 'Links' are simply coastal strips of land between beaches and the old agricultural areas. Because of their sand base, not a single arable crop could successfully take root in the infertile soil and people such as Hamish and Gordon hadn't the foresight to build grotesque blocks of retirement flats looking out over the distant watery horizon. It is my assertion that these two men had chanced upon a delicious mixture of heaven and hell.

Links as Heaven

Any golfer who has stepped onto a links course on a warm summer's day will have affectionate memories of fast-running fairways; slick, firm greens and flags hanging as limply as a tea-soaked ginger biscuit. All seems right with the world. Waves lap gently onto the nearby shoreline, birds hover in an azure sky, whilst blooming heathers and iridescent yellow gorse confirm nature's beauty. The only thing that stands between a golfer and their finest round is a sudden desire to write florid poetry in praise of God's creation.

Links as Hell

I can safely say that those golfers more familiar with links courses have no desire to play in such sublime conditions. To assume that there is satisfaction to be gained from a toothless links course is to misunderstand the essential nature of an amateur player's character. Golfers thrive not on pleasure but on unadulterated pain. Masochism is their *raison d'être*, the source of every contented moment. Male golfers, in particular, wish to have their virility put to the test, to shoulder arms against the warring elements. Links courses will grant them all their subconscious desires. Invariably, coastal courses show their teeth more often than a snarling Rottweiler with a bad attitude towards anything that smells like a postman. If you should chance across a links course on a still, sunlit day, it is likely to be the wagging tail before the ferocious bite. As the tide begins to turn, dark rain clouds will be gathering in the distance; balmy breezes will be preparing to send the flags into a frenzied dance and the clawing rough will be growing before your eyes. Soon, the shimmering gorse and soft-hued heathers will be demanding to consume your errant drives, the once picturesque sanded bunkers will darken into deep, open-mouthed caverns of despair. And as the light begins to change, the previously inviting fairways will begin to reveal every capricious bump and hollow, ready to destroy the well-struck shot with a shrug of contempt. Hell has arrived. Yet, for many golfers, it is a hell truly made in heaven.

Do I have proof for these claims, that the measure of a golfer's satisfaction can only be judged in relation to the degree of self-inflicted pain?

For the necessary evidence, I suggest that you need look no further than the burgeoning number of amateur golf touring parties that litter the courses of Britain. Where are these players to be found? On the flatlands of Cambridgeshire, the undulating plains of Northamptonshire or the soft rolling hills of the Scottish Borders? To search in such places would be fruitless.

Look, instead, towards 'the edge', to the coastal fringes of the windswept shoreline. It is only here that you will witness the true golfers, those who stand on the 1st tee buffeted by a biting north-easterly gale, who huddle under contorted umbrellas, their bodies swathed in layers of heavy-knit sweaters. But ignore these outer signs of misery and examine their expressions. Instead of despair, you will quickly notice the contradictory air of untainted bliss; a collection of faces that confirm my hypothesis that a golfer's contentment is gained only from suffering.

Such a list of facts could easily be translated as evidence of golfers' madness (and in my own experience, this is often true), but there are deeper reasons for this incongruous reaction to misery. T-shirts bearing the motto *No Pain No Gain* (worn by those wishing to impress others with their clean living and inevitably truncated life span) offer only a hint of explanation.

All untalented sports men and women are riddled with fantasies. Beer-bellied rugby players dream of playing at Twickenham; uncoordinated village cricketers lust after the green sward of Lords; puny American footballers imagine themselves making a touchdown in a Super Bowl final; handicap golfers have visions of strolling around the fairways of St Andrews. Only in this latter case is fantasy likely to turn to reality. Given a bulging wallet, I can pick up the phone and, within days, find myself teeing off on the Old Links, firing irons at the pins of Turnberry, putting on the silky greens of Carnoustie or (given the cash *and* the right social connections) pitching out of the deep bunkers of Muirfield. I can tread in the footsteps of Nicklaus, Faldo and Woods; sense the long-lost shadows of Hogan, Sarazan and Vardon, and feel history beneath my feet. No other sport allows you such intimacy with your heroes or the chance to test yourself against all that a links course can throw at the unwary competitor.

But it comes at a cost. Green fees at these championship courses tend to be prohibitive. Though I'd welcome their loose change, this book has not be written for the minority of millionaires but for the other 99.9 per cent of club golfers who want the challenge of high-quality links golf without having to remortgage their house or sell their spouse to a passing slave trader.

With a few notable exceptions (we all enjoy the occasional treat), my spotlight has fallen on eighteen of the UK's finest links courses – all of which were required to meet the following criteria:

- They had to be truly 'links' in nature, predominantly treeless, heavily bunkered and terrifying to the naked eye.
- They had to be established courses perched 'on the edge' of the coastline. If a golfer needed to ask, 'Where's the sea?', the course lost all chance of inclusion.
- The watery grave of the ocean had to be an integral part of the golf course – either visually or as a hazard that needed to be avoided. Nothing strikes more fear into a swing than the sound or sight of a crashing wave.
- In the main, selected courses had to be financially accessible and welcoming to all players – be they corporate high rollers or a cash-strapped private visitor driving a second-hand Ford Fiesta.
- All courses had to supply the required level of pain to players of any standard. Measured on my official 'Misery Meter', scaled between 1 and 10, any reading lower than 6 led to immediate exclusion. Pleasure is therefore assured at all selected courses.
- Each course had to reach a high standard of quality and condition, and preferably enjoy a degree of welcome eccentricity.
- Any course that showed the slightest inclination to favour 'target golf' was omitted from my selection. True links courses should present the golfer with a minimum of at least three choices for every shot played. As a man who is easily confused by the choices on a McDonald's menu, I remain surprised by my love of links golf. But my passion has never faltered.

It is more than 3,000 miles around the coastline of Britain. As agreeable as the journey might seem, I have no wish to add to the current pollution problems by encouraging convoys of frantic golfers to search out their ultimate links experience. The legwork has been done. Trust me. I'm a fellow masochist. You won't be disappointed by any of the agonizing pleasures delivered by any of the selected courses.

When Shakespeare's despairing King Lear found himself caught in a storm without a large striped golfing umbrella or a set of Gortex waterproofs, he ranted at the elements:

> *Blow, winds, and crack your cheeks! Rage! Blow!*
> *You cataracts and hurricanes, spout!*

As a king (he claimed) more sinned against than sinning, you can understand his self-pitying pessimism. Had a golfer uttered these poetic words whilst standing on the 1st tee of a wind-ravaged British links course, their optimistic expression would tell a different story. Despite the numbing cold, the dripping rain and the nearby raging sea, you can be sure that they were looking forward to one of the most satisfying days of their golfing life.

THE MODUS OPERANDI

or

How the Author Bravely Subjected Himself to 'The Terror of the Unknown'

Despite my strict criteria, the selection of the final eighteen courses was never going to be an easy task. Inevitably, the list would attract criticism for its omissions. To avoid the inevitable brickbats or to assist if you are on a golfing 'tour', at the end of each chapter are some *Recommended Alternatives*, within fairly easy reach of the selected course. But what is guaranteed is that you will be presented with a tour of British seaside links courses that will satisfy every golfing palate. Rather than offer an all too often tedious description of each hole, this book's objective is to give you a true 'feel' of the nature of the courses.

To achieve this aim, the author took the perilous decision to request that each club visited supplied two or three volunteer members who would join me in a game and give an insight into the qualities and pitfalls of their course. At the planning stage, this seemed to be a well-thought-out strategy. In reality, I found that I had subjected myself to eighteen terror-filled moments when, in the company of a group of complete strangers, I was forced to stand on the opening tee and expose my inconsistent swing to public scrutiny. If nothing else, it verified my qualification for writing this book. As suggested in the Introduction, the need to enjoy morbid gratification in suffering ego-sapping emotional pain is a prerequisite for a true links golfer who gains satisfaction from living life 'on the edge'.

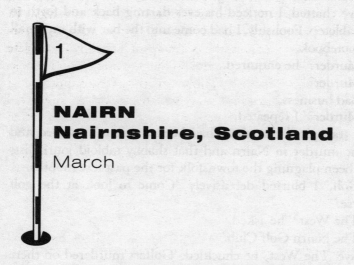

NAIRN
Nairnshire, Scotland
March

Minutes after taking rooms in a pub bed and breakfast, I became aware of the true nature of this small Scottish town. As would soon be confirmed, the landlord's demeanour suggested that the cost of my stay would be completely outweighed by his generosity. Having 'freshened up' (an obligatory habit adopted from the American branch of my family ménage), I strolled down to the bar, intent on enjoying the first single malt of my short stay. A finger tapped me gently on the shoulder.

'Which room's the whist drive in?' asked the elderly man as I turned to face his line-worn features.

'Whist drive?' I responded. 'I don't—'

'Wrong Thursday, Archie,' interjected the landlord. 'The card game's next week.'

'Bit early then?' smiled the crumpled figure. 'You'll take a drink with me?'

He proved to be a welcome companion, an old sea salt who

had once earned his living in the now defunct fishing fleet. As we chatted, I noticed his eyes darting back and forth to the tabletop. Foolishly, I had come into the bar with my small red notebook.

'Murder?' he enquired.

'Murder?'

'Bad business.'

'Murder?' I repeated.

It transpired that there had been a recent, unsolved and tragic murder in Nairn and that shabby tabloid journalists had been plaguing the townsfolk for the past few months.

'Golf,' I blurted defensively. 'Come to look at the golf course.'

'The West?' he asked.

'The Nairn Golf Club.'

'Aye. The West,' he chuckled. 'Golfers murdered on there every day. It's a tough old bugger.'

'Let me buy *you* a drink,' I muttered, confused by his answer.

'You do the drinking, I'll do the buying,' he insisted.

'But . . .'

'The first drink wasn't a loan,' he laughed in reply.

This type of hospitality was to follow me for the next two days. Having spent much of my life on the golf courses of southern England, where offers of drinks are on a strictly reciprocal basis, I had to adjust quickly. I had clearly flown into a foreign country, a land where a week's delay for an expected game of cards was no more than a minor irritant. In the frantic streets of London, a five-second hold-up often seems to result in demands for psychiatric counselling. The town of Nairn is slow and sleepy; a little weary and well worn; laid out long and languid along the shores of the Moray Firth.

Having visited the area on a number of occasions, I also knew that this slumbering town contains one of the finest links courses in Britain.

Details of the golfing fare must wait, as I would advise you to savour the dish slowly. The menu of pleasure is presented the moment you wind your way along Seabank Road (there's a clue), towards the stylish red-bricked clubhouse. The grey waters of the Moray Firth bank the road and give you a delightful chill of anticipation. There's no hint of diffidence in Nairn's introduction, the grandeur of its setting announcing its quality with total self-confidence. And, if you can, arrive early to wander around the haute couture professional's shop; take coffee in one of the most comfortable and scenic bars in British golf; grab a putter and step onto the magnificent practice green, which sits directly outside the clubhouse window. The speed of its surface may well frighten you to death but it will give you a chance to whet your golfing appetite as you glance out over the waiting course. I can't recommend this unhurried approach enough. Like a fine wine, Nairn shouldn't be suffocated by impatience. It needs to be given time to breathe and is a course that should linger on the palate.

Though familiar with what Nairn had in store, I had forgotten the relevance of the old man's reference to the golf club as 'The West'. Slowly, I began to recall the dark secrets implied in his answer. The nearby battlefields of Culloden have cast a long, historical shadow. Until fairly recently, the town had been split into two distinct areas, clearly defined by language and social class. To the east lies Fishertown, a collection of ancient dwellings built below sea level. So often did this part of the town suffer flooding that these Saxon-speaking mariners must have been well prepared for the advent of the submarine. To the west, and on higher ground, are the grander dwellings of what was once known as Upper Town. The Gaelic-speaking owners certainly had their 'baps' buttered on both sides. They experienced no flooding, lived in exquisite granite houses and, in 1887, enjoyed rights to an ideal bit of land, on which they were to build an outstanding links course. Twenty years later, down-town Fishertown constructed their own course at Nairn Dunbar, a challenging but strange mixture of links and semi-parkland, which satisfies no one apart from its dedicated members. They even promote their golf course with a postcard displaying two men with their socks tucked into their jeans, putting out on a green whose backdrop is the local caravan park. The social division is still clearly cemented into the town and it is interesting to note that the superior 'West' course, which I had come to visit, chooses to employ in its title (what I'm informed is) the emphatic definite article. Clearly, '*The* Nairn Golf Club' is willing to have no truck with any hint of abbreviation. And once you've played the course, you'll understand why.

I woke early the next morning, the sound of numerous single malts still ringing in my head, but fresh enough to take on the challenge of *The* Nairn golf course.

'Fine day,' I said as the landlord heaved a mountainous breakfast onto my table.

'Tide's coming in,' he answered, smiling genially. 'Wind's freshening.'

'Hope my swing holds up,' I muttered nervously.

'Swing slow,' he countered. 'Swing slow.'

He was a man with a handicap lower than the fingers of one hand with no thumb, and I nodded my reply with an earnest gratitude. Half an hour later, I was taking the short walk down to the links. It was a bright sunlit day with a hint of menace in the distant heavy clouds, but not a breath of the predicted wind. Yet as I approached the clubhouse, it was as though some ancient Gaelic god had turned on a giant fan. Peering over the Moray Firth, I could already see white horses breaking into a canter and the club's flag unfurling into a frenzied Scottish reel. My stomach began to churn. And I knew the reason.

As a child, I once tried to replicate the culinary demonstration of a seaside stallholder who professed to be the most talented omelette maker in Lancashire. As a result, I was violently ill for over thirty-six hours and, to this day, cannot tolerate the smell of these foul pancakes. The highly agreeable odour of 'The Nairn Golf Club' has exactly the same effect. The whiff of softened leather and polished wood, seasoned by the salt air, sends my stomach into a quiver of despair. Like the omelettes of my childhood, it is a stimulus to my doom-laden response.

On the first two occasions I played on this course, it devoured my spirit as an aperitif, my soul for the main course and my plums for a pudding. Nairn has a voracious appetite for the naive, over-optimistic golfer, yet will offer no reward for temerity. Some years previously, I had stepped onto the 1st tee fired with groundless enthusiasm. I had, unwisely, entered the annual open competition, unaware that I would be formally announced onto the tee; that the eyes of numerous competitors would monitor my every nervous twitch, and that the Moray Firth, like the sirens of Greek mythology, would be luring my ball towards the waiting, watery grave.

It is this terrifying memory that plagues my swing every time I take my stance on Nairn's 1st tee. The mumbled, hypocritical prayers of all agnostic golfers often accompany my shaking body. Sadly, these invocations to the gods have little effect, and only remind me of my first encounter with a well-known Nairn 'Starter'. This redoubtable man's main hobby appeared to be striking fear into any nervous visitor who is not in possession of a Scottish lilt. Due to play a three-ball with two unknown partners, there was only one other golfer present. Quickly checking the list, I identified the missing party and, having heard of the official's reputation, approached the starter with caution.

'Any sign of Mr J. Knox?' I asked nervously.

'I know of only one J. Knox,' he answered abruptly, 'and he was last seen preaching in the streets of Edinburgh in 1572. You'll have to play a two-ball.'

As rude as he sounds, we became great friends over later years and he turned out to possess one of the driest wits I've ever encountered on a golf course. The bonding of our relationship was confirmed when I once noticed an uncontrollable horse gallop across the hallowed green of the adjacent 18th hole. Asking if there was a local rule concerning the repair of horseshoe marks on the putting surface, I was informed, with studious gravity, that any decision would be dependent on whether the rider's feet were in the stirrups at the time of impact.

My two companions for my most recent round at Nairn fortunately arrived on time, and, unexpectedly, turned out to be two delightful Welsh expatriates. They had been members for many years and knew every blade of grass on the course. With my landlord's words still fresh in my ears, I swung slowly and saw my drive bore down the middle of the fairway. The sirens of the Moray Firth sighed their disappointment as I tried to disguise my look of surprise. As I strode forward, I could only think of the Right Honourable Viscount William Whitelaw, CH, MC. Because I'm a naturally political animal, it's not unusual for me to recall such parliamentary detail, immediately after a successful golf shot. Viscount Whitelaw (or 'Margaret Thatcher's Willie', as he became affectionately known) was Nairn's President until 1999. He was often heard to remark that it was quite possible to drive your ball into the sea from the first seven tees of the golf course, a feat that (though he was a very talented golfer) he achieved on more than one occasion. With my own ball lying smack in the middle of the fairway, I suddenly felt as if I'd just won a general election.

It seems to be the case that Nairn revels in the great and the good who have trodden its fairways. Even their website invites you to check out 'The Notable Guests At Nairn'. These include the wrinkled Hollywood stars Jack Nicholson and Michael Douglas, the ex-prime ministers Harold Macmillan (who famously arrived at the course in a pair of hand-patched trousers) and Ramsay MacDonald (who saw politics as a punctuation, to, his, golf, game.), the ousted King Edward VIII (before he was banished from polite society) and Field Marshal Earl Haig. In the latter case, the deep bunkers of Nairn were probably the nearest the field marshal ever got to the Somme trenches.

The fact that this list of celebrities tends to be male dominated comes as no surprise. In the early days, the grudging acceptance of emancipation was confirmed by only allowing women members into the clubhouse – once the thermometer had fallen below zero. To be fair, and thanks in some part to the notoriously assertive Mrs Winnie Whitelaw (Willie's mother), the club now enjoys a strong, and much warmer, ladies' section.

Having successfully negotiated my second shot towards the 1st hole, I was immediately reminded of Nairn's greatest defence. When the Walker Cup was played at Nairn in 1999, a number of the American players were convinced that the greens were faster than Augusta. As I don't own anything resembling a Green Jacket or have $50 million in my bank account, I can't verify this claim. But is anything faster than an ice rink that's been sprayed with engine oil? What's even more extraordinary is that you can pitch a ball onto the surface, and it will stop dead without leaving any apparent indentation on the closely cropped grass. Manic games of Hunt the Pitchmark are a common sight amongst first-time visitors keen to make an impression. Their troubles have only just begun. Get a little heavy-handed with your putting stroke and you could be playing your next shot from the outskirts of nearby Inverness.

Like many links courses, Nairn (roughly speaking) has nine holes out and nine holes back. If you have a violent slice, and given the proximity of the sea, it's probably best either to start on the 8th or to carry a dozen spare balls. It was once said that three of the first seven tees are so close to the sea that you could flick a cigarette butt into the Moray Firth. Given the current puritanical attitudes to tobacco, this claim can now be tested with a frenetically gnawed piece of nicotine-replacement chewing gum. If done successfully, you may be surprised to find the discarded item snapped up by a dolphin suffering fag end withdrawal symptoms.

If you are fortunate enough to play at Nairn, *never* hurry these first seven holes. Give yourself time to delight in your surroundings. The distant Black Isle and Ben Wyvis range loom across the wide Firth and, if it's your lucky day, the now nicotine-free, balletic dolphins will be putting on their daily show of playful pleasure. If a group is pushing you from behind, wave them through and enjoy the moment. This isn't an invitation to play slowly and irritate the hell out of the members, but a suggestion that Nairn has far more to offer than a golf course. Extraordinarily, perhaps uniquely, the sea can be viewed from every hole on the golf course, even the more inland back nine. (One diminutive member was not convinced by this claim but anyone over five foot seven can take my word for it.)

It is always a subjective choice, but on the outward half, two holes are worthy of special mention. The par-three 4th, even for a man of my limited ability, is no more than a flick with an eight iron. If there is even the hint of a southerly breeze, a well-struck seven iron could see you fishing your ball out of the Moray Firth. Sound easy? Not quite. For many years, wildcats have set up home in the nearby gorse and unnervingly watch your every move. The green is hidden from view and is about as narrow as a bootlace. But worse is to follow, though glancing at the card will tell you all you need to know. It remains unclear which of the two whiskered, pancake-hatted course designers (Old Tom Morris or James Braid) named this hole 'Bunker'. Whoever gave it this title revealed a feeble ability for unimaginative thinking but a greater talent for ill-omened prophecy. Nestled up against the front of the green is a sand trap that makes the notorious (now sadly emasculated) St Andrews Road Hole bunker look like Harold Macmillan's little local difficulty.

Some years ago, I was drawn to play in the Nairn Open with a delightful, tea-stained and incomprehensible man from the Orkneys, and an equally agreeable player from the south of England. We had all started well but the Englishman, clearly fired with confidence, was two under par after the first three holes. I watched him reach for a nine iron as we stood on the 4th tee. I shuffled. I winced. I did everything within the rules of the game to suggest he had made a serious error of judgement. He struck the ball beautifully, covering the pin as it arced towards the flag. He nodded his approval. I hung my head in dismay and reached for a seven iron. My own ball was soon flying into the biggest lateral water hazard in Scotland.

And there is a moral to this tale. I walked onto the 5th tee, recording an acceptable five on my own card and a thirteen on that of my distraught companion. His first three attempts to hit out of the bunker were met with stoic resolution; his next four attempts with wide, dewy-eyed horror and by the time his tenth shot sailed onto the green, he appeared to be pleading for his mother. The man from the Orkneys just smiled and a self-righteous wildcat purred its delight.

The 5th is not a challenge you wish to face having just eaten up your whole handicap on a short par three. 'Nets', as the next hole is known, has everything you could demand from a true links course. The drive must negotiate the sea to the right, gorse and heather to the left and myriad bunkers within the fairway. If all these hazards are avoided, the second shot to the raised, bunker-defended green needs the weaving skills of a Harris tweed crofter. The sight of it returned me to thoughts of Nairn's once segregated Fishertown. As the herring fleet dropped anchor and drifted into folklore, local fishermen eked out a living catching salmon on the shores of the Moray Firth and repaired their nets along the land bordering the fairway. It allowed the Nairn members to tell their wives they were going fishing for the family supper, sneak their clubs out of the back door and buy healthy but net-damaged salmon from the real fishermen who waited their arrival on the 5th green. I imagine that such deceit was not a problem in the colder months, but in the height of summer, fish-toting golfers must have run round the next thirteen holes, followed by swarms of crazed and hungry flies.

My companions, on this present visit, informed me that the front nine holes of Nairn are the easier of the two halves. I remain to be convinced. In my short experience, there is no more than a scintilla of difference and I found them equally demanding. The dangers of the second nine come from between the ears. Arrive at 'the turn' with a good card in your hand and you are likely to commit Nairn's cardinal sin: you find yourself indulging in premature self-congratulation. If flexible enough, you might even want to slap yourself on the back. That's fine. But on *no* account must you *relax*. It would be wiser to cover your grips in Vaseline or take a one-legged stance over your next drive. Do what you like, but *don't relax*.

In many ways the back nine enjoys wider fairways and you begin to feel that you can really open your shoulders. There are perils in such temptation and *'Oh Lord, the whins await'* is a useful melodic mantra to adopt on every future back-swing. Whilst these five words may sound like a line from an old Presbyterian hymn, they are no more than a self-invented swing tip, carefully constructed in a three-beat rhythm. This can be a useful remedy, which allows highly strung players to swing back, down and through in a more rhythmical if not musical manner. In truth, it has never really met with any success, but on the frequent occasions when my shot is accompanied by a crude and blasphemous curse, I find the comfort of absolution in this repetitive religious chant.

'Whins' is the locally adopted Nordic name for the gorse bushes that 'await'. Whilst they offer little visual threat, any misdirected drive would be as attracted to these hazards as the eyes of a retired brigadier would be drawn to a pair of seamed nylons strutting across the floor of his gentleman's club. This clawing gorse is so dense and impenetrable that should you be foolish enough to hunt for a missing ball, it would be wise to enter the bushes with a full set of provisions. They are card killers, more heartbreaking than the ending of a pubescent romance, more dispiriting than an exorcizing priest. At Nairn, he who whins loses.

Stand on the 10th tee, concentrate and remember Macbeth's torment. There is good reason why this hole was given the name of 'Cawdor'. On more than one occasion have I played this hole, convinced that the whins that moved against me would vanquish my spirit. If you should slice to the right or pull to the left, cross all your fingers, touch the nearest piece of wood and, if you happen to be carrying a bag of salted crisps, throw the whole packet over your left shoulder. I'm not in any way superstitious, but I'm terrified of curses delivered by wart-riddled witches.

Survive the next few holes, and Nairn will quickly remind you that the summit of torment has yet to be conquered. The mountain in question is the 13th or 'Crown', the one bit of jewellery Lady Macbeth never successfully held in her blood-stained hands. Marked down as a par four, players of average skill, such as myself, should take this figure with the pinch of salt you've just thrown over your left shoulder. Such is the steepness of rise to the blind green that the club has, for many years, left a battered copper water scoop in the small spring that runs down from the nearby farmland. In a breathless state, I've often sipped this reviving potion, ignoring the liquid's suspicious swine bouquet, infused by the rutting pigs in the fields above the green.

Once having putted out (allow a minimum of three putts), walk over to the 14th tee, rest on one of the wooden benches and soak in the prospect of one of Nairn's finest holes. If I could bribe a local planning officer, I would happily live on the 14th tee for the rest of my days. You will find yourself at the highest point on the course, gazing out over the Firth to the distant mountains, the waiting green nestled into the natural contours of the heathered land. If you feel no surge of pleasure in the undiluted beauty of this setting, it's time to give up living.

The name given to this long par three only adds to its attraction. Mysteriously, *'Kopjes'*, as it's known, confirms Nairn's peculiar relationship with Africa. Once again, the clues are to be found in the dark history of nearby Fishertown. Strangely, the long-forgotten fishing smacks were known as 'Zulus' and, in the later Boer Wars, a number of Afrikaans words began to filter into the local dialect. Amongst them was *Kopjes*, a Dutch term for an advantageous look-out position. Dull history? Not if you were a young man from Inverness, decked out in a bright red uniform, with camouflaged Boers taking potshots at you from their *Kopjes*.

I was reminded of this African inheritance as I prepared to take my own shot to the waiting green. Two of the four players in front of my own group were wearing garish red sweaters and were taking an interminable time over their putts. In contrast, I was suitably decked out in a sartorially elegant beige outfit, which blended into the surrounding terrain.

'Anyone got a rifle?' I asked.

I received no more than a mumbled and slightly nervous response.

To reach the green of 'Kopjes' requires a well-struck shot that will carry your ball more than 200 yards over the deep guarding bunkers. This is the easy bit. The green itself mimics a deep-frozen sea swell, with any putt from more than 10 feet only likely to be successful if the player possesses a Doctorate in Applied Mathematics. Intent on impressing my playing companions with my numeric skills, I took four putts from the edge of the green and walked off with a false air of academic qualification.

As we wandered down the 15th fairway, our heads now bent against a strengthening easterly wind, I confirmed my intellectual talent by introducing into our conversation my prowess with the *Brio Labyrintspel*. Following my threat to shoot two members on the 14th, this was met with a wary silence. I pressed on regardless. The *Labyrintspel* is a child's game I first played in a dingy Amsterdam café whose smoked-filled air would have sent a sniffer dog into a state of apoplectic frenzy. The game's mechanism is highly complex and involves two wooden boards, which swivel on two different planes. The object of the game is to manoeuvre a large ball bearing around a labyrinth of sixty holes. It would be easier to drink the Moray Firth with a teaspoon. Throughout my *Labyrintspel* career, I have never managed to get that damned ball beyond hole fifty-seven.

In response to this admission, one of my fellow players offered a reply of glazed eye interest.

'Fascinating,' he mumbled. 'But what's that got to do—'

'With Nairn?' I interrupted.

'Well . . . yes.'

'Everything.' I smiled.

The problem with *Labyrintspel* and Nairn is that as soon as you catch a glimpse of the finish, you know you're in trouble. The last three holes (in theory) are not difficult. But stand on the 15th green, catch a sight of the distant clubhouse and your game can be ruined by the anticipation of stumbling over the line. The moment you step onto the 16th tee you must gird every loin in your loinery and concentrate harder than a Boer sniper taking aim from his *Kopjes*.

Ignorant of my own advice, I walked onto the 17th tee having recorded my first eight on the card. In relative terms, this was not such a bad result. Some years previously, during an open medal competition, I had encountered a lonely, middle-aged Aberdonian weeping in the clubhouse. His voice was muffled with tears and the only words I could make sense of were, '*Sixteen! Sixteen! Sixteen!*' Adopting what I hoped would be seen as the expression of a non-judgemental Samaritan, I offered a few words of comfort and an assurance of confidentiality. His sad story soon gushed from his quivering lips.

Standing on the 16th tee, five under his handicap, he had watched his first four drives disappear into the dreaded 'whins'. Once he had a ball in play, his tenth shot found the burn in front of the green, his twelfth thinned into a bunker, his thirteenth and fourteenth left him still in the sand and he was fortunate to hole a twenty-footer for his sixteen. Having finished his sorry tale, he turned to me for sympathy.

'Can you swim?' I asked.

'No,' he answered quizzically.

'Excellent,' I responded quickly, keen to avoid the queue building up at the bar. 'Tide's coming in.'

It was in that moment that I realized how unwise it might be to offer my services to the Samaritan's hotline. Had I ever done so, I fear there may have been catastrophic effects, including a rapid depopulation of golfers in my local town. I'm not the most unsympathetic of people, but whenever I make an enquiry about how someone else has played, I want no more than, at most, a two-word answer, e.g. *Not good*; *Great*; *Not bad*. Barring the quarterly conversations with my hairdresser (who doesn't really care where I've been on holiday), I can think of nothing more tedious than fellow golfers assuming that a passing question about their game is an invitation for a shot-by-shot response. In truth, unless you're Tiger Woods or Ernie Els, no one gives a damn. Golfers are, by definition, competitive, self-absorbed and mercenary individuals, who have absolutely no interest in the plight of other hackers. Away from the golf course, they may well prove themselves to be altruistic saints, but once that bag's over the shoulder and the glove is on the hand, they enjoy nothing more than seeing the opposition's ball plug into the face of a bunker.

I will therefore resist giving a full account of the extraordinary finish to my round at Nairn. Suffice it to say, I was clapped off the par-five 18th green by a group of men in matching sweaters who (falsely) assumed I had just made an eagle, requiring no more than a final six-inch putt. Casually raising my hand in gratitude (to what transpired to be the assembled Carnoustie scratch team) I sauntered back to the locker room, unwilling to shatter their illusions.

With only two hours to spare before making my flight home from nearby Inverness, I grabbed a quick lunch in the club's restaurant. You can always tell the first-time visitors at Nairn, as their table manners are universally appalling. This isn't the result of a poor upbringing but the fact that the view from the panoramic windows is so stunning that they find it impossible not to dribble with delight. Between courses, my pen hovered over my notebook. What was it about Nairn? What makes it so unique?

I suddenly became aware of a contradiction. On first appearances, it has all the hallmarks of stuffy formality – a grand entrance, an atmosphere of convention, a desire to promote its history – the celebrities, royalty and political grandees who have deigned to play the course. In reality, this is no more than a masquerade for its friendly informality. Pay a green fee here and you'll feel as if you've just become an honorary member. It's an exquisite golf course, which can have justified pride in every one of its eighteen sublime and testing holes.

Arriving at the airport later than intended, I was informed that the flight was going to be delayed by almost two hours. Normally, such an announcement would result in seething frustration. But Nairn had entered my blood. I felt like a man who had turned up for his card game a week early. Somehow, it just didn't matter.

Recommended Alternatives

Moray (Lossiemouth): A high-class, wild, wonderful and windswept brute. The 18th is truly unique.

Fortrose & Rosemarkie: Situated on the Black Isle; views to die for; the sea at every turn. Great fun and tougher than you might think.

Hopeman: Quirky classic links, but a delight and not to be underestimated. The par-three 12th alone is worth the very reasonable fee.

If you're looking for a respite from the rigours of links golf, **Boat of Garten** is a MUST. Stunningly beautiful.

TREVOSE
Cornwall, England
March

I knew it was early March, because I'd checked my calendar. The morning I left for Trevose, I stepped into my car and the bank of unnecessary technology informed me the temperature was minus 6 degrees. Something was wrong. Had God forgotten to replace the dead battery in his seasonal alarm clock? I checked my personal, physical barometer. The fingers of both hands looked as though they had been bleached in an industrial cleaner. I'm told it's called Raynaud's disease, a badge of honour for many hypochondriac (mostly male) golfers. I prefer to call it 'bloody cold fingers'. I gripped the wheel as best I could, fired the reluctant engine into life and headed off along the frost-glittered roads.

Three hours later, I arrived on the outskirts of Exeter, in need of caffeine. Wherever you travel from, Cornwall is a long way. Look on the map and this beautiful, sea-washed county appears as a giant lamb chop, surgically transplanted onto the carcass of the mainland. The warming beverage at the service station proved to be so expensive that I assumed it must have come from a rare Brazilian coffee plant, clearly in danger of extinction.

'*Cuanto!*' I exclaimed, certain that the use of schoolboy Spanish would confirm my expertise.

'What?' came the dismissive reply.

I sipped the watery coffee with the care of a man who has just opened his last bottle of vintage Krug. As I left, I glanced through the local paper on the nearby newsstand. The temperature had struggled to minus 3, but the headline date still suggested it was March. If some divine being was really responsible for these arctic conditions, He or She had obviously overslept. I pressed on towards the waiting Trevose.

The decision to take a short cut only confirmed the seasonal time warp. A blizzard swept down from the summit of Bodmin Moor, the snow blanketing the shivering heathered hills. In a moment of panic, I reached back to the rear seat and rustled through my golf bag. Had I remembered to pack a few iridescent, yellow balls? Without them, Trevose may prove to be unplayable.

I should have known better. If I had paid more attention during my geography lessons, I would have recalled that the majority of seaside links courses enjoy the benefits of a microclimate. As a man who finds a meteorological map about as comprehensible as a James Joyce novel, I have no idea why these things occur. What I do know is that a golfer should never despair until they stand on the 1st tee of a coastal course. Two miles inland, it can be raining in feline proportions and with the combined power of the residents of the Battersea dogs' home. Step onto the golf course and you can be bathed in sunlight.

Should you ever be tempted into golf at Trevose, take

the narrow coastal road down to nearby Harlyn Bay and stretch your motorway-weary legs. Cornwall is not shy in announcing its beauty. On a high spring tide, the giant azure Atlantic waves display their power with shameless confidence. Giant rollers, which I'm assured begin their journey in the Caribbean, foam onto the waiting beach. I couldn't smell the coconut oil, but even on a numbing March afternoon, you sense that the West Indian tempo of life has been exported to the Cornish coastline.

Within ten minutes I was approaching the Trevose Golf and Country Club humming Bob Marley songs with a chilled body and an equally chilled-out demeanour. Glancing up from the narrow bottom road, the clubhouse, with its accompanying array of flats and bungalows, dominates the skyline. At first appearance, it resembles an over-elaborate wedding cake whose recipe has omitted the self-raising flour. A line of stark white buildings appears to stretch across the horizon, their virginal walls a complete antithesis to the rather dour and featureless golf course that stretches out towards the coast. Things looked promising.

One of the great appeals of links golf is that it confirms the adage that the best presents often come in the worst packages. Wooded and manicured parkland courses often flatter to deceive. They look pretty, pristine, pleasing to the eye, only to disappoint when you begin to tread their fairways. In contrast, once you've unwrapped a links course, it will, almost always, begin to reveal its worth. Coastal golf is a voyage of discovery. Trevose was to prove no exception.

Unlike most golf courses visited, Trevose has its own accommodation, a grand array of flats, chalets, bungalows and cottages. As I was to learn soon, this is not a members' club but a full-blown business venture, in which golf is only part of the offered package. I have visited such places before.

In general, they tend towards the impersonal and give such clubs a soulless character in which its visitors are treated as little more than contributors to the owner's coffers. I feared the worst as I located the reception office and made my entrance.

I was weary, dishevelled, with the undisguised grumpiness of someone who, apart from my quick stop at Harlyn Bay, had been trapped in an airless car for almost six hours. Even if I had been greeted by a charitable nun, she would have been in danger of receiving a withering response. I approached the desk.

The face that welcomed my arrival had no hint of the manufactured 'Have a nice day' attitude. Instead, the expression suggesting the young woman had just been re-acquainted with a long-lost favourite cousin. I was disarmed within seconds.

'You're staying in a hotel?' she asked cheerily. 'You can have one of the bungalows. Cheaper. Much nicer.'

This was too good to be true. I gave her a sterner test.

'Tea-making facilities?' I asked.

'Of course.'

'Milk?'

'Individual long-life cartons.' She grimaced. 'They're disgusting. I'll get you a jug of fresh milk.'

That was it. Trevose could do no wrong. Hotels and golf clubs prove themselves not by grand gestures but by attention to detail. Within seconds, the delightful receptionist had read my *if you give me long-life cartons of milk, I'm leaving* expression, and come up with the goods. I signed in, dropped my bags in the bungalow, slipped on my spiked shoes, grabbed my notebook, placed a ball in my pocket and headed for the golf course.

It has always been my habit to walk a 'new' golf course

before I play it. Apart from saving you at least five shots and avoiding later embarrassment, it's the best way to truly take in the demands and vagaries of the terrain. This is particularly true of links courses, where you are often faced with blind shots into greens and hidden bunkers. The light was already fading as I headed off down the 1st hole, breaking into a run as I searched for the distant green. The word 'run' is a slight overstatement. Having already spent six hours bent double over a steering wheel and employing an ex-rugby knee held together by the most expensive bits of wire and plastic known to the medical profession, my investigative tour was conducted with more of a strutting hobble. But I'm not offering a limp excuse and I covered the ground in an hour and a half – just in time to avoid being swallowed by darkness.

It was enough to prepare me for what lay ahead the next day. Trevose was clearly going to be a true challenge but a delight to play. The holes themselves are rarely picturesque, yet from almost every tee you are given a sight of the swelling Atlantic Ocean. On the westerly edge of the course you are breathing in the clear, crisp, salted air, your drives and putts interrupted only by the sound of waves crashing onto the sanded beach of Constantine Bay.

But it was something else that really captured my interest. In early March, as most golfers would know, the greens of any course tend to look tired and worn, waiting patiently for the spring growth that will return them to their summer glories. The greenkeeper at Trevose must have contacts in high places. Very high places. Winter had apparently bypassed Constantine Bay and the putting surfaces looked as if they had just been plucked from a May-blossomed month. As soon as I reached the 18th, I tested my theory.

Extracting the golf ball from my pocket, I stood on the edge of the green and gently rolled the dimpled sphere towards the hole. Though I had chosen a good line and pace, the ball slipped past the hole and then began to accelerate at an alarming speed, finally coming to rest in the light rough, some 20 yards away. The dollar-rich green jackets of Augusta ought to take a trip to North Cornwall and ask Trevose for a few tips.

'Tomorrow could be interesting,' I whispered into the strengthening wind.

With hardly enough energy left to lift a fork, I headed for the clubhouse to sample a light meal in the restaurant. The season was still to get into full swing and my only company in the bar proved to be a small golfing society made up of twelve women of a 'certain age'. A wide-screened television, suspended high on the wall, treated us all to the latest episode of *Songs of Praise*. I bent my head reverently, but furtively tuned into the group's conversation. As a counterpoint to the religious transmission, they were singing their own songs of derision.

It started positively enough, with Trevose being given unanimous high praise. Only when the diaries were produced and future matches organized did the vitriol rise to the surface, the criticisms orchestrated by the ubiquitous 'SASH', commonly known as the 'Self-Appointed Society Humorist'.

'What about Newquay?' came a voice.

'Rather stick pins in my eyes,' responded the SASH.

General laughter.

'Penzance?' offered another.

'Prefer to chop my arms off.'

Guffaws.

'Whitsand Bay?'

'Have more fun sawing my own head off.'

Sighs.

This one-joke humorist seemed determined to reduce her body to little more than a quivering torso. The expressions on her companions' faces suggested they were now praying that she would offer to cut her tongue out with a rusty knife. I retired to the restaurant and was served (delightfully) with local fish (delicious) and a house white (good quality, great value).

One thing you must prepare yourself for in this area of Britain is that all bar and restaurant staff under thirty are likely to have long blonde hair, and are only working in order to raise enough money to buy a new surfboard. It's advisable, when eating out, to carefully check the weather forecast and the tides. If there is the slightest chance of a 5-metre wave hitting the nearby shoreline, there's a fair chance that you will die of hunger and thirst. Surfers know their priorities and there's no competition between a group of famished golfers and an Atlantic high roller. As surfing 'dudes' represent my alter ego, they have my unreserved support.

I slept fitfully, woken early by fast-green nightmares. Throwing the curtains open, I was met with a clear, inviting day, the flag by the 1st tee unfurling in no more than a gentle breeze. Breakfast was taken in the restaurant and served by a beaming waitress who (if I'm not mistaken) was wearing a full wetsuit under her black-and-white uniform. The wind was obviously due to strengthen well before I began my round.

My meeting with the general manager had been arranged by phone and I had no idea what to expect. I was in for a pleasant surprise. I was greeted by a man clearly uninfluenced by stereotypical, fuddy-duddy golf club secretaries. Instead, I found myself in the company of an enthusiast with

Hollywood looks and a set of teeth that wouldn't look out of place on a Steinway Grand. I immediately made a note to visit my dentist and continued our conversation with no more than a tight-lipped smile.

It transpired that I was in the presence of the latest member of the Trevose dynasty. His grandfather, a certain John C. Gammon, had formed the present club back in 1925, after making his fortune in reinforced concrete engineering, especially in the Far East. In need of a quiet haven for his holidays, Mr Gammon discovered Trevose. Most of us in such a position would have bought a cottage. John C. Gammon bought himself a golf course.

The grandchild Gammon was now the custodian of this inheritance and I pressed him for more information. Under his father (Peter Gammon – a self-confessed but popular benevolent autocrat), Trevose grew into a top-class links course, which appears to be in extremely good hands. Don't take my word for it. Not long before my visit, the blazered powers of golf had just invited this club to host the Brabazon Trophy or English Amateur Championship. They won't be disappointed.

'Fixed you up with the Misfits,' said the manager cheerily, as our conversation drew to a close. 'Hope that's OK?'

'Misfits?'

'Monday morning roll-up. Nice bunch. You'll enjoy it.'

It's never easy for a golfer to be thrown in with a large group of strangers and I warmed up with the dedication of a young professional about to hit his first shot in the Open Championship. I was given a warm welcome as I waited patiently on the practice putting green and was quickly informed of the procedure.

'Drop your ball in the official bag,' I was told, 'and wait for your name to be drawn out.'

The 'official bag' turned out to be a used, plastic Tesco bag, tied to a stake by the 1st tee. I relaxed immediately. Or I did until my name was called out to play in the second group. I instantly realized the implications.

Within ten minutes, I was hunched over the ball trying to look as cool as my alter ego. Twenty-four pairs of eyes burned into my confidence as I took the club back and ripped into the drive. Silence. I searched the horizon. Nothing.

'Anybody see it?' I asked nervously.

'Bit of a slice,' came a voice from the back.

'Right,' I murmured. 'Thanks.'

A 'bit of a slice' turned out to be a generous and sympathetic appraisal. My shot had moved through the air in such grotesque parabolic proportions that, had I seen its flight, I may well have given my excuses and headed straight back to Exeter. Fortunately, my second shot proved far better, the ball spearing over a hill towards the waiting green. Sadly, I never saw it again. I could only mumble my apologies as I shuffled, droop shouldered, towards the next tee. Things were not quite going to plan. And there was to be little respite on the 2nd, my drive hooking wildly into the bushes on the left. Had I been playing only for my own score, I would have been content to dismiss such a start as 'just a bad day at the office'. Unfortunately, I found myself embroiled in a team event, which required a slightly greater participation. I hacked out onto the fairway, eventually leaving myself a simple 'tap in' putt for a bogey five. I missed.

To remedy a crisis of this nature, I would normally revert to the method of juxtaposing deep prayer and satanic swearing. I glanced sideways, wondering how my partners would react. Their expressions suggested that they were happy to give me free licence, if only for the sake of the team score. I let rip, the sentence exploding from my lips proving to be a cleverly constructed union of profanity and reverence. I was to drop only one more shot before the turn for home.

Whoever had dipped their hand into the rustling Tesco bag on the 1st tee had done me a great service. Trevose, like much of Cornwall, is awash with retirees and escapees and my companions were no exception. I had been joined by an ex-RAF education officer (a delight and full of tales), an ex-high-powered city slicker (with an admirable philosophic approach to golf) and an ex-1980s international pop star with a low handicap (who proved to be equally fine company). In this latter case, I was presented with something of a problem. The reason for joining these groups is to gain access to local, unwritten golfing fables. Yet I feared that one hint of my motives might see me cast as a tawdry newspaper hack, intent on celebrity character assassination and making a fast buck. He had no need to be concerned, but I would have understood his fears. Employing discretion, I kept my mouth firmly shut and made a note *not* to include the word WHAM in my report.

The area around the 4th green and 5th tee is probably Trevose's highlight. It is a corner of the golf course that must grind every visiting golf society to a standstill. From here the roaring ocean is in full view, the stretching sands of Constantine and the wonderfully named Booby's Bay tempting you onto the shoreline. I was informed by one of my companions that during the 1930s, the disgraced Edward VIII flew his own flimsy plane to Trevose, for a quick eighteen with the locals. He must have stood on that 5th tee for an eternity, glancing longingly across the Atlantic to dream of his slinky American divorcee. Assuming my most regal pose, I tried to replicate the occasion. Unfortunately, I was able to conjure up no more than the image of Hillary Clinton in a bikini and turned away as quickly as possible.

My pre-match putting practice was paying positive dividends. The reason for this alliterative phrasing is to test any reader with loose false teeth and also to reaffirm my claim that Trevose enjoys some of the best greens in Britain. They are truly extraordinary and not for the faint-hearted. In high summer, I would suggest a large Scotch before playing and a hip flask in the bag. If they get any slicker, the general manager may need to employ a counsellor to comfort emotionally broken golfers. I was fortunate to avoid these traumas on the 6th by holing a nine iron from 120 yards. This is, however, not a reliable technique for mastering the true but tricky greens of Trevose.

Get to the turn without having a nervous breakdown and you enter the second 'sausage'. Unlike many links courses, Trevose is constructed in two distinct loops, the first nine holes hugging the perimeter and wrapping itself around the second inner nine. The effect of this is that the final three holes come as something of a surprise, as the course suddenly turns back to the waiting clubhouse. In a medal, with a good score on your card, this finish must make the nerves jangle. Though not the most scenic part of the course, the last three holes represent a real challenge and were possibly my favourite part of the round. A long par three is followed by a short par four, with a treacherous green guarded by a deep burn, whilst the 18th requires an accurate drive and demands a second draw shot into a narrow slanting putting surface. It's a finish that must have destroyed many promising scores. Unfortunately, my 'Misfit' team failed to land the spoils, though we put in a respectable points tally – without coming to blows. It was time to move on.

As I headed away from Constantine Bay I began to reflect on my time at Trevose. There's a certain snobbery amongst golfing aficionados regarding the merits of Golf and Country Clubs. They stand accused of lacking tradition, of paying only lip service to their membership and in general of providing only mediocre courses. In all honesty, I have often found these accusations to be warranted. Trevose is the exception. The dynastic management seem to have struck exactly the right balance between commercialism, high standards and tradition.

I had enjoyed my visit, played well and felt exhilarated by the experience. By way of celebration, I headed for nearby Padstow and Rick Stein's world-renowned restaurant. Parking up on the quayside (twenty-four-hour payment demanded and access denied to the toilets), I glanced across at the warm glow from the windows of Rick's haute cuisine eatery. This was not my goal. Profligate spending has never been my bag and I strode out towards the moored fishing boats, straining against their ropes in a rising tide. To my right was the real object of my desire, the lights burning in Rick Stein's fish and chip shop. Snow was already in the air and my hands were whitening by the second. I checked the date in my newspaper. It was still March.

I ate well that night, the battered cod teasing every taste bud. Raising a cup of tea to the pleasures of Trevose, I looked out across the estuary. It was almost dark by now but clear enough to make out the mountainous sand dunes on the far riverbank. St Enodoc beckoned.

Recommended Alternatives

Saunton: One of my favourite links in Britain. The sea is only visible from the 1st tee but it is an unadulterated pleasure to play. A must visit, and beautifully presented course.

Royal North Devon: A little trapped in its own traditions but if you want links golf in the raw, definitely worth the trip. The clubhouse is like stepping back in time.

Thurlestone: More down-land than links but the clifftop setting and quality of the course will provide a real test of your swing.

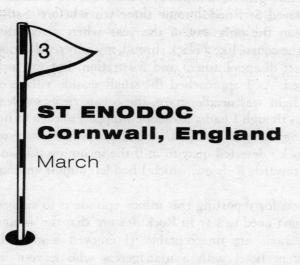

ST ENODOC
Cornwall, England
March

I have loved only three women in my life. One, I met and married (only a fool would leave his wife off such a list); the second was a face across a crowded bookshop (her image captured me from the front cover of a literary novel), and the third (sadly never seen) is the subject of an amorous soldier's poem. My wife will remain nameless but the writer Virginia Woolf and the poetically adored Miss Joan Hunter Dunn will always pluck my emotional strings.

These wistful musings had invaded my thoughts the night before my visit. The confines of a Padstow fish and chip shop rarely have such an effect. But on this particular occasion, I had glanced over the Camel Estuary towards the curvaceous sand dunes of St Enodoc, my mind flooding with unrequited passion. Perhaps the malt vinegar was too strong or the bread too thickly buttered. Whatever the cause, the effect was immediate and I began to scribble a dreadful romantic rhyming couplet onto the paper napkin. The result was a piece of literary genius, destined only for the café's dustbin.

I had played St Enodoc some three years before. Sadly, I had chosen the only day of the year when a sea mist blanketed the course like a black shroud, my only recollection one of abject disappointment and frustration. But my luck had changed. As I approached the small seaside village of Rock, the light was needle sharp, the ocean views so clear that I felt as though I had a telescope strapped to each of my eyes. Passing the golf club entrance, I purposely drove on towards Rock's deserted quay to sniff the incoming tide and stare back towards Padstow, which I had left almost an hour before.

My reason for reporting this minor episode is to suggest that you don't need to stay in Rock. It's not that the various accommodations are unacceptable. (I enjoyed a night in a magnificent hotel with a manageress who let out an extraordinary nasal snort every time she laughed.) But lodge in Padstow and you'll be making the most of your journey to St Enodoc. A small ferry service (£3 return, continuous daily sailings, m'dear) will skim you across the estuary in ten minutes. You will be dropped at the old Rock quay, from where it's a ten-minute stroll up to the golf course or a thirty-minute gasping hike if you haven't brought your trolley. What better way to start and end the day? (Late-evening golf is not recommended, as once it goes dark, the river taxi skipper will probably have taken to his bed with a copy of *Ferry Monthly* and you'll be stuck on the wrong side of the estuary.)

There's something strangely exotic about the entrance to St Enodoc golf course. A narrow lane rises quickly from the equally narrow main village road, the bordering native shrubs interlaced with shock-headed palm trees. The white balconied clubhouse has a colonial feel, sitting high above its golfing plantation. Though not architecturally dramatic, it exudes the sort of understated style reminiscent of its 1930s origins, as if challenging the brashness of the modern era. Given the warm glow of a summer evening, it wouldn't be difficult to imagine bob-haired ladies floating through its portals in long-flowing ball gowns, hanging on the arm of stiff-collared beaus. Yet, despite this slight whiff of empire, it's a building that seems to offer an open invitation to all who come to its door.

Ready to walk the course, I made myself known to the 'authorities'. Expecting a stuffy brigadier, I straightened my shoulders and polished the toecaps of my brogues on the back of my winter corduroys. The secretary rose to greet me.

'Stephen,' he began. 'Have a seat. Coffee?'

He was tanned, immaculately dressed and about as stuffy as a favourite uncle who takes his nephew for his first drink. To add to my surprise, his words were delivered with the natural amiability that accompanies a Southern States accent. Which State, I have no idea, but I'd hazard a guess at Missouri. I make no claim to being an expert on American accents. My assumption is based on the fact that the wonderfully named Tuck Clagett admitted to having grown up with Tom Watson. I was impressed.

It's said that we are never more than three links away from anybody in the world. Barring the odd Aboriginal hermit, I have found this claim to be true. And now I had shaken the hand of a man who had shaken the hand of Tom Watson, who had shaken the hand of Jack Nicklaus, who had shaken the hand of Tiger Woods, etc., etc. I already felt like a better golfer.

It transpired that this genial American had taken a circuitous route to his present position, surfacing from the ski slopes of Colorado to live and work in one of the most enviable places in Britain. As I left for the course, it struck me that this must be a man who could enter a Missouri craps game with his last dollar and leave with a bulging wallet.

I had two reasons for walking St Enodoc's rolling fairways. The first was to clear my misty memory. Having previously witnessed this demanding course in a thick fog, I had little recall of its blind shots, contours or greens. And despite a rooted, agnostic nature, my second motive was to go to church. These two incentives may seem poor bedfellows, but, as I would soon discover, stride across these sublime links, and you will feel that you have been granted a preview of eternal bliss.

Unusually, the opening hole is a par five and should you be fortunate to hit a decent drive, the second shot presents you with the whole of St Enodoc's golfing menu. From here you are treated to a view of the estuary with the ocean beyond, the two guarding headlands shading the sanded bays. If paradise is like this, I don't want to be turned away. I'm going to behave for the rest of my days and volunteer to run an inner-city soup kitchen.

In many ways, the first few holes tell you everything you need to know about the course. The coastal views from tees and greens come in a continual stream of pleasure whilst the use of natural contours begins to develop a familiar theme. I know little about the current winter craze of snowboarding, apart from spending an inordinate amount of time watching my offspring being patched up in hospital casualty departments. Yet, by the time of reaching the 9th hole, it was impossible not to draw comparisons between St Enodoc's topography and the half pipe chutes used by the baggy-trousered 'boarders'. Many of the fairways lay at the base of tunnelled dunes and salty grasses, errant drives climbing the ominous surrounds until gravity returns the ball to the safety of the tight-cut, level ground. I made a mental note to wear my widest trousers for the next day's match and only converse in mid-Atlantic 'boardese'.

Once past the turn, heaven's symbol comes into view. The 10th is a truly wonderful hole, the green only reachable (at least for me) with two well-struck woods. The second shot not only requires length but also draw – the type of shot I only ever achieve through lack of ability and complete good fortune. The thirteenth-century church of St Enodoc nestles to the right of the green, oblivious to the pain or pleasure of the passing golfers. It is a place of unadulterated beauty and tranquillity, its tilted, lemon squeezer spire casting shadows across its incongruous golfing landscape. Many years before, the church had succumbed to nature, buried, like its grave-yard inhabitants, by the wind-blown sands from the nearby shore. For some time, the local vicar was forced to enter his place of work through a trap door in the roof, oddly, the same technique employed by a burglar who once broke into my garage and walked off with my golf clubs. But, by the end of the nineteenth century, the God-fearing parishioners of nearby Rock had thankfully resurrected the church and, to the relief of their roof-scuttling parson, were once again able to use the front door.

To the best of my knowledge, the setting of an active church within the confines of a golf course is unique amongst British links. Because of its isolated position, no tracks or lanes lead to its heavenly gates. Would-be worshippers must cross the course, guided by a series of bleached-white stones, trusting in God that they can avoid a sliced drive or a violently pulled iron. I suspect, however, that the majority of visitors who run the gauntlet of the flying golf balls pass through the wooden lich-gate entrance on a literary rather than religious pilgrimage. Within this sloping graveyard lie the remains of the poet John Betjeman, a man worthy of praise if only for supplying his readers with accessible verse. He must have enjoyed the irony of demanding that his body took its final rest in such an inaccessible place. You can almost hear his wry schoolboy chuckle as the pilgrims trudge across the surrounding fairways and pick their way along the snaking white markers.

St Enodoc Golf Club might also be unique in enjoying the praise of a Poet Laureate. Betjeman's 'Seaside Golf' relates his delight at playing the 13th. Oddly, it's probably the least attractive hole on the course, yet the final lines of his simple verse successfully compress the delights of St Enodoc.

> Lark song and sea sound in the air
> And splendour, splendour, everywhere.

Like Lapsang Souchong, it's not everybody's cup of tea, but Betjeman always seems to pull the three-card trick, hiding his royal talents amongst the plain and common words. It's the very reason I fell in love with Joan Hunter Dunn, the girl who caught the poet's eye at the local tennis match. Who else but Betjeman could construct a simple line like 'The warm handled racket is back in its press' and evoke such a sensual response in a talentless golfer wandering through a graveyard?

I couldn't resist a quick look around the church. Unfortunately, I was wearing golf shoes; the metal spikes an insurance against losing my footing on the treacherous sandy turf. Slipping them off quickly, I placed them neatly at the side of the ancient porch. An aged verger, tending a nearby grave, cast a suspicious eye as I creaked the door open.

My stocking-clad feet stepped silently across the stone-flagged floor and I began to collect brochures I would never read and postcards I would never send. Working my way quickly around the vaulted space, I stopped briefly at the lectern, which supported an old, leather-bound Bible. Glancing at the open page, I hoped to reveal some obscure golf reference, perhaps a passing mention of St Titleist.

The Book of Esdras was to prove a disappointment, the flimsy tissue page revealing no more than a list of good people with unpronounceable names smiting and begetting another lot of bad people with equally indecipherable titles. And it was at this moment that the verger peered round the door, his eyes darting around his territory, tracing the erratic dampened foot marks of my shoeless feet. It was clearly evidence of my ill purpose. His sudden entrance had shocked me and I could feel the blood drain out of my face, the pallor of my skin almost albino in appearance. Instinctively, I tightened my belt, the constriction of leather around my waist offering a strangely satisfying, searing pain. I left quickly, rushing out into the darkening light.

I ate once more on local fish that night, the sole proving my salvation from my hotel's snorting host. With a good night's sleep behind me, I threw back the curtains to reveal yet another Cornish spring blizzard, the distant hills swathed in crusted snow. The chances of taking on St Enodoc seemed lost and I breakfasted in such a morose manner that the waitress almost burst into tears. Yet, just as I buttered my final slice of toast, there was a glimmer of hope. A shaft of sunlight appeared as if from nowhere, the unexpected lustrous beam glinting through the prisms of my marmalade.

Letting out a small grunt of pleasure, I tipped the waitress heavily and headed back to the golf course.

By the time I arrived, I was faced with a bitterly cold day but a Mediterranean sky. Rummaging through my golf bag, I realized I needed a new glove and a bag of my favourite white tee pegs (golfers are notoriously superstitious about these things). Rushing into the professional's shop, I was met by a snoring dog and an equally laid-back professional. I slowed down, immediately respecting and adopting the West Country philosophy of life. Ten minutes later, I had a new glove, a bag of tees and had become the unexpected owner of a brand-new nine wood.

'How did that happen?' I murmured, as I sauntered (with a relaxed Cornish air) to meet my waiting opponent.

The secretary had kindly fixed me up with KG (I respect his privacy), a member who had, with no regrets, moved from London many years before. Fortunately, he was a man of similar handicap and proved to be excellent company. On meeting, he informed me that, due to a poor (and false) weather forecast, a large society had just cancelled their booking. We had the course to ourselves and as I hit my first drive, with the sun now beating onto our faces, I couldn't help but think that the organizer of that absent society must now be chewing his head covers.

Armed with the knowledge of my pre-round inspection, I began well, using the contours to employ my half pipe snowboarding technique. By the time we left the 5th green I was two up and coasting. Naturally, and like the majority of mid-handicap idiots, I thought it was time to relax. You could almost see KG's eyes sparkle.

On the front nine, the 6th hole deserves a more detailed mention. It is here that you are faced with a blind second shot to a sheltered bowl of a green, only successful if you have carried the giant Himalaya Bunker. It is, without doubt, the steepest and biggest sand trap I have ever encountered. I'm no quantity surveyor, but I'd guess that there's enough sand in that hazard to keep the world's fastest bricklayer in raw materials for the next ten years. Luckily, I avoided its waiting jaws but should you ever find yourself in this mountainous trap, don't go in there without a Tibetan Sherpa.

For those who are fortunate enough to play St Enodoc regularly, I would guess that the six holes that circle the church (isolated on a thin spur at the north end of the course) would be seen, at least in relative terms, as the least attractive section of the eighteen holes. The rest of the course is far more wild and rugged, teasing you with unseen hazards, clinging wiry rough and steep-faced bunkers. Yet the gentler church section provides the more enquiring, occasional visitor with many of St Enodoc's hidden treasures. Betjeman's grave and poetic legacy are only part of its story.

From this area you are given sight of Doom Bar at the mouth of the estuary, a treacherous sandbank, which has seen many ships founder on its concealed barricade. The 12th hole has been the scene of courageous golfers interrupting their game to dive into the waves of Daymer Bay and pull survivors out of the fast-flowing currents; of rocket lines being fired to fishing vessels listing in the frequent winter storms. And standing guard over the churchyard and the surrounding buried heroism is Brae Hill, a dark, half-wooded knoll. I might have passed it by until my partner (sadly, about to square our match) pointed to its summit. A group of muffled walkers had gathered at the top, their unheard voices signalled by their frosted breath.

I was told that this is not an uncommon sight as you stand on the 11th tee. Year after year, poetry pilgrims trudge to the top of Brae Hill and pay homage to English bards. I imagined them chanting in unison as though summoned by the bells of St Enodoc, peering over the famous 13th and echoing Betjeman's words:

> *How straight it flew, how long it flew,*
> *It cleared the rutted track*
> *And soaring, disappeared from view*
> *Beyond the bunker's back.*

If they had seen me hit my own drive off the 13th, they would have ditched Betjeman and moved on to a dreary piece of Dryden. I was losing concentration, my mind wandering with thoughts of chanting poetry buffs and tales of heroic derring-do. It wasn't long before I found myself one down to KG with the holes running out. I steeled myself for the finish.

The 15th proved to be the gateway to the final holes and it felt as if we were re-entering the promised land of the true St Enodoc. This short but delightful par three seems incongruous to the natural links of the rest of the course. It appears suddenly, as if discovering a small oasis of calm in a desert sand storm. The tee shot requires a precise iron to a raised bunker-guarded green, the ball needing to climb high over a waiting, stream-fed lake. Once putting, you gain a sight of the finishing 'stretch' and realize that crossing the stream over the picturesque dry-stone bridge is akin to rowing across the Styx on your journey to an exquisite Hades.

Though I finished strongly, KG had done his job and we exchanged handshakes on the 17th. And to celebrate his victory, I was invited to take my final drive from the 'tiger tee', high above the narrow fairway. The disappointment of my loss disappeared the moment I climbed onto the raised grass platform. From here you are treated to a 360 degree view of your surroundings; to the south, the metal-spanned bridge over the Camel River; Padstow, shaded by the clawed headland of Stepper Point, and Daymer Bay, welcoming the incoming tide. To the north lies the full panorama of St Enodoc, the treacherous rolling land, which has given you so much but has probably destroyed the bubbling optimism of the 1st tee.

In the traditional manner, I paid my losses with a beer and a sandwich and was pleased to find that the interior of the clubhouse had managed to avoid the colonial feel of its mildly austere exterior. Instead, I was met with a surprisingly cosy and informal atmosphere, and staff who uniformly confirmed the overall sense of welcome. A table of twelve male members (a tricky term to use) sat close by, discussing the merits of each other's recent game. The night before, I had sat in the hotel bar skimming St Enodoc's Centenary History. It contained a description of the club's membership, which included (amongst many others) 'two a penny' headmasters; a bomb disposal expert; barristers and crooks; surgeons galore and, delightfully, a winner of a 'Spot the Ball' competition. Even more strange was a claim to have a 'spy' in their midst. He can't have been much of a secret agent if they knew he existed.

I looked for signs of the spy's presence amongst the twelve members at the adjacent table. There wasn't a hint of a false moustache amongst them and I think the elderly man with a copy of *Teach Yourself Morse Code* sticking out of his back pocket was just trying to tease me.

But it was their earnest conversation that really caught my attention. They spoke of the exasperation of shanking a chip to the green, the misery of missing a 2-foot putt, the embarrassment of slicing high and wide of a broad fairway. It's the stuff of all golfers' chatter, often delivered by high-ranking professional men whose actions had decided the fate of lesser mortals. Put a golf ball on a tee and even a prince is transformed into a golfing pauper, where nothing is so important as making a par to win the match.

Inevitably, my thoughts returned to Betjeman. In his slightly patronizing introduction to *The History of St Enodoc Golf Club* (which he terms a 'delightful little book') he perceptively talks of crickets chirruping, indifferent to the missed drive and of sheep who look on passively as a headmaster struggles to get out of a bunker. And, of course, the old Poet Laureate was right. In the grand scheme of things, golf really doesn't matter a jot and nature must chuckle at the importance it holds in a player's life. Chirruping crickets and passive sheep are far more interested in survival than worrying about maintaining their handicap.

Yet, I suspect, Betjeman's philosophy only proves that (as he was happy to admit) he wasn't 'much of a golfer'. It's a game that transports you to another world the very moment you tie the laces on your polished spiked shoes; a mythical land of absurd illusion and hope, where the rules of everyday life are suspended until the final putt. Like my futile adoration of Virginia Woolf and Miss Joan Hunter Dunn, it's a game of fantasy, played out in idyllic settings. If St Enodoc had been a woman, there would be a new name added to my lovelorn list.

Recommended Alternatives

Saunton; Royal North Devon; Thurlestone. (See end of chapter 2, pages 53-54)

NEFYN
North Wales

March

There are certain small passages in life which, when taken together, present you with a taste of the future. At the time, these seemingly incidental, isolated moments have little meaning, yet they soon evolve into jigsaw vignettes, gradually revealing the larger picture. Not until I struck my first drive at Nefyn did I begin to understand the symbolic nature of the day's events. The ball sailed high into the distance, a perfect shot framed by the blue waters of Caernarfon Bay.

'That'll do,' pronounced my playing partner, as I stood back in self-admiration but damned by his faint praise.

The opening hole is 450 yards and requires a second, accurate full shot to the green. With the ground running away and the breeze over my right shoulder, a four iron soon nestled in my hand. I puffed, I blew, then steadied myself over the shot. Like my drive, it sailed high and true, nestling at the back of the green and no more than 20 feet from the waiting pin. Though surprised by this uncharacteristic display of ability (I'm a notoriously inept iron player), I retained an air of calm and quiet satisfaction. I glanced at my partner, hoping for a glimmer of veneration.

'Nice shot,' he shouted from the other side of the fairway.

I smiled my acknowledgement.

'What were you aiming at?' he added quickly as he walked towards me.

'Aiming at?'

'Good shot, wrong flag,' he declared. 'You've just hit the eighth green.'

So there it was. The picture was formed. A culmination of strange, minor occurrences, which, at the time, hardly seemed worthy of note. Yet all the clues had been there, all the evidence that my short stay in Nefyn was to be submerged in a soup of madness.

The insanity had started at Chester. And then Oswestry. And then Chester. And then Oswestry. And then Chester once more. It will be clear (or not) from this graphic description, that having battled up the M6 motorway for nearly five hours, I then began an exhausting circular tour of the Welsh borders, as if trapped in a tarmac maze that seemed determined to keep me in England. I can only assume that the bewildering road signs were designed by an idiot or that it's a cruel but cunning strategy aimed at imprisoning travellers in Cheshire to boost the flagging tourist industry. At one point, I became so frustrated that I began to place identifying chalk marks on trees, hoping that it might help me to avoid being trapped in Oswestry for eternity.

If I had been carrying a 30-mile ball of string, I think I may have broken out earlier, but it was an hour before I finally breached the defensive wall and found myself, unintentionally, heading through the stunningly beautiful Snowdonia National Park or Parc Cenedlaethol Eryri. Should you ever find yourself in the position of an Oswestry refugee, you'll know you're safe when the garage petrol attendants speak to you in Welsh. Thankfully and delightfully, North Wales is the heartland of the endangered Celtic language and when all hope appears lost, the Welsh melodic tongue is music to the despairing soul.

My Welsh education began as I pumped what seemed to be the equivalent of the annual Saudi Arabian oil stock into my thirsty car.

'Do you know the quickest way to Nefyn?' I asked.

'Nefyn?' quizzed the genial attendant.

Oh God! I thought.

'You mean Nevin?' he sung.

Being a quick-witted pupil, I soon realized that the Welsh language does not recognize 'f' as a 'ph' as in the 'English *philistine*'. Nefyn is not Nefyn as in *'effing prat'* but Nevin as in *'verisimilitude'* or *'va va voom'*. If Nefyn were Nephyn it would be spelt Neffin. The ffriendly garage attendant must hafe thought I was an *'eving* idiot', or something of that description.

I was feeling quite bilingual as I pulled out onto the road and headed for the coast. An hour later, Nefyn welcomed me with open petals. It had been a long, cold, dreary winter and though already almost April, not one English daffodil had dared to brave the icy eastern winds. Nefyn & District Golf Club (as it is more properly known) had a treat in store. Perhaps they've just got braver flowers in Wales but whatever the reason, bright yellow blooms danced on the air, waving their greeting from the borders of the long track that led up to the waiting clubhouse. Even the car park was flanked by open fields, the frost-bitten winter pastures providing a playground for week-old prancing lambs. It was a sight that raised my emotions, excited my poetic bent and stirred my gastric juices. But it proved only to be an interlude of sanity before hints of madness returned once more.

At first sight, the old clubhouse looked as tired as a man who had circled Oswestry for two hours. Desperate to find the gentleman's convenience (not an uncommon bladder panic after a stress-ridden drive), I went in search of relief. Unfortunately, I was unable to access the interior of the clubhouse due to a proliferation of locks with secret codes. With a sense of growing urgency, I queried the nearest passerby.

'Gents?' I pleaded.

Employing such brevity in my request almost proved my undoing. The response was clearly helpful, friendly, welcoming, understanding. It was also delivered in Welsh. And before I could stress the gravity of the situation, my intended saviour had turned the corner and disappeared from view. Fortunately, his accompanying hand gestures had been delivered in universal sign language and within seconds I had located the bright blue unisex port-a-loo.

But just as I approached the relieving door, I heard the crunch of golf-spiked shoes. Employing the side step of a Welsh fly half, the woman swept past me, grabbed the door handle and slipped inside. I only caught a glimpse of her face but I clearly remember her pallid skin and windswept hair.

Now in crisis, but assuming the woman had a distressing bowel problem, I waited patiently, hopping from one foot to the other, pacing up and down and even, at one stage, chanting a calming mantra. Seconds passed. Minutes passed. Still the door remained closed. It wasn't looking good. But just at the point of no return, she reappeared in a haze of perfume, her image miraculously transformed into a bronze-faced, highly coiffeured, ageing Hollywood starlet. I rushed forward, half expecting to be met with a fully staffed beauty parlour and with a faint hope that I would reappear as a George Clooney clone.

Disappointed, still dishevelled, but a little more composed, I went in search of the secretary. My finest golfing sweater seemed to have absorbed the highly scented interior of the port-a-loo beauty parlour and I knocked warily on the door. He must have had a poor sense of smell, as a delightfully loquacious man met me without any hint of suspicion. He was also extremely bright, as he had managed to secure his office on the top floor of the clubhouse with probably one of finest views of any British golf course. As our conversation unravelled, madness returned once more.

'Which course would you like to play?' he asked.

'Er, Nefyn,' I replied naively.

'But you have a choice.' He smiled, before beginning his explanation.

With the ever-growing interest in golf, it is not uncommon for many clubs to find a bit of land and build an extra nine holes. This takes the weight off a single, eighteen-hole course, by offering any combination of two of the three nine-hole circuits, which, for the sake of clarity, could be termed A, B and C. This means you have access to any of three combinations, namely, AB, AC, BC. (If you are tiring at this point or losing concentration, take a break for a heavily sugared cup of tea.) In total, therefore, there are twenty-seven available holes. In a bizarre version of this scheme, Nefyn possesses twenty-six holes in which all play the first ten and then choose whether to take on the final eight holes on the 'old' or 'new' course. It reminded me of Woolworths' well-established *Pick and Mix* sweet counter.

'What's the difference?' I asked.

'Between the old and the new?' smiled the secretary. 'Easy.

God made the old course and we made the new. The old course is pretty but we don't think God was a golfer.'

It could have been the response of a Welsh bard and his lyrical description soon had me warming to the links of Nefyn but puzzled by the detail. Feeling more confused than an illiterate fourteen-year-old attempting a *Times* crossword, I decided to search out a course planner in preparation to walk the course. But, just as I was leaving, the office phone sprang into life and I waited as the call was answered.

'No bookings,' sang the secretary. 'First tee free until four o'clock.'

There was another muffled question.

'Bit dull and cold. But dry,' he added. 'Just a gentle breeze.'

A howling gale almost took me off my feet as I walked out into the sort of temperature that would put a smile on a polar bear's greasy lips. It's well known that if a country yokel tells you it's about a mile to the nearest pub then you are probably facing a two-hour hike. Links golf weather forecasters share a similar ability to subvert the truth. Any conditions that barely allow you to avoid frostbite, drowning or being blown over a cliff edge are likely to be described as 'fine golfing weather'. The secretary had proved himself a man who shared my sentiments. Determined to play the traditional old course on the next day and with my fingers numbing in the easterly wind, I limited my initial investigative foray to the eight new holes.

And, in truth, I found them a little disappointing. They were well constructed, well designed, cleverly bunkered and in admirable condition but, like the weather, a little dull. The main drawback was that they had become detached from the nearby seascape and hazardous cliffs. As I returned to the clubhouse, I looked out towards the spit of land that supports the final holes of the old course. This was the real Nefyn and as darkness began to sweep over the rolling links, I knew where I belonged.

A strangely bizarre day was building to a crescendo and it came as little surprise that the owner of my small hotel turned out to be a young French woman with a touch of delicious *je ne sais quoi*, married (I presume) to an ex-Welsh racing driver who had reinvented himself as a chef.

Nefyn itself proved pleasant enough but did have the feel of a one-sheep town. Waylaying a local resident in the street, I enquired about local restaurants and was immediately directed to Pwllheli, some seven miles to the south. As a result of this brief encounter, I ate in the hotel that night and, as you'd expect from an ex-racing driver, the meal came very quickly. Refuelled by a large Scotch and Welsh lamb, I took an early night and dreamed of the waiting old course.

I rarely sleep for more than five or six hours in unfamiliar beds and I woke early to a bright sunlit day, the first signs of spring shrugging off its winter blanket.

My breakfast came even faster than my dinner, the *œufs au bacon* delivered with a Gallic giggle, the rashers and sunny eggs arranged as a smiley face.

'To celebrate spring,' she laughed as the plate hit the table.

I was suddenly in very good spirits and even better when I arrived back at the course to be presented with a cloudless sky and a truly gentle breeze. It was only minutes before the secretary introduced my volunteer opponent, an immaculate octogenarian, decked out in the finest pair of plus-fours I've seen since the late Payne Stewart graced the fairways. Though I only had to give him five shots, I knew I was in trouble the moment his vice-like grip gave me the handshake of a twenty-year-old body builder. Clearly a past winner of a Fernando Rey look-alike competition (think *The French Connection*), he had a steely competitive manner and a strong Yorkshire accent. As I'm a man with Lancastrian roots, there would be no quarter given.

My prophecy was fulfilled by the time we turned towards the last eight holes of 'the Point' and, despite playing fairly well, I was already four down. The first ten holes had taken us out to the west, the majority of tight fairways hugging the rugged clifftops above Caernarfon Bay, the deep waters swallowing two brand-new golf balls without the slightest hint of apology. It's treacherous stuff and if you've got any tendency to fade your shots, it's worth playing the first four holes with the cheapest balls in your bag.

But my driving grew in strength and distance, only to be met with variations of the praise I had received on the very first hole. 'That'll do' was followed by 'That'll be all right' succeeded by 'That'll be OK' and finally, following a searing drive which bisected the fairway, a congratulatory 'Aye'. He was proving to be the master of understatement and with every successive shot, I hit the ball harder and harder, determined to gain his admiration. It was a strategy destined to prove my undoing.

You may well conclude from this description that I was not enamoured by my opponent's company. Nothing could be further from the truth. He proved a delight to play with and his seemingly terse comments were always delivered with a twinkle in his youthful eyes. It suggested an attitude to the game of golf that all amateurs would do well to adopt. We all like to win, but in the end, and in relative terms, it's just a hill of beans. And I had to face the truth. The man had my measure.

The 5th hole deserves a special mention. A short, fairly nondescript par three is transformed into a thing of beauty by the demands of the shot to the green. The long narrow tee juts out on no more than a ledge-like spit, the sea raging against the surrounding rocks more than 60 feet below. As we walked forward, I was told that many years before, a visiting golfer, new to the course and playing my opponent in an important club competition, had appeared nervous as he strode onto the waiting tee. Mumbling something about chronic vertigo, he had suddenly run for the safety of a nearby fairway, refused to take his shot and conceded the hole. Despite being only one down at the time, he found the experience so disturbing that by the time they reached the 11th he was forced to concede the whole match.

Latching quickly onto the opportunity (I was already two down), I waited until my opponent was ready to strike and posed a polite, caring question.

'Dizzy?' I asked.

'Steady as a rock,' he replied, simultaneously firing his shot into the centre of the waiting green.

'Bugger,' I mumbled, as my own ball buried itself deep into a greenside bunker. Resisting the urge to throw myself over the cliff edge, I strode on towards the old course finish.

I have a strong piece of advice for anyone who encounters the eight peninsula holes for the first time: buy yourself a set of horse blinkers, place on your head (as best you can), and do not remove until your final putt on the 18th green. What you are about to face when you stand on the 11th tee requires extreme measures and there will be no need to feel embarrassed by your rather strange, equine appearance. You will be embarking on Nefyn's barking schizophrenia, and will be given confirming evidence of the course's split personality. You will be striding into madness.

Why the horse blinkers? Without them, four down at the 11th is a guarantee of looming defeat. With them strapped around your ears, you may just have a small chance. The problem that lies ahead is not the minuscule greens, the rising ground, the blind shots or the tight narrow fairways. That is the easy bit. Your biggest enemy comes from the barrage of breathtaking beauty that accompanies your every step around what the members call 'The Point'. American visitors have been heard to declare that it out-pebbles Pebble Beach and deserves sainthood more than St Andrews.

Whether you accept their point about The Point, there is no argument that without restricting your vision, your concentration will fall to zero. But it's probably a price worth paying. Playing badly, but giving yourself time to absorb the surroundings, is always preferable to hitting eight straight pars and missing the enveloping natural beauty. Nowhere is this better seen than on the 14th tee, which nestles on high ground below the now disused coast guard station. The clear deep waters wrap themselves around the whole peninsula, seals preen themselves on wave-washed rocks whilst cormorants dive from the clifftops. To the north are golden beaches guarded by the nearby Rival Mountains and in the far distance the snow-capped summit of Snowdon glints its superior height. And despite the old peninsula course lying high above the bay, the sea still fights to reclaim its former possession. The 16th (The Pot) is a long par three, guarded not only by bunkers but by a giant pit whose eerie base disappears into the granite cliffs. When the tide is high, the sea is forced upwards as though a giant beached whale is blowing its final breath.

And it was here, amongst whales and seals and looming rocks, that I finally offered my companion a hand of congratulation. Another two brand-new balls had disappeared into the foaming sea. I had lost the will to play golf. It had become an interruption to my pleasure, a hindrance to the privilege of being cocooned in nature. Emotional? You bet I was. I doubt I had felt such undiluted satisfaction since an old curmudgeonly boss of mine sneezed in a meeting and shot his false teeth across the boardroom table.

We wandered back amiably along the clifftops, the wind freshening as the clubhouse came back into view. The Ty Coch Inn, which lies in an isolated cove below the 16th green, tried to tempt me to its door. But I had to resist. South Wales beckoned and I could manage no more than a hurried lunch of Welsh broth and a quick return to the still scented port-a-loo. The secretary came to join us.

'You were wrong,' I said accusingly.

'Wrong?' he replied.

'About God. About God and the old course,' I answered. 'God *must* be a golfer. Only someone playing off single figures could design anything as good as that.'

Offering a final word of thanks, I jumped back in my car. Recollections of my visit flashed into my mind, as I turned onto the road for Pwllheli. Oswestry mazes, French hoteliers, smiling breakfasts, Welsh racing drivers, the octogenarian Yorkshireman, lyrical secretaries and a sublime but eccentric golf course. It had been madness from start to finish but a gift of lunacy wrapped in a parcel of pleasure. What more could a golfer want?

Awr iach, golgfeydd. Mae'n hynod o brydferth. (Believe me, that's an unreserved Celtic compliment.)

Recommended Alternatives

Conwy: A bit flat for my liking but stunning views and a good challenge. Gorse over the final 'stretch' makes for a very challenging finish.

Royal St David's: Dunes, castles, sandhills in every direction. If you think the front nine is tough, wait till you turn for home. It gets far worse, but all the better for it.

Holyhead: If you fancy the short trip to the Isle of Anglesey, it's worth the effort. Tricky fairways, rocks and ball-clinging heather make it a true test.

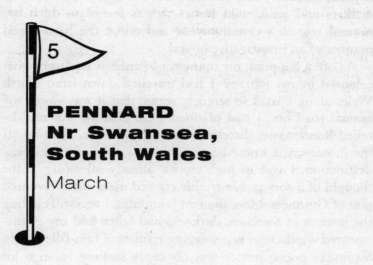

PENNARD
Nr Swansea,
South Wales
March

It's often claimed that when we meet someone for the first time, our assessment of their worth and compatibility is formed within no more than five seconds. It's also suggested that we are invariably right in the conclusions we draw. My own experience only confirms the theory and suggests that it has far more credence than you would expect to find amongst the modern plethora of glossy magazine psychobabble. The moment I arrived at Pennard, I drew my five-second conclusion. Twenty-four hours later, I had blown the theory out of the water. It might work in the frenzied atmosphere of a speed-dating evening or the nail-biting confines of a job interview, but a links golf course needs a far more intimate examination.

What did become immediately clear, however, is that Pennard cannot be described or understood in the simple terms of greens and fairways, clubhouse and facilities. It is, instead, a country tale of commoners and cattle; wandering walkers and wild, wild horses. I was forced to ditch my normal role as a casual voyeur and adopt the hard-edged manner of an investigative hound.

As often happens, my opinion of Pennard was somewhat coloured by my journey. I had travelled down from North Wales along a road so serenely scenic that it was worth my annual road tax. I had planned well, printing out my detailed Routemaster directions some days before. Turning off the motorway, I knew I was within twenty minutes of my destination. I was in high spirits, already salivating at the thought of a cosy pub, a freshly cooked meal and a favoured pint of Guinness. More than an hour later, I was still circling the interior of Swansea, darkness had fallen and my grime-smeared windscreen was weeping rivulets of rain-filled tears. Swansea's poetic justice was obviously seeking revenge for some unknown misdemeanour.

Frustrated, exhausted and quietly cursing, I pulled up at the side of the road, the only person in sight a crumpled, hooded, bearded figure. Reason dies in the face of exasperation and I rolled down the window.

'Any idea how I get to Pennard?' I asked with an anxious smile.

He mumbled something about mumbling and I repeated my question.

'Mumbles,' he insisted. 'If you want Pennard you want Mumbles.'

He was obviously a village idiot lost in the city and I began to close the rain-spattered window. Suddenly, a wiry hand thrust itself onto the closing glass. My mind exploded with the sound of shrieking, scraping, Hitchcockian violins.

'You'll never find it in this weather,' he shouted. 'I might as well jump in and show you the way.'

Madness overtook me and I decided to trust the five-second personality assessment test. He passed. I opened the door. I prayed, and then drove off into the night, checking my wallet was still in my back pocket.

The fact that I am able to relate this tale of Pennard confirms that my body was not found floating in Swansea Bay the following morning. I survived and, as luck would have it, my tramp-like passenger managed to renew my ever-flagging faith in humanity. Despite being transported more than a mile from his original position he seemed quite content to walk all the way back.

'I was only out to buy a loaf of bread,' he smiled as he left the car, dismissing my effusive thanks. 'Nothing else to do really.'

I can only think that he was a founder member of the Swansea Joy Riders and Loaf Buyers Association, but whoever he was, he proved to be a thoroughly decent man. The hint of a personal hygiene problem was not enough to dull my gratitude.

The mumbled Mumbles turned out to be a small coastal town only five minutes south of Pennard and less than three minutes from my waiting hotel. I'm told the locals still think of it as a village, but despite its charm, it's big enough to be heaving with ritzy restaurants and a few dubious slot-machine arcades. Whatever its status (be it brash seaside resort or a fine dining oasis), it appears to be a gateway to the glorious sea-washed Gower Peninsula. Even in my manic state, I swore this rugged coastline would one day feel the heavy step of my well-worn hiking boots.

Despite knowing that I was close to my lodgings, it took me another half hour to locate the hotel. The hostelry proved to be down a steep unlit track and required the skills of a bloodhound to finally approach its door. I was met amiably, but with words I had no wish to hear.

'Sorry. Chef's night off.'

I dined on a large Scotch, a packet of plain crisps, a thirst-inducing bag of salted peanuts and stumbled wearily upstairs. My eyes closed quickly but I stayed awake long enough to hear that my precious, relegation-doomed football team had gained a valuable three points away from home. A contented smile guided me to welcome oblivion.

The morning paper lay on the breakfast table as I entered the echoing dining room. Only one place had been set and it was clear that I was the only guest in the hotel. At my side was a miniature Hammond organ and I prayed that, like the chef, the organist was having a day off. The thought of munching toast and being serenaded by a reluctant pianist singing 'My, My, My Delilah' filled me with horror. I reached for the newspaper and turned to the sports section. One glance and I knew I had slept under a duvet and false pretences. The myopic sports presenter had read the football scores incorrectly and my team had plunged to the bottom of the league.

As I drove into Pennard Golf Club my teeth couldn't have been more gritted than if I'd peppered my breakfast with course grain sand. My mood was black, my pen sharp, my mind geared for negative critical appraisal. And it was bitterly cold, an icy gale bending the flags almost double, the grey, cloud-filled skies taking all definition out of the contoured sandy fairways. Standing by the red-brick clubhouse I glanced in every direction. There was no sign of a coastline, no evidence of the sea. I made yet another five-second assessment. I hated Pennard.

Quickly changing into my golf shoes, two sweaters, rain trousers, waterproof top, woollen hat, thermal gloves and knitted scarf, I prepared for my walk around the course. Like the tide I had yet to see, I was at a very low ebb. Fortunately, as an old music hall comic might say, I was grabbed by the Diddlies. My notebook and I were suddenly invited to accompany a three-ball, who were just about to strike their balls from the 1st tee. Curiously, one was a retired doctor, another a local baker and the third member seemed reticent to reveal his occupation. I made a note that he was probably an itinerant candlestick maker and that I had been caught up in a bizarre nursery rhyme.

They all proved to be reasonable golfers and, given the severe conditions, quickly gained my admiration. The course seemed long and treacherous, the greens capricious, the putts unmakeable. On one occasion the wind had reached such a level that the good doctor's putt horseshoed round the hole and was then blown back, 2 yards beyond his feet.

The sea finally came in sight at the 6th but, though whipped into an angry rage, it seemed distant and melancholic. Even the ruined castle at the edge of the 7th fairway looked as though it would have preferred to be back in the twelfth century. I was in good company but depressed by the un-seasonable winter winds and the seemingly featureless course. I strode on, notebook in numbing hands, sure that when my turn came the next day, I would not enjoy the experience. I was filled with foreboding and if sixboding was a recognized condition, I surely had it at that moment.

Kindly, my three companions invited me for a drink and it was during the resulting conversation that the secret of the Diddlies was revealed. This is Pennard's expression for the well-established weekly 'roll-up' and a term that, despite my persistent questioning, appears to have no known derivation. I can only guess that as my own course has a similar society known as the 'Swindle', the term Diddlies has its roots in the term 'diddle' or 'cheat' . . . an unusual choice for a game, that rightly prides itself on unquestionable honesty.

On my way out, the secretary, a thoroughly likeable man

who seemed as cuddly as my late teddy bear (who met his end in very suspicious circumstances), informed me of the next day's arrangements. Three members, including the doctor, had volunteered to make up a four-ball and would be on the tee at 9 a.m. I tried my best to look enthusiastic and hurried to the car.

Just in case the hotel organist decided to show up, I ate in the local pub. Things didn't really improve. The food was acceptable but, as is the danger when a lone stranger comes to town, I was cornered by a local storyteller, a man intent on telling me his rather mundane, beer-breathed life story. Assuming I was hard of hearing, he told me his life story again and then once more for luck. I consumed my supper far quicker than my body would allow and just to finish the dispiriting day, spent half the night with chronic indigestion.

In fairy tales, I would wake to a sun-kissed morning and full of the joys of spring. But life is rarely so kind. Instead, I was revived by the sound of giant raindrops hitting the hotel roof with the power of a machine gun. It might have been March but there was no sign of spring in my step. Another solitary breakfast was taken in the thankfully organist-free zone and, taking a deep breath, I returned to the waiting torment of Pennard.

I was immediately met by the doctor who, offering his apologies, said that the weather was so bad he would have to pull out of the four-ball. At a guess, he was probably frightened of catching pneumonia and didn't trust his own physician. But I didn't blame him. The rain was now of such intensity that no known man-made fabric was going to save me from being turned into a wet sponge. I was even tempted to ask the reluctant doctor for a bottle of antidepressants but lost my nerve at the final moment.

'Up for it then?' came a voice at my side.

It was delivered with a strong Yorkshire accent and accompanied by an even stronger handshake.

'Just three of us then,' he added in a jovial manner that failed to match the storm-filled skies. 'Drop of rain. We'll be all right. Let's go for it.'

I doubted if the threat of a nuclear holocaust would keep this man off the golf course and I hurriedly donned my wet-weather gear.

Two very strange things happened in the next ten minutes. Though trussed up like a pre-packed turkey, I hit my opening drive straight down the middle of the fairway and my second iron shot into the heart of the green. And then, as I prepared to putt, the rain suddenly stopped. By the time we reached the next tee the wind dropped, the temperature rose and the sun broke through the leaden skies. The 3rd hole is called 'President'. They should rename it 'The Road to Damascus'. I looked across the waiting links only to realize that I was in the middle of a stunning, challenging golf course, edged by golden gorse and cliff-topped seas. My five-second theory was in tatters. I had been fooled by appearances. I had become a believer.

There were two major concerns preying on my mind before we began our round. The first was that I was to play with a Yorkshire man and, what's more, a Yorkshire man who, I was informed, had spent his life in PVC. I'm no puritan, but my sexual tendencies have rarely strayed from the straight and narrow. (Admittedly, there was one occasion when I played a Barbra Streisand record, but that's about as far as it goes.) The fact that he appeared on the tee in a highly respectable Gortex rain suit came as something of a relief.

My second concern was that the other member of our trio was the head greenkeeper. Given my impressions of the previous day, I felt I was destined to spend eighteen holes lying through my heavily gritted teeth. As I was about to discover, there would be no call for mendacity. The fairy tale was coming to life.

In the space of twenty-four hours Pennard had transformed itself from the dampened, truculent ugly duckling to the graceful swan gliding through the natural terrain of the Gower Peninsula. As all good links should do, its fairways follow the inherited undulations of the land, the greens built on the given layers and folds of their deep clay base. And it was these greens that finally won me over to the glories of Pennard. They share the salt-worn look of many links courses but have the borrows of Augusta and the speed of Nairn and Trevose. But more than any other feature, they are universally well designed, their bowl-like construction gathering the ball onto the tight-mown surfaces.

The developing course shifts easily through its gears, accelerating towards a middle section that is visually stunning and thrilling to play. Though not necessarily my favourite on the course, the 7th or 'Castle' hole, might be termed its flagship and, it is said, the cradle of the course. The drive requires an accurate shot between both the ruins of the thirteenth-century church and the equally ancient remains of Pennard castle. The history of this small Saxon outpost is lost in time but is noted as a fine example of inept medieval design. Whichever architect put pen to parchment, he managed to have the arrow slits facing in the wrong direction. With skills like that, he was clearly a man ahead of his time and could have made a fortune building twenty-first-century housing estates.

But it is here that the fairy tale (or tales of a bunch of fairies known as the Tylwyth Teg) went into folklore. It is said that on (as always) one dark and stormy night, a young woman begged shelter in the castle. Denied access by the inevitable wicked Baron, she cast a spell on his family and persuaded the Tylwyth Teg to do her dirty work. As in all good fables, the wind blew for a year and a day and buried the church and castle in a mountain of sand blown over from Ireland. If the old Baron had been a little more politically correct, he could have avoided the curse by building a wine bar with velveteen seating and Guinness on tap. Though the 'sand fairy' (as she became known) had her revenge, she also (unknowingly) created a golf course. Who needs James Braid or Old Tom Morris when you've got your own fairy?

The positioning of Pennard castle came, as estate agents would say, with a lovely aspect but, I suspect, with no en suite, fitted kitchens or double garage. What it gave those nervous, thirteenth-century Norman warriors was a panoramic view of Three Cliffs Bay and an early warning of having their dinner disturbed by face-painted Saxons or my ancestral hairy Vikings. Fortunately, my pillaging gene has been well diluted over successive generations and the locals had no need to fear my presence.

What this area of the course supplies for the golfer is one of the finest vistas in British golf. The sands of Oxwich Bay lay in the distance, washed by the surging tides of the Bristol Channel, whilst the high sharp lines of Three Cliffs towered over the rocks below. Like many seaside courses, it's hard to keep your concentration, but the sanded hummocks and dunes grow in severity from this point and will make you pay for a wandering mind.

I concentrated hard as, to my surprise, I was holding my own against two very competent golfers. As those who have faced me in competition will know, show me a lark rising in the sky, a woodpecker flashing across a green or a wave crashing onto the shoreline and I immediately become a spent force. (If I find that anyone has read this admission and asks me to play for money, they will be met with a blunt refusal.)

By the 10th I still had every chance of taking the money. Though Pennard members may not agree, this was one of my favourite holes. The drive must be carefully placed on a narrow strip of land held between impenetrable rough and a crossing stream. The second requires a shot to the base of a heavily bunkered raised green and a final delicate shot onto the putting surface. A kestrel hovered in the sky. My third shot hovered over the green only to disappear in the bunker. I shook my fist at the bird but marvelled at its flight. The dangers of my poetic nature could not be contained.

I finally crumpled on the wonderful 17th. Three grazing cows peered at me from the nearby rough and in the distance two wild horses, showing no regard for etiquette, galloped across the 16th fairway. It was all too much and though my fourth putt was a good one, it was time to concede defeat. It was also time to raise the matter of commoners and cattle, wandering walkers and wild, wild horses. As a guest of a club, you soon learn to be aware of the boundaries of conversation. In my brief chat with the Diddlies, every time the word 'cow' or 'horse' entered the conversation, I sensed a certain frisson of unease. The game now over, I challenged my two companions to reveal the story.

It seems that rights of access and grazing have been a thorn in the side of members and local residents since time immemorial. Detail is unnecessary, but as the tale was recounted, it seemed reminiscent of a Wild West range war in which disputed pasture led to some bad blood and an increase in the population of Boot Hill. In essence, the commoners of Pennard claim an ancient right to grazing, walking and equine freedom. The committee or council of Pennard Golf Club beg to differ, especially as, for many years, they were forced to surround their greens with electric fencing. I only wish I'd been there when I was twelve years old. At the time, our favourite hobbies were running away from charging heifers and daring each other to stick our tongues on battery-fed wires.

'So why no fences now?' I asked innocently.

'Took them down,' came the reply. 'We realized the greens had been cut so short, the animals weren't interested.'

It seemed a pity that the youth of Pennard had been denied my electrifying, childish pleasures.

We had lunch soon after, a delicious and freshly prepared plate of beer-batter cod. I let the prickly question of grazing rights fade back into history and treated my playing partners to my extensive knowledge of fish and chip suppers. I could see them glazing over as I spoke and quickly bade them farewell. On the way out, I popped into the pro's shop.

'Enjoy it?' I was asked.

'Enjoy it?' I responded. 'Loved it. Loved every minute of it.'

'Thought you would,' answered the professional knowingly.

He was a knowledgeable man and one of the most genial professional golfers I had ever encountered. I suspect he had put me to his own five-second assessment test when I first walked into his shop. He had seen the apprehension in my eyes, noticed the reluctance with which I wandered onto that 1st tee. He knew I would come back with a new perspective on the glories of Pennard . . . and he was right. Halfway across the Bristol suspension bridge, I realized I had left my golf shoes in the changing room. They say it's a sign you want to return. They were right about that, too.

Recommended Alternatives

Royal Porthcawl: Tough and pricey classic links but pure class and should be played at least once. Constant sea views. If your swing's not in top gear it could tear your heart out.

Ashburnham: Maybe not well known but a classic nine-out, nine-back links exposed to the wind. Noted for its good greens and tricky borrows.

Pyle & Kenfig: An unforgiving but superb links course laid out in two contrasting loops. One for your golfing list.

6

BRANCASTER
Royal West Norfolk
Golf Club
Norfolk, England
April

This is the story of a room. In truth, it's the story of a room and a very brief conversation. When combined, these two facets of my visit told me everything you need to know about the nature of Royal West Norfolk Golf Club.

I had trailed across the flatlands of East Anglia, peering through my windscreen at the sour and sombre skies. April had promised much and delivered little, the chilling easterly winds growing in intensity as I approached the coast and wound my way through the narrow marsh-flanked roads. Though it was some years since I had taken this journey, weary grey cells enjoyed their resurrection and prompted my faded memory. There is no sign for the golf course, only a small, bleached, wooden board with the words 'To The Beach' clinging to its splintered surface. I recognized it immediately and, with good reason, gingerly turned the wheel of my suddenly reluctant car.

Are German manufacturers so clever that they can *Vorsprung Durch Technik* an emotional response? Many years before, my former, ageing motorcar had turned into this road only to be met with another affluent piece of Germanic kit driven by a man who was having a nervous breakdown. Perhaps arrogant stupidity and Porsche 911 owners make good companions, but whatever the case, he had ignored the warning signs of a flooded road, put his foot on the accelerator and sent his car into a watery grave. I should explain.

Royal West Norfolk Golf Club (RWNGC) is (as far as I know) unique in being accessible only at certain times of the day. Fail to check the local tide times and you could find yourself trying to run your engine on ecologically friendly but highly corrosive salt water. You might make it through in a grotesque American military Hummer but anything sleek and low slung is destined for the scrap yard. As will become clear, RWNGC is an island course whose sanded beach boundaries and marshland interior are regularly invaded by the swirling eddies of the treacherous North Sea.

Being neither a Porsche driver nor arrogant, and only occasionally stupid, I made it through this time without any trouble. My silky-voiced satellite navigation system thanked me for being so careful, whilst my engine purred with relief. I pulled into the car park.

At least I think it was a car park. Whatever I pulled into was a strange mixture of empty, deserted builder's yard and stony beach. And it was here that I became involved in THE important, brief, yet clue-filled conversation. As I gathered my highly professional, journalistic paraphernalia (a small red notebook and chewed Biro), a rusting Volvo pulled up beside me and disgorged its driver and two nuzzling black

Labradors. The elderly man was clearly a club member; his actions relaxed and assured, his demeanour clear of the facial tension that only visitors display. I took my chance with the usual banality of a stranger.

'Clearing up,' I offered. 'Still cold though.'

His reply was somewhat muted, but he seemed pleasant enough, and whilst we never developed the conversation into the philosophy of life, our words were exchanged in a friendly, easygoing manner. Realizing I would soon be encountering the club secretary, I pushed the boat out a little further.

'Tell me,' I asked, 'do I refer to the club as Royal West Norfolk Golf Club or just as Brancaster?'

He cast me a knowing smile before offering his reply.

'Royal West Norfolk or Brancaster?' he mumbled. 'Not the sort of thing we fuss about.'

His response made no real impact at the time, yet within thirty-six hours it was to prove of vital importance. For the moment, it was enough to send me in search of the secretary with a little more confidence. I turned towards the club-house.

I use the term 'clubhouse' loosely. Though once failing miserably to qualify for the Royal Institute of Surveyors, my knowledge of architecture could be written on a pinhead with a thick-nibbed fountain pen. Despite this ignorance, I would hazard a guess that this startling edifice was a progeny of (perhaps) a Georgian builder with Gothic leanings. It is Bleak House, set amongst a stark, Dickensian, Norfolk landscape.

High above the entrance and gnarled (possibly) oak swinging doors, a simple, weatherworn clock pointed its skeletal black fingers to one o'clock. At the base of its pock-marked face, the words 'English Clock System' gave the only clue to its maker or its ultimate significance. I stepped in, now with more ginger in my step than you'd find in a Kerala curry. Immediately to my right, another heavy wooden door announced its interior with the small inscription 'Smoke Room'. My knees creaked in close harmony with the ancient timbers, and in I went.

I would understand, at this point, if you were suffering a slight impatience whilst you waited for a detailed description of the waiting golf course. But I make no apology for the delay; my defence built on the premise that you will never fully appreciate the fairways and idiosyncrasies of this golf course until you have experienced the Smoke Room.

It would take the artistic skills of a Caravaggio to depict its impact. Perhaps Rembrandt would be a more appropriate choice, as the shaded light conceals the shadowed detail of its interior. But, in brief, the room is tired, wooden, worn – in parts decrepit. Paint cracks from its decorated timbers, six dusted light shades hang on long wires from the high vaulted ceiling, whilst a small insignificant bar nestles in the corner. The floor is covered in a simple green threadbare carpet, which provides a home for six plain wooden tables surrounded by a whole array of hard college chairs. To enter the Smoke Room is to walk into a Jules Verne interior, a land that time forgot. It is an anachronism in the twenty-first century. It is also a place of sublime beauty and unadulterated charm, which wraps itself around you with the warmth of a school matron's buxom embrace. As I suspect its members always do, I would defend it to the death. This is the engine of the club and the rhythmic heartbeat of Brancaster Golf Club.

Half circling the Smoke Room are twenty-five ancient lockers (still in regular use by ancient members), the owners' identities roughly scrawled on tiny parchment labels. Knights of the realm rub shoulders with mere commoners, whilst doctors and clergymen attend to the physical and spiritual needs of their surrounding members. The narrow locker doors stand erect in line, like sentinels guarding the club's tradition and propriety. And should these custodians of decency be caught napping, a reserve army stands ready to defend the cause. Hanging high above the two glowing coal fires are a number of simple wooden boards, inscribed with a list of past captains. But this is no ordinary commemoration of club officials, no place for mere mortals to find an eternal home. Reflecting the nature of the nearby lockers, admirals of the fleet sail into history with brigadiers and generals; air chief marshals fly towards heaven with viscounts and professors whilst members of royalty sit patiently with medical consultants. Their presence follows you round the room like a *Mona Lisa* smile. (No one apparently knows how the captains are elected, though I think there's a bit of a clue in the collection of military and ancestral titles.)

Checking that my newly bought shoes were suitably polished, I approached the hutch-like bar and ordered a sandwich and a beer. So immersed was I in the atmosphere that I felt as if I had betrayed convention and probably should have asked for a thick broth, a jug of ale and paid with a golden guinea. Proffering a ten-pound note, I wandered back to my seat.

'Your change!' came the barmaid's cheery but over-loud cry.

As her words rang around the room there appeared to be a collective splutter of disapproval amongst the gathered members. Two elderly gentlemen tried to raise themselves from their table but keeled over in a sweating faint.

An embellished story? Of course it is. But it serves my purpose. I was beginning to understand that Royal West Norfolk, despite its connection with the great and good of English society, should not be mistaken for a club that wishes to build its reputation on pompous tradition or the thoughtless maintenance of an outmoded status quo. It would be easy to throw brickbats at the members, who sit at the apex of the social hierarchy; who view plus-fours as de rigueur; who never cast corduroy trousers till May is out or consider anything other than a full brogue shoe as the attire of a scoundrel. To take a cheap shot at such behaviour would be to completely misunderstand the Brancaster philosophy.

Fortunately, I had been given all the clues during the first hour of my visit. My brief conversation in the car park and the admittedly apocryphal barmaid's tale had already solved the puzzle. Brancaster simply doesn't fuss about anything and is quite happy to operate within the dictum of 'if it ain't broke, don't fix it'. If there were such a thing as a Royal West Norfolk dictionary, I am certain that the word 'change' would be omitted from its lexicon and banned from usage.

The contents of the Smoke Room only reinforce this view. They don't really fuss about anything. The list of celebrated captains is just a statement of fact and should not be seen as bragging one-upmanship. Apart from one or two unremarkable paintings, very little else adorns the panelled walls. Grand competition boards are noticeably absent; beaming photographs of present captains and presidents nowhere to be seen; self-congratulatory silverware is kept to a bare minimum, whilst there is no sign of rules or dictatorial restraints on dress and behaviour. A Brancaster member clearly knows how things should be done and, on gaining that membership, inherits its history. Why make a fuss of such things? Should you ever be fortunate enough to enjoy the Smoke Room, sit back in those college chairs, rest your hands on the kingly round tables and let your fingertips absorb those laissez-faire traditions. You will require no commands from brigadiers or admirals of the fleet. You will know instinctively.

Minutes later, and still in a Smoke Room daze, I was joined by my Brancaster mentor. He slipped into the 'bar' with the ease of a stockinged foot reacquainting itself with a favourite shoe. A guided tour soon followed, the first port of call being the 'Dressing Room', reminiscent of boys' prep school, cricket pavilion locker room. Lockers are not provided, the only concession to comfort a simple, scarred wooden bench with brass hooks on the rail above. Two small showers are the only sign of modernity though, I was informed, are rarely used.

'Brancaster men prefer to bathe at home,' I was told with some solemnity.

And then up the winding staircase, to the simple dining room (plain food, sticky school puddings, no speeches, no available toilets) and the delicate Charles Whymper water-colours. No need to fuss about them. They were simply superb. Finally we stepped onto the stunning Millennium veranda – built because they 'thought they had to do something or other' to celebrate the passing of a thousand years. I was informed that the majority of the membership would rather have adopted the more usual Brancaster philosophy of simply carrying on as if nothing had happened.

But the verandah was constructed, and it gave me my first real view of the course, stretching out on a narrow, featureless tongue of marshland. To the south-east, Brancaster Harbour (or Staithe, as it's locally known) lay in the distance, the un-rigged yachts rising and falling on the rain-filled horizon. To the north, the wild deserted beach could be seen hugging the shoreline and meandering out towards the 9th green, at the point of the island. It looked ominous and threatening, as though laying down a challenge to my feeble swing. I stared hard at its fairways, dismissed its rough with a cursory glance and stared steely eyed at the waiting greens. The course refused to blink an eye and gave me no hope of its submission to my fragile skills.

Returning to my hotel, I rummaged through my suitcase and threw out any form of clothing that suggested either non-Brancaster overenthusiasm or any hint of 'trying too hard'. Suitably dressed, I dined (shabbily but smartly country) in the company of 'T.H.', my delightful clubhouse mentor and storyteller. As you must always do on the wild Norfolk coast, we filled our stomachs with offerings from the nearby sea. Razor clams and halibut (and all at a third of the price you would pay in a starched-cloth city restaurant) followed the local mussels.

I was beginning to think that I had a guardian angel. As had happened on many occasions at other visited courses, the following morning I returned to the clubhouse to see the leaden clouds parting in welcome, the sun turning the menacing links into a thing of reassuring beauty. Larks danced in the air whilst swooping gulls squawked their pleasure at the signs of spring. I can hardly tell a peewit from a vulture but never fail to enjoy the sight of birds celebrating their freedom in an open sky. This part of Norfolk is famed for wildlife and migrating flocks of exotic birds and they were to accompany us around the course for the rest of the day.

It was still bitterly cold and the crystal-clear air flooded my lungs. Sensing a renewal of my flagging energy, I hurried over towards the 1st tee to confront my unknown companions.

But before you walk onto the course, it's important to absorb the setting for your opening salvo. The old clubhouse may well be the most isolated in Britain. It sits almost on the beach itself and to gain access to the links you have to walk across a sandy gully that leads directly onto the shore. Once you have crossed this narrow strip, you will be met with a large wrought-iron gateway, its pillars engraved with the names of Brancaster men who lost their lives in the two world wars. It is not a thing of beauty, or ornate in any manner. As you would expect, the gates and inscriptions are simple and unfussy and yet more powerful because of their modesty.

Seconds later, my heart sank to my highly polished golf shoes. As you turn into the course you are immediately met by a large white sign, which must have struck fear into many unsuspecting golfers. *Foursomes and Singles Matches Only*, it declares. *No Four-ball Matches Allowed Without the Consent of The Secretary.*

T.H. approached.

'We're playing foursomes?' I stuttered.

'Of course.' He smiled. 'Don't like four-ball matches at Brancaster. Never have done.'

'Why's that?' I asked nervously.

'Well, all that *everybody putting out business*,' he laughed in reply. 'Too damned cold to hang about. We like to get on. Fast play. That's the thing.'

'Right.'

In case you are unfamiliar with the foursomes format (sadly, it is rarely played these days), it involves two pairs of players who take alternate shots on each hole. It is a magnificent game when you are both playing well but a contest of nightmare proportions when one member of the pair is 'off his game'. Sending your partner's perfect drive into the face of a bunker or the depths of a skin-ripping gorse bush is not always met with a look of approval. It is a heavenly game, which can soon dissolve into hell.

Our opponents, who were to prove perfect company

for the resulting match, soon joined us. One was dressed immaculately but in an understated manner; the other in a pair of plus-fours and gartered socks, which would have had Baden-Powell purring with delight. I stepped forward onto the tee, my brown corduroys and plain blue sweater seemingly gaining looks of approval.

As with many opening shots in the company of strangers, my swing was a little hurried and lacking in rhythm.

'Anybody see it?' I asked with my usual myopic uncertainty.

'Down the middle. Fine shot,' came the reply.

I glanced towards my opponent who nodded his contentment with a pleasant Brancaster dismissiveness. Over-enthusiasm was obviously considered an unacceptable, emotional response at Royal West Norfolk Golf Club.

Only a drive, I thought. Best not to fuss about it.

I suspect that, rather like J. M. Barrie's dire warning to those children who doubt the existence of fairies, every time a Brancaster man hears a shout of 'You're the man!' during an American golfing tournament, one of the members dies. Fortunately, as I *do* believe in goblins, pixies and leprechauns (especially when backing a horse at an Irish racecourse), I began to relax, ready to play our match in a suitably unexcitable manner.

The night before, I had glanced at an old centenary pamphlet. Inserted in its pages was a map of the course headed with the words, *A Century of Not Much Change* Wonderful. As I strode forward and admired the marshland views, I felt certain that should the ghost of the very first captain, 'The Great Horace' (it's a long story) have joined me on the opening fairway, he would have assumed that it was still 1891 and that he had just woken from a long nap in the Smoke Room.

Unusually, the 1st and 18th fairways are shared, as are the 2nd and 17th. But it's a huge expanse of land, once used to hide the armoured tanks that were destined to track their way up the Normandy beaches. Essentially, it is a classic links layout with nine holes out and nine holes in, the front nine hugging the marshes whilst the back nine follow the contours of the shoreline. But you are never far from the sea, and the sound of waves crashing onto the waiting beaches provides an ocean backdrop to every shot.

Whilst Brancaster is not long in yardage, it is definitely short on respite. Rarely, if ever, are you faced with a shot that doesn't require careful thought. As early as the 3rd you are introduced to its characteristic heavily guarded greens. Not only are you facing bunkers but high-mounded areas supported by gigantic railway sleepers that send terror into anyone with a tendency to thin or top their irons from the tight sandy fairways.

Then just when you think you have started to outflank the enemy, Brancaster links calls on nature and unleashes its main battalions. Having set a number of tight criteria for the courses I chose to visit, by the 7th hole I was beginning to wonder if my inclusion of Royal West Norfolk might have been an error of judgement. But standing on the 8th tee, my fears were soon allayed. And my terror soon increased. Like Macbeth's ill-fated Birnam Wood, creeping towards Dunsinane, so the tidal waters of the North Sea surge come to meet the usurping golfer. When the tide is high, the salty waters snake onto the course with the stealth of a viper, marooning the fairways in a series of shallow treacherous lagoons. The 8th hole is a spectacular example, the opening drive demanding a long carry over water, the second another teasing 'lay-up' shot over another tidal hazard and a final approach onto a small sloping green. Negotiate a par five on this hole and you'll feel like Jack Nicklaus in his prime. But don't relax. The magnificent 9th requires you to repeat the process, only this time, the green is guarded by a curving bank of railway sleepers that seem to taunt you with its wooden smile.

Though there is much else to enjoy, this eastern apex of the course stands out as Brancaster's finest point. In fact, 'The Point' is exactly how the members refer to this section of the course. From here you glance over to Brancaster Staithe, and out to the wide horizons of the white-flecked sea. Nearby, an inscribed bench seat is dedicated to The Old Bailey Judges Golfing Society. If I had stood on the 9th green, accused of indulging in undiluted pleasure, I would have been found guilty on all counts.

The day before, my companion, T.H., admitted that when he'd made his final putt, he would happily have his ashes scattered around this green. If there's room, I might join him, though the events of the next few holes suggested that he was very serious about his intent to enjoy a Brancaster burial.

T.H. had struggled over the front nine and whenever he did find a swing I managed to return the compliment by knocking our ball into every available hazard. We were soon four down and heading for an early handshake and a miserable toothless defeat. Yet something strange happened at that 9th hole. I managed to put our third shot 15 feet from the pin. T.H. strode onto the green, his once hunched shoulders suddenly drawn back, his step a little lighter. Something about his manner had changed. The putt dropped in with a satisfying metalled rattle. Three down and nine to play.

As you will now realize, I find tales of other people's golf matches to be tiresome in the extreme and, in the Brancaster spirit, I have no intention of becoming overenthusiastic or to make any fuss about the outcome of our game. All that needs to be said is that by the time we arrived at the par-three 15th we were only one down, T.H. was now playing well and I was facing one of the biggest bunkers I've ever encountered. To stand on the 15th tee and look towards the towering railway sleepers is reminiscent of facing the gaping mouth of an approaching sperm whale, ready to filter your ball out of the air as if it was no more than a passing shoal of plankton. I tried to draw the ball around the waiting mammal and for once in my life managed to scamper the ball around its waiting lips. All square.

You might well expect me to finish this short tale with the result of our match, to relate the heady excitement of our victory or the final missed putt of defeat. I am about to disappoint you. This is Royal West Norfolk. This is Brancaster and I had absorbed its way of life. A chap isn't going to make a song and dance about losing or winning. The game's the thing and the spirit in which it's played. You must work it out for yourself.

We shook hands on the final green and took a contented lunch in the Smoke Room. I had been in good company and played well enough. What more could I ask?

I checked the tide times and prepared to make my escape along the narrow and sometimes flooded road. Changing quickly in the prep-school locker room, my eye was attracted to the only notice pinned up on the timbered wall. It was no more than an old and torn scrap of paper. Turning down its curled edge and faded print, I was expecting to see the result of a recent competition, perhaps a notification of altered handicaps. I should have known better. What faced me was no more than a tattered wine list, displaying four unassuming reds, four very palatable whites, and all at surprisingly reasonable prices. Like everything about Brancaster, it was simple, unpretentious and never changing. Pure bliss. Who needs a long ostentatious wine list when there's enough pleasure to be gained from a few good dusty bottles that have stood the test of time? No need to change. No need to fuss.

Like one of Snow White's dwarfs, I'm informed that Brancaster may have to face a short life. During various parts of its history, the protective sand dunes have eroded, the North Sea surges growing in power as global warming tightens its doom-laden grip. Whole tees have been known to disappear in a wild winter storm, the snaking gullies sometimes bursting onto the low-lying fairways. Is nature finally forcing change on a course whose unwritten motto is, *We like it as it is*? Over the years, valiant members have stuck their fingers in the dam of progress and so far held the tide at bay. I only hope they discover a permanent remedy for their watery illness. God, I hope they find a cure. Royal West Norfolk Golf Club is a place for Peter Pans who still enjoy school puddings and fire-burned toast with lashings of jam. It's an adult fairy tale. I don't want to fuss about this, but I like it – *just as it is*.

Recommended Alternatives

Sheringham: Don't be fooled by the rather dull start. The course explodes into pleasure as you climb up to the clifftop holes. Great fun and testing.

Hunstanton: Perhaps overshadowed by Brancaster (what isn't?) but still a course you won't forget easily. Superb greens that can be slicker than Augusta. Foursomes or two-balls (rather than four-balls) are often preferred. Fine links course.

Royal Cromer: Clifftop holes and some steep inclines – so get into training. Very exposed on seaward holes but great to take on. If you're feeling fragile, pray for a calm day – but it's more fun in the wind.

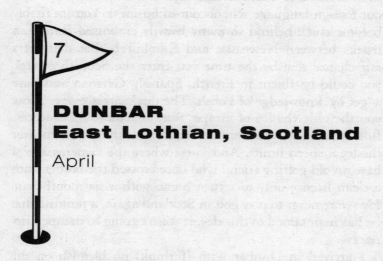

DUNBAR
East Lothian, Scotland
April

'I love a good line of washing.' It's an expression that permeated my Lancastrian youth and has left me with the visual antennae of an obsessive laundry maid. Why these words have rooted themselves in my unconscious, I have no idea. But within 800 yards of Dunbar Golf Club, I had spotted the flapping sheets and enough dancing undergarments to condemn a devout Scottish Presbyterian to everlasting damnation.

'That's a lovely line of washing,' I instinctively muttered, as I manoeuvred my car along the narrow coastal track towards the looming clubhouse. It seemed insignificant at the time, yet it was to prove vital in my understanding and appreciation of the waiting links.

Only 40 miles north of the English border, I had been welcomed to Scotland by a population of the most devious speed cameras I had so far encountered. The trick appears to involve providing a narrow main road interspersed with short sections of dual carriageways. It is a system that could put foreign language schools out of business. You inevitably become stuck behind so many heavily embossed European trucks between Newcastle and Edinburgh that there is a fair chance that by the time you enter the Scottish capital, you could be fluent in French, Spanish, German and have a 'get by' knowledge of Polish. The dual carriageways allow you the only chance of escape. But, to achieve this successfully and safely, you must accelerate quickly and often over the legal speed limits. And guess where the cameras are? I have an old golfing friend who once crossed the border with a clean licence only to return home with a six-month ban. He swore never to play golf in Scotland again, a promise that he has maintained to this day. It wasn't going to dampen my resolve.

I arrived in Dunbar with (I think) no blemish on my driving licence but slightly aggrieved by the lack of national hospitality. The town did little to raise my spirits, the red sandstone houses, dour and gloom laden, were set against a still wintry sky.

Pressed for time, I sought out the golf course, which lies only about a mile from the east edge of the town. Thankfully, the line of washing came to my rescue, waving its welcome in the stiffening wind and raising my flagging spirits. Like many Scottish courses, the initial introduction is a low-key affair, free of the growing 'nouveau pomp' electric gates and over-elaborate clubhouses, which have become the hallmark of many English parkland courses. Dunbar treats you to a rough narrow track, a fairly unkempt but large practical car park and a small white bungalow clubhouse. Come over the border and pretentiousness is quickly left behind. I began to relax.

It was already mid afternoon and I hurried into the clubhouse to pay my respects to the secretary and grab a very late lunch. Thankfully a Scotch pie was on the menu. Despite their dubious contents, these pastries remain a favourite treat. I doubt if even the original baker has ever truly discovered the constituents of this savoury dish. Your first bite into the grey innards of a Scotch pie should be regarded as a leap of culinary faith. Murmuring a brief prayer, I took my seat in the long main bar, tucking myself on a small table at the very end of the room.

'Visitor?' came a passing, friendly, East Lothian voice.

'Playing tomorrow.' I smiled through pie-crumbed teeth.

'Know about that seat you're sitting in?' he asked.

'Not the captain's?' I spluttered. 'Should I move?'

'No,' he chortled. 'Stay where you are, laddie. Enjoy the view.'

'The chair?' I queried.

'Nearest to the sea in any British clubhouse.'

I turned quickly and glanced over my shoulder. He was probably right. No more than twenty yards from my steaming Scotch pie and half pint of Belhaven best, the tide was swelling onto the rugged red-stone shore.

'Firth of Forth?' I asked.

'We call it the North Sea,' he chuckled. 'If you've time, take the John Muir walk. Good way to get a feel of the course.'

It transpired that John Muir was a Dunbar boy 'done good'. As a young man he found himself in California and introduced the Americans to the concept of conservation and, in time, the establishment of protected national parks. Such was his prowess that he and President Theodore Roosevelt would trek off on camping trips like two ancient Boy Scouts. Nowadays, this would involve a bag of kindling wood, a box of matches, thirty security men with nailbrush hairstyles and reflective sunglasses, a briefcase with a nasty red button and a whole fleet of surveillance planes chewing up the ozone layer. Sadly, times change, though gratefully, not the intrinsic layout of this admirable golf course.

By chance, my visit coincided with the 150th anniversary of Dunbar Golf Club, firmly cemented in my memory by a fine new sweater bartered for at the isolated professional's shop, which sits beside the 1st tee. A glance at the card began to reveal some of Dunbar's unique features. To the best of my knowledge (I'm sure you'll let me know), it's the only seaside links course that opens with two par-five holes. And in all honesty, and despite their well-constructed links design, they feel like a bit of a disappointment, laid back from the coastline and played in a loop that brings you directly back to where you began. It's as if the course is teasing you and gives the sensation of a rather stuttering start to your campaign.

Don't be fooled. The pleasure is all to come. You turn towards the sea at the 3rd, a superb par three, played off a high tee towards a well-guarded green that nestles in full view of the clubhouse window. Known as 'Jackson's Pennies', it gains its name from an ancient member who would give young boys a penny every time they recorded a two on this tricky hole. Like Theodore Roosevelt's camping trip, it's a sad indictment of our loss of innocence that if he was still alive today, Mr Jackson would probably be hauled in front of a local magistrate and charged with dubious solicitation. And as it happened, I was privileged to see a young golfer achieve a simple tap-in birdie. Though tempted to maintain Mr Jackson's fine tradition, the fear of arrest made me resist searching my pockets for a bit of loose change.

Unlike marathon runners, who 'hit the wall' at 20 miles (in my own case, every time I passed a pub or a cake shop), you meet this obstruction not long after crossing the starting line. Entrance to the 4th tee is gained by stepping through a small opening, cut into a high stone wall, which, incongruously, borders the waiting fairway. And it's from this point that Dunbar announces its intentions and waiting hazards. To the left, the clear blue sea breaks onto the shore whilst the craggy flinted stones of the towering wall threaten the slightest hint of sliced drive. Only a few feet away, John Muir's boot-worn coastal path stretches out into the distance, and I stepped out to discover what lay in store.

It soon becomes obvious that, despite the curious opening two holes, the majority of the course reflects the classic links design. A thin strip of land reaches out towards a distant headland, following the line of the coast but, unusually, is bordered by another series of menacing stone walls that mark the old boundaries of the Duke of Roxburghe's deer park. You are therefore playing on a funnel of land that will happily punish the smallest loss of concentration.

With the light fading, I quickened my pace along the coastal route. Without detailing the holes encountered, it can be generally stated that the golf course gets better the further you move away from the clubhouse. Yet, as it gets better, in some respects, it also gets worse.

This is no criticism of the golf course, as the holes are beautifully constructed and in magnificent condition. Each one makes constant demands to fire long irons over flowing burns and land pitch shots onto small greens bordered by a shoreline that seems delighted to receive your ball into its watery hazard. But step along the 9th fairway and Dunbar soon reveals its blots on the landscape. At first your eye is caught by a distant, stark white lighthouse, rising, steeple-like, from a rugged spur of land that juts out into the North Sea. But let your eye wander a few degrees west and the looming geometric blocks of Torness blind you to the surrounding beauty. For a second, it seemed reminiscent of my car engine, which, on the rare occasion I raise the bonnet, reveals nothing more than a flat lump of metal that gives me no idea what is going on behind its smooth silvery surface. But Torness couldn't fool me. I had passed it earlier, slowing down to avoid yet another speed trap. It gave me enough time to read the small sign at the side of the road and check whether all my electronic Volkswagen car 'gismos' included a Geiger counter. There was a time when the slightest ticking noise in a car would be explained away with the words 'it's probably your tappets'. These days, you have to be a little more knowledgeable.

Torness is a nuclear power station carefully disguised by gallons of powder-blue paint. Despite the hot reactor within its walls, there's something about powder blue that always sends a cold shiver down my spine. The imagined beauty of two-headed gannets flying over my head and cuddly six-legged lambs grazing in a nearby field did little to allay my growing fears.

Turn towards the 9th green, alerted by a strange smell of ozone, and blot No. 2 comes into view. The Blue Circle cement works seems to stretch over many hundreds of acres, the limestone quarries gouged out of the coastal hills leaving grey open wounds in the otherwise picturesque landscape. Whether it's reminiscent of a desolate Iraqi city, I have no idea (I rarely go further than a Greek island these days), but it appears to be a target for deafening RAF fighters doing dummy bombing runs. I just hope they don't make any mistakes, such as loading up the real thing and having a crack at Torness.

The odd thing is that I rather liked it. Don't know why. The bleak industrial wasteland reminded me of a scene from *Get Carter,* a gritty north-eastern gangster movie in which Michael Caine loads dead bodies onto the giant shingle transporters. It seemed so far removed from Dunbar's historic links, yet somehow, they live happily in each other's company. Perhaps it's a pervading sense of death and destruction that lingers on the land. It was in this area that Cromwell camped his beleaguered army in 1650 and waited to be slaughtered by angry battalions of kilted Scots, who held the high ground on nearby Doon Hill. It should have been a formality for their commander General David Leslie, who, being busy during the week, decided to dispose of Cromwell on the Sunday.

Unfortunately, the Presbyterian elders suggested that fighting on the Sabbath (like glancing at undergarments on a washing line) would be a mortal sin that could see them all condemned to hell.

General Leslie had little choice and issued the instruction (I paraphrase): *Have a wee nap, lads. We'll attend to our slaughter tomorrow.*

This proved to be a bit of a tactical error. Cromwell, quite literally, caught them napping and sent the Scots to hell rather earlier than they had anticipated. The moral of this tale for all Scotsmen is never to listen to sanctimonious Presbyterian advice when you're about to hit an Englishman. It can only end in tears.

Oddly, having first arranged my game on Sunday, I had been forced to switch to Monday morning. The portents looked good, especially as I was about to take on three men from East Lothian. Like Cromwell, I crept off the course at dusk, headed for my hotel and made preparation for the battle ahead.

Because of my horseracing background, I tend to gamble on hotels. Quick flick through the Internet, quick phone call, quick decision. On this occasion I found myself lodging in a gloomy sandstone building that was halfway through a full renovation. Brimming with frighteningly muscular, hard-drinking contract workers, it at least confirmed the economic benefits of having a nuclear power station and limestone quarry close to the town. After a wholesome bar meal, I retired to bed. I was exhausted. It had been a long day. It was to be an even longer night.

Whilst running the bath (I couldn't work out how the newly renovated shower worked), I took the chance to have a little putting practice. With a glass mug laid on its side, I holed out six times out of ten and stepped into the waiting hot water with growing confidence that my short game was intact. The new owner had been kind enough to include the installation of Jacuzzi baths into his renovation master plan. I pressed the button and began to bubble away happily, my enervated muscles relaxing in warm delight. My head dropped back, my eyelids dropped down and my body dropped into sleep.

I can only describe my awakening as being similar to being caught in a car wash in the middle of a tropical hurricane. Jets of water were not only hitting my face but also the brand-new carpet, the freshly painted ceiling, the gleaming brass light fittings and (though I'm hesitant to reveal my intimate secrets) my waiting cotton pyjamas. I was caught in the crossfire of twenty water cannons and whichever way I turned, found myself knocked back into the emptying bath. Finally locating the Stop button, I hauled myself out and unsuccessfully attempted to dry myself with the sodden bath towel.

As luck would have it, I was able to don a pair of woollen long johns (for those bitter Scottish mornings) and a thermal vest. I climbed under the thin duvet cover, curled into a survival position and attempted to get some sleep. An hour later, I could stand it no more. The bed covers felt as heavy as a Kleenex tissue and the recently renewed radiators refused to respond to all my alliterative urgings. The state-of-the-art, button-laden phone/fax machine proved completely inoperable and I rang the manager from my mobile.

'I'm cold,' I stuttered. 'Can you . . . ?'

'On my way,' he replied.

Five minutes later, a bemused hotel manager dressed in shorts and T-shirt faced a shivering guest in long johns and vest. To his credit, he made no comment as he squelched across the bedroom carpet to examine my inadequate duvet.

'All new,' he exclaimed. 'And they've all got a tog value over twenty.'

'But I'm cold,' I pleaded.

'With twenty togs!' he cried.

It was as though the repetition of tog values would immediately raise my body temperature by 10 degrees. Deciding to speak his language, I stood my soggy ground and increased my demands.

'More togs!' I pleaded. 'I need more togs!'

The following morning, preparing to hit the first drive of the day, my body was still rigid with cold, the muscles screaming as I tried to turn my shoulders to the required 90 degree angle. I doubt I even made it halfway, the ball searing off to the right in a tangent that seemed to deny all mathematical logic.

'Bit of a "loosener",' I offered, embarrassed by the inanity of my excuse.

Recording an opening eight on my card seemed not to impress my companions who remained politely quiet. The 2nd showed signs of improvement, though a seven on a par five rarely results in congratulation. As we approached the 3rd tee, there was a definite look of 'why did we bother?' on the three Scottish faces. But something was stirring. At last, the blood was beginning to flow in my veins, the hands had relaxed their vice-like grip and my hips were starting to show signs of movement. 'Jackson's Pennies' waited my arrival.

Inevitably last to go, my five-iron shot arced through the air, clearly destined to drop straight into the hole some 173 yards away. Clipping the rim, it ran 12 feet past, leaving me a very real birdie chance. Determined to cement my golfing credentials, I weighed up the putt carefully, trying to imagine an upturned glass mug ready to receive the ball, and the ghost of Mr Jackson rushing across the green to thrust a bright new penny into my hand.

Naturally, I missed. The green proved far quicker than the heavily watered bedroom carpet and I had to be satisfied with a solid par. Sadly, one member of the opposition holed out for a birdie and we strode through the 'wall' towards the 4th tee, already three down.

I would like to tell you that things got better. So here goes. Things got better. Though my partner and I finally succumbed on the 16th, we put up a stern fight and enjoyed a sunlit day on Dunbar's links. The pleasure was enhanced by my companion's knowledge. A naturally chatty man, he possessed an extensive knowledge of the course, detailing its history as we fought our way back into the game.

It was from his lips that I learned of Torness, the Blue Circle limestone quarries and the ill-fated Battle of Dunbar. And in many ways, the narrow strip of land that contains the 6th and 17th holes typifies the true nature of these historic links. The two fairways are held in the corridor of the high estate walls and the North Sea shoreline. The short 6th ('Broxburn') demands a careful drive, which avoids both the wall to the right and a wide flowing burn just before the green; whilst the 17th ('Fluke Dub') requires you to land your drive on an island fairway between two burns whilst avoiding the rock-strewn beach that contains the fish pools that give the hole its name. And it's from here that you gain your first real sight of Bass Rock to the east and (I think) Edinburgh's distant skyline to the north. It's a setting that couldn't fail to raise even the highest handicapper's game.

But if I were to choose one hole, it would be the 12th, a long par four, which, for the average golfer, requires two woods to reach the narrow bunkered green. Once more, the waiting sea threatens your drive, whilst a misjudged second shot will find you in the depths of a pot bunker or wading through the waves to retrieve your ball. 'The Point', as it is known, is, like all the finest links holes, an unfussy challenge of simple design but demanding of all your golfing skills.

As admitted, we shook hands on the 16th, having sent my tee shot high over the deer park wall (I swear the wind dropped just as I made my backswing). Having negotiated the 17th in a spectacular fashion that only happens after you have conceded the match, we had a moment's wait on the 18th tee. It proved to be a hole that had produced its own modern history.

If you have any doubts about the validity of my regard for Dunbar, it can be confirmed by the fact that it is regularly employed as a qualifying course for the Open Championship. In 2002, a certain Steve Elkington had stood on the 18th tee with a healthy lead over his fellow hopeful qualifiers only to send his first two drives sailing over the deer park wall and out of bounds. He had endeared himself to the Dunbar membership with three days of greeting all and sundry with the Antipodean address of *G'day, mate*. Recording an eight on his card (as I had done on the 1st), and to the dismay of his growing Scottish fan club, he appeared to have blown his chances.

But fortune was on his side. Not only did he qualify for the Open by a single shot but reached a play-off final against Mr Ernest Els and was granted honorary membership of Dunbar Golf Club. He probably remembers the course with great affection, though I doubt many nights pass by without a nightmare encounter with that 18th hole.

Having paid my extensive losses (£1.25), I headed back into town, a fresh line of washing waving its farewells as I manoeuvred down the track. Fearful of more Presbyterian sanctions, I quickly averted my eyes away from the frilly undergarments and reflected on my game. I realized that, like the billowing sheets, I had been hung out to dry, defeated by two Dunbar members whose local knowledge had seen them comfortably home.

With a few hours to spare and terrified of returning to the car wash madness of my hotel bathroom, I wandered down to the old harbour. It proved to be a beautiful and natural setting, access from the sea gained from a narrow inlet between high rising cliffs. Yet its most extraordinary feature were the names given to the surrounding cobbled streets. To my great surprise, Cromwell's name appeared to emblazon every signpost as I made my way through Cromwell Court towards the Cromwell Quay. It was as if the Roundhead general hadn't only massacred the Scottish army, he had also captured their soul and made the townsfolk betray the memory of their luckless army. High above the nearby Victoria Dock, a flock of nesting kittiwakes shrieked their disapproval of my personal invasion. Thousands of flapping wings turned the cliff face into a wall of vibrating sound, unwilling to yield to the intrusion of flashing cameras and long-lense binoculars. It seemed like a metaphor for my visit, for my experiences of the fine enclosed course at Dunbar; a delightful walled oasis of history and rugged nature, amongst the threats of a sterilized nuclear age.

Recommended Alternatives

Muirfield (Honourable Company of Edinburgh Golfers): One of the finest links courses in world golf and playable if you've just won the lottery – or have the right contacts.

Gullane: Exquisite and unique links. Choice of three courses. Play Gullane 1 if you get the chance. If the wind blows, you'll need to keep your rhythm and your nerve.

Kilspindie: Great views and scary bunkers. Short but traditional links and well worth a visit.

KINGSBARNS
Fife, Scotland

May

The day before playing this Fifeshire course, I was struck by a sense of foreboding. During my preliminary inspection, I sauntered, notebook in hand, between the 11th and 15th greens and sensed what polite society would term 'a need to respond to the call of nature'. My newly enforced health regime of consuming a minimum of 2 litres of water per day has undoubted benefits, but also a number of unsurprising consequences.

As chance would have it, I stumbled across a small wooded glade, its beauty enhanced by a picturesque trickling stream, which did little to alleviate the urgency of my situation. Quickening my step, in search of a discreet refuge, a rustic cabin hove into view. It seemed a perfect spot to maintain my dignity and conceal myself from the inevitable ladies four-ball, which always seems to appear seconds after you are beginning to sigh with relief.

I need not have worried. As I approached, it soon became

clear that I had happened upon a 'convenience', a 'lavatory', a 'toilet', a 'privy', or whatever euphemism you choose to employ. However, the sign above the door stopped me in my hurried tracks. Nailed to the surface of the wooden hut was a small plaque with a single word that had me spluttering with indignation and the odd expletive.

'*Restroom! Restroom?*' I grumbled. 'In Scotland? It's a bl***y lavvie!'

I need to explain the true reasons for this momentary show of rancour and the subsequent feelings of apprehension. It wasn't the word Restroom that upset me but the implications of its use.

I was in Fife, in many ways the home of traditional golf, of the 'Old Course' at nearby St Andrews, of tough links courses, of golfers who whip round eighteen holes in three hours and despise the growth of modern manicured fairways and target golf. In short, dyed-in-the-wool links golfers are always wary of the Americanization of their rooted traditions.

Now don't get me wrong. If you're an American reading this piece, I have no wish to offend. I have good friends in California and Dakota; relatives in Seattle and Boston; love homemade apple pie and have been known to put marmalade on my bacon (well, only once). But such is my love of links courses that I instinctively reject any hint of change, any compromise with the demands made by the new breed of modern golfers in logo-festooned clothing, carrying a bag full of graphite-shafted Pings, Callaways and Nikes. I like my golf tough and *un*compromising, and, given the chance, would happily play with Prosimmon woods, hickory-shafted spoons and a couple of mashie-nib'licks.

What concerned me most of all was that Kingsbarns is the 'new kid on the St Andrews block'. Though its history dates back to 1793, the present course was only opened at the start of the present millennium. In golfing terms, it is akin to a four-year-old being given full membership of a long-established and crusty gentleman's club. Inevitably, it's an uneasy alliance, which requires the young pretender to earn its stripes and prove its worth.

I soon came to the conclusion that Kingsbarns can only truly be understood in this context. Within minutes of driving into the St Andrews area you become aware, not only of golfing history but of the fact that it is emerging as the Costa del Golf of Scotland, a narrow strip of barren undulating land that teems with (presently) seven golf courses, all of high standard and all submerged in visiting golfers, intent on absorbing its folklore and mythological tales. Walk down any street, and you are bombarded by golfing memorabilia. The Royal and Ancient Golf Club dominates the town, drawing you back to its austere architecture from every point. The sometimes cobbled roads are littered with tourist traps, every shop appearing to entice the unwary visitor with 'authentic' Scottish produce such as handbooks informing you *What's Under a Scotsman's Kilt* or *How to Hunt for Wild Haggis*. 'Genuine' traditional golf clubs burst from every window, the St Andrews crest adorns every towel, tie and teaspoon, whilst the famous faces of the golfing gods smile out from every book cover.

Do I have the nerve to criticize St Andrews? You bet I do. There's a manifest danger of golfing overkill, a distinct odour of potential tackiness, which needs to be reined back before it's too late. As yet, the treacherous Rubicon of plastic modernity has yet to be crossed, but there's a distinct feeling that they've already dipped their toe in the water.

So this is the context. But why choose Kingsbarns and ignore the 'Old Course' of St Andrews? There's a simple reason. The 'Old Course' just doesn't meet my strict criteria for selection.

I'm told that one of the great disappointments of first-time visitors to the home of golf is that the sea is barely visible from the course (they have been fooled by wide-angled, long-lens television coverage), and that there is so much traffic on the links that it could easily be mistaken for a golfing motorway. To be fair, and to its credit, it remains an Open Championship venue highly accessible to all comers who are willing to take their chance in the daily ballot and its staff could not be more welcoming. In stark contrast, the more southerly Muirfield (or The Honourable Company of Edinburgh Golfers, as it pretentiously prefers to be listed) continues to discourage the casual golfer and is more reminiscent of a stuffy English golf club than the majority of the more characteristically friendly Scottish venues. Kingsbarns, with its long winding driveway and equally imposing clubhouse, could easily have fallen into the same trap of pomposity. As well as the incongruous 'Restroom' toilet, a giant Rolex clock crowns the portico entrance, both acting as symbols and guarantors of its affluent nature. But, as I was to discover, it's here that any similarity thankfully ends.

There's an old joke (but perhaps worth repetition) that you know when summer has arrived in Scotland because the rain is warm. Though still in May, summer beckoned and I had spent the previous week rubbing high-factor sun cream into my wintry pallid skin. Sadly, my investigative walk around Kingsbarns was conducted in three sweaters, waterproof trousers and carrying a wide umbrella, which sagged under a deluge of heavy and very cold rain. My luck had clearly run out.

Or so I thought. As I turned into the club's driveway the next morning, a thick dark cloud hung over the course. I may be mistaken, but I think Moses was in the car in front, as, within seconds, it seemed that some celestial deity parted his stratocumulus curtains to let in the light and allow the gods to sniff the morning air. By the time I parked my golf bag by the pillared entrance, I was bathed in bright sunlight.

From this position, you can glance over towards the 18th green. The day before, feeling wet and shivering with cold, I had scurried from the course without giving the final hole much attention. Yet every new visitor to Kingsbarns should give themselves time to take in its demands. In many ways it will provide the perfect preparation for what you are about to face. Even from a distance, it's clear that the drive needs to be placed well to give you any chance of hitting the green in two. Even then, a longish iron needs to be struck well, as the putting surface sits on a plateau, guarded by a deep gully and a fast-flowing burn.

But that's the easy bit. Once on the green and depending on the daily pin position, you can be putting uphill, downhill, across quickly breaking borrows and, more than likely, at a pace that suggests your golf ball is hooked on 'speed'. I logged this information as best I could and strode into the surprisingly small clubhouse.

It proved to be a sumptuous but relaxed affair, which reminded me of the drawing room of a country estate mansion. Deep leather armchairs seemed to be haphazardly scattered, rather than formally arranged, and it was clearly designed to accommodate more weary sleepers than you'd find in the Rip Van Winkle Golfing Society. The changing room, on the first floor, was equally well equipped with its own leather-furnished lounge. Oil paintings of golfing heroes litter the walls and you are treated to magnificent views of the course and distant sea. Oddly, the resplendent bathroom even supplied bottles of mouthwash and I could only assume that halitosis was endemic to the furry-tongued inhabitants of the St Andrews coastline. Never one to turn down a free gift, I gargled for two minutes and went back downstairs to meet my playing companions.

Handshakes were exchanged and I offered my name with as much exhaled air as I could muster. They were clearly impressed by my dental hygiene and we soon slipped into easy conversation and enough shared humour to suggest that it was going to be a good day.

Sadly, this temporary optimism lasted about two minutes.

'Handicaps?' I asked genially.

'Five,' answered one.

'Six,' replied another.

'Scratch,' declared the third. 'And you?'

'Oh God!' was all I could manage.

Even without my trusty abacus, I was able to calculate that the combined total of my companions' handicaps still fell short of my own (though not by much – I do have some pride).

And then it got worse. Failing to find my bag where I had left it only half an hour before, I broke out into a sweat of such magnitude that it managed to conceal the previous 'post-handicap-declaration' perspiration. Until my host offered a quick word of reassurance, I was convinced that my clubs had been stolen.

'Caddy's taken it,' he said with a smile.

'Caddy!' I exclaimed, unable to disguise my growing anxiety.

Surrounding the 1ˢᵗ tee stood six waiting figures, solemnly lined up in greeting. They reminded me of a recently seen picture of Puritan scaffold attendants who lined the steps as Charles I climbed to his bloody death. Four young caddies, the caddy master and a benevolent starter met me with warmth in their hands but pity in their eyes. Refusing the last rites, I asked for my driver.

As a guest of the club, I was granted the honour and gulped my way to the loneliness of the waiting, symbolic block. With a deep, mouth-washed breath, I turned my shoulders, prayed for salvation and hurled myself at the waiting ball.

'Shot!' came a chorus of nine voices, in such perfect harmony that they would have done credit to a Welsh male voice choir.

To my astonishment, the ball flew long and true, with the only draw I had managed to hit in the last five years. I walked back to my congratulatory audience with an unconvincing air of calm, careful to remove any sign of surprise from my quivering facial muscles. We were underway and, for the moment, life felt good.

I had spent the previous evening looking through the course design notes, produced by the managing director a year before Kingsbarns was officially opened. Though difficult to paraphrase, it became clear that the primary intention was to use the bordering sea to its best advantage and that the amphitheatre setting and natural topography would be retained in the final course layout. With such a claim, they had set themselves up for my critical eye and provided a target for my acidic pen.

Yet, what made the greatest impression was that the document seemed dominated by philosophy rather than factual detail – a mission statement rather than a list of technical specifications – and at first I assumed that many of the words must have been plagiarized from Socrates or Plato. As a pseudo-academic who once dallied with metaphysics (it's another long story), what's left of my inadequate intellectual ability suddenly prompted my memory. I had once made a vain attempt to read *Design Argument*, David

Hume's virtually incomprehensible philosophical treatise. This eighteenth-century Scottish scholar, appropriately born in nearby Edinburgh (and a man who obviously shared my fervent scepticism), contended that though the world may well confirm some sort of random design by an all-powerful being, there's nothing wrong with the present inhabitants offering Him a helping hand and giving what's on offer a damned good tweak. (Yes, I know it's over simplistic but I don't want any complaints from young, over-smart, acne-ridden philosophy students.)

What really stirred this vague memory of David Hume's rantings was Kingsbarns' perspective on golf. They wanted players to be (I quote), *emotionally free* to enjoy *the majesty of the site's sea aspect*; to enjoy the game in *anticipation and hope-fulness* rather than in *despair and anger.* Though maybe a bit flowery, I share their golfing sentiments and before I had hit a single shot, they had me on side.

Put even more simply (than my explanation of David Hume's philosophy), within the space of five holes, I began to fall in love with Kingsbarns. It wasn't the sort of mindless affection suffered by pubescent adolescent boys whose hormone-flooded veins quiver at the sight of a shapely female form. My amorous feelings were built on the sort of inductive reasoning that would have most hardened academics slavering with delight. The course is truly beautiful; the never-ending seascapes breathtaking; the fairways tough but fair; the greens challenging but never over elaborate. Every landing area, be it fairway or green, seems to gather the ball in a friendly embrace and then tempt you into bravery. In the words of Kingsbarns' *Perspective on Golf,* I found myself playing in *anticipation and hopefulness* and rarely in despairing anger.

On my previous day's walk around the course, I had noted

the 11th green with the single word 'Madness'. The plateaux and contours seemed unreadable, the swinging breaks almost ridiculous. But playing the course proved to complete my conversion. On every chip and putt, though undeniably difficult, the necessary line soon becomes apparent, though, as always, the gap between theory and execution proved to be an insurmountable void, but always an enjoyable challenge.

I was playing well. Embarrassingly well. My young caddy (who played off six), gave me perfect lines, perfect club selection and perfect, morale-boosting encouragement. Needless to say, I began to develop an overblown belief in my own questionable ability and played the 12th as if I had never hit a golf ball in my life. And if you are ever fortunate enough to play Kingsbarns, try and maintain your concentration on this hole. It's not that it's a particularly difficult par five. The reason you should hold your game together is that it's probably the finest hole on the golf course, the fairway sweeping in a giant arc around the North Sea shoreline; the bumps and hollows typical of a classic links design; the long narrow green heavily guarded by bunkers. You could play this hole all day and never tire of its imposing beauty and the demands it makes on even the finest golfers. Don't (as I did) waste the opportunity.

'Wondered when your handicap would kick in,' laughed my scratch opponent.

It was said without the slightest hint of malice and, instead, delivered with a comforting arm around my shoulder and a broad cheery smile. I had found myself in wonderful company, my partner never failing to praise a well-hit shot or to sympathize with the occasional 'duff'. It had become a highly competitive game played in a fine spirit.

Unfortunately the professional golfer had underestimated the brittle nature of my golfing temperament. If I had been plugged into a golfing *neurotico'meter*, I would probably have found myself certified as mentally unstable and been admitted to an Edinburgh clinic. My game shattered into fragments of slices, shanks, fat shots, thin shots and, if I had ever reached the greens, would probably have missed a one-inch putt.

This sad state of affairs appeared to have no end. As we approached the quirky par-three 15th (and having nothing else to do as the others completed the 14th), I glanced once more at the course guide. The notes for this hole began: *'Tighten yer kilt, laddie'. A good round can be derailed here.*

As I already felt derailed, I thought it couldn't get any worse. Then I saw the 6-yard gap between a copse of trees and the waiting, foaming sea. Apparently, I was expected to fly my shot through this needle's eye and land it on a long narrow green some 165 yards in the distance.

Having given up any intention of ever hitting a long iron again, I whispered, *'Nine wood,'* to my caddy and ignored his look of dismay. He knew I was suffering and his expression suggested that my condition had advanced from 'critical' to 'terminal'. You can guess the rest. My second drawn shot in five years pierced through the gap and sailed high onto the green. I was back in the game.

What is it about golf that can see one good shot transform you from a pessimistic wreck into a man oozing with optimistic bravado? Deny it if you will, but we're a fragile breed who can take life-changing decisions without blinking an eye and yet find ourselves with the constitution of a jelly as we hover over a 3-foot putt. It's always struck me that if you want to find out about yourself, play golf. If you prefer to spend a life in denial, take up stamp collecting.

We arrived at the 18th all-square, but unusually for a final hole, it had been given a stroke index of four. I had a shot in hand and was armed with the benefit of having studied the demands of the hole when I first arrived at the course. Both my partner and I hit good drives, easily close enough to make the green in two. Five minutes later, our opponents were safely on the raised green, my partner in the watery burn and I was in deep rough still 80 yards from the pin. We were heading for defeat with a whimper.

Yet another poor shot saw my ball nestle in a grassy hollow with only the slightest view of the fluttering flag. It took all my skill (and there's not a great deal to call on) to persuade the dimpled sphere onto the putting surface. With the 'enemy' safely home in four, I was left with an 8-foot putt (an angler's description) to save our small wager and my own dignity. With the eyes of caddies and players burning into my neck, I steadied myself over the putt and sucked salt air deep into my lungs. The ball rolled forward and . . .

I can only offer a clue to those final moments but I can still remember sleeping well that night with my wallet at my bed-side no slimmer than it had been on the previous morning. It had been a truly memorable day.

Before sipping the final drop of a fine single malt, and switching off my bedroom light, I reached once again for the Kingsbarns brochure. It informed me that the American Kyle Phillips had designed this new addition to British links golf. Later research revealed a man who doesn't look old enough to design Lego bricks yet has a golfing CV that stretches back for many years. Given my initial fears of the Americanization of traditional links courses, I began to reflect on my visit. Had I been wooed by the enjoyment of my game? By the caddies and great playing company? By the ritzy clubhouse and the Kingsbarns tartan 'goody bag' of badges, ball markers and course guide? Had the whisky and hot dogs at the starter's hut blinkered my view from the truth? Was

Kingsbarns no more than a parody of tradition, a counterfeit links course plagiarized by an American designer?

I thought long and hard about the answers to these questions and no more so when, the next day, I went on a pilgrimage to the Old Course at St Andrews. As usual it was seething with visiting devotees, the starter announcing each game through a Tannoy that was clearly striking fear into every combatant. Unable to find a slot in the ballot, I wandered down the open roadway that runs by the side of the famous 18th hole, towards the 'Valley of Sin'. A procession of four-balls stopped to record their visit with a picture on the shrine of the Swilken Bridge.

As I watched one group strike their drives, a ball flew over my head, hit the stone stanchion of a nearby hotel, shot back across the road between two startled motorists and finally came to rest in the middle of the fairway.

'Nice shot,' I offered with friendly irony, as the errant golfer approached. 'Good round?'

'Yeah. Good thanks,' came the reply. 'Bit slow.'

'How long?' I queried.

'Not too bad.' He smiled. 'About five hours.'

Feeling grateful that my name hadn't been drawn out of the ballot, I wandered back towards the ancient clubhouse to watch yet another group of golfers strike their nervous drives down the 1st hole.

'Five o'clock game, play away please,' came a tannoyed voice.

You could hear the knees knocking from twenty yards, their swings hurried and graceless as crowds of tourists willed them into embarrassment. A group of waiting caddies huddled in conversation by the starter's hut and I took my chance. I wanted answers to my questions and I wanted to hear it from the horse's mouth. They were a tough but affable lot and before I could speak, one of the men turned towards me.

'Playing?' he asked.

'Couldn't get in,' I replied.

'Tried Kingsbarns?' he asked.

'Kingsbarns!' I exclaimed. 'Why Kingsbarns?'

'Better than this,' he whispered. 'Best course I've ever played.'

The horse had spoken and I had the answers to my questions. Looking back, I knew the answers already. If I hadn't approached Kingsbarns with my usual sceptical prejudice, I'd have been able to see the course for what it was. Take away the luxurious trappings, the hot dog offerings and the 'Restroom' signs and you are left with a stark reality. Kingsbarns does *not* represent an act of American piracy or a counterfeit of Scottish tradition. Its layout can hardly be faulted. The sea, visible from every hole, fires your spirit; the iridescent gorse and tight rolling fairways provide a perfect landscape, whilst the riveted bunkers and contoured greens will make you drool with pleasure. It is a true links course in every sense and a thing of sublime beauty. It should be admired by even the most xenophobic of golfers who consider that nothing worthwhile has occurred since Britain lost its Empire. Kyle Phillips might have 'tweaked' God's creation, but you'll never spot the human hand of intervention. The philosopher David Hume would have loved it. And so did I. This course *is* the real thing and they've achieved their stated mission. Go to Kingsbarns and play in anticipation and hopefulness. You won't be disappointed. If you are, take my earlier advice – throw away the golf clubs and take up philately.

Recommended Alternatives

St Andrews (Old Course): The shrine of links golfers. If you really want to appreciate the home of golf, play it in a strong wind and under storm-filled skies. Truly unique.

St Andrews (Duke's Course): Many think it's better than 'The Old'. Certainly tougher, more scenic and more heartbreaking. You might miss the tingle of tradition but it's magnificent to play.

Crail: Often missed by the golfing tourists. Seascape views and great greens. Put it on your itinerary.

NORTH BERWICK
Lothian, Scotland

May

Though I'm an Englishman, this was a return to my virginal Scottish roots. I mention this, not to lay false claim to a tartan heritage, but to place on record that many years ago, North Berwick was the first Scottish golf course I ever played. I remember it as a boy might recall his first scented kiss: a moment of trepidation laced with consuming pleasure. This East Lothian links had lodged itself in my mind as a small corner of golfing heaven.

Two weeks before renewing my acquaintance with the course, I had, on no more than a whim, tried to locate another fragment of my past. The Internet colossus that is Friends Reunited had often tempted me with its promise to exhume my personal history. And so, one lazy morning, I found myself taking the first tentative steps into the treacherous quicksands of reminiscence. No sooner had I tapped on the computer keyboard than I began the struggle to break free of my buried past. An inner voice was telling me that I might be entering dangerous territory. How many times have you had chance encounters with forgotten, youthful friends, only to find them creased and tired, their once carefree natures blemished by time?

In my own rose-tinted recollections, the links of North Berwick had somehow developed its own catalogue of saintly mythologies and unchallengeable odysseys. Would they prove too fragile to be put to the analytic test? Preconceptions tend to offer far more comfort than stark reality and I approached this small golfing hamlet terrified of shattering my long-held illusions.

At first, the town makes little impression, especially if approaching from the east. It has that rather dowdy feel so reminiscent of many British seaside resorts. The high street, normally the hub of a thriving community, looked dreary and unimposing, the profusion of charity shops suggesting that the town may have seen better days. But making my way west in search of a hotel, the houses suddenly grew in stature and gave me the first indication of North Berwick's affluent core. And, as I was to find, the clue to its true nature can be found at the quirky little railway station where the line comes to an abrupt stop, only a short stride from the centre of the town. From here, it's no more than a thirty minute journey into Edinburgh and, given the grandeur of the houses to the west, the passengers take their skills to the city and return with some fairly hefty wage packets.

North Berwick lacks the vulgarity of many of Britain's music hall coastal towns – in most cases, there's far less to them than meets the eye. In North Berwick's case, exactly the opposite applies. If the high street is the dowdy auditorium, wait until the curtain goes up. Step onto the shoreline and you'll start to get the real picture. You'll be presented with a natural set design that will convince you that your ticket was worth every penny. Wide sweeping beaches stretch out along the coastline, the circling horizon dotted with rugged islands and jutting outcrops. To the east lies Bass Rock, its towering cliffs shimmering in a snowcap of breeding seabirds, whilst to the east, the island of Fidra peeks a craggy fin out of the dark waters of the Firth of Forth, the beacon of its clifftop lighthouse guiding seafarers away from the waiting rocks.

It's said that Robert Louis Stevenson was inspired by this seascape; the looming silhouette of Fidra providing the fictional setting for his piratical adventure novel *Treasure Island*. If he had been writing today, I suspect Stevenson's hero, Jim Hawkins, need not have travelled so far to discover the pirate booty. There may be no Blind Pew or his gang of dastardly brigands, but North Berwick's real treasure is to be found on a narrow strip of the mainland that provides a buffer between town and shore.

Unlike the wonderful Kingsbarns or the austere Muirfield, don't expect any sort of grand entrance to the links of North Berwick. You can almost stumble across the clubhouse, which occupies the site of a nineteenth-century toll house. The small, but impressive sandstone building nestles amongst private houses, the only available car park being a narrow roadway that runs along the edge of the white rails, bordering the 18th fairway. Yet understatement is perhaps the clubhouse's finest quality, and obviously close to the heart of those members who had once rejected any talk of extending its facilities. The changing rooms are small, the bar simple, the dining room opulent but reserved. Like a cosy den, it has the sort of warmth that only comes with age-worn use and can't be built to order.

To maintain the sense that you are treading in Robert Louis Stevenson's footsteps, I would suggest that you begin your visit by going on a North Berwick 'Pro's Shop Hunt'. I can't offer you a pirate map but I can supply some cryptic, *Treasure Island* clues.

Hunting the North Berwick Pro's Shop:

Look for a place that can't be seen.
Search not for what is 'on' but that which is 'under'.
The name of its owner you'll hear from an angry
    librarian.
From the clubhouse entrance, pace 200 strides to the
    north and a sign you'll be given.
You may find a 'Black Spot' but only on a Ping.
If you see a one-legged pirate with a parrot on his
    shoulder you have spent far too long in the bar.

I have always felt slightly sorry for David Huish (pronounced 'Hush'). This admirable and talented man once led the Open Championship into its third day and is probably one of the longest serving club professionals in Britain. But this is not the object of my compassion. The club's gratitude for the professional's commendable service seems to be slightly muted by the fact that his shop is barely visible to the naked eye and appears to be almost totally submerged below ground. I'm sure a retired miner would feel at home, but for a golfer to be denied any view of some of the finest scenic landscapes nature can offer, it has always struck me as scant reward for a lifetime's service.

In contrast, the nearby starter's circular, stone-built hut enjoys the greatest position in North Berwick. A slight twist of his neck allows a view down the 1ˢᵗ fairway, a swing of the shoulders provides an eyeshot of Fidra Island, whilst a swivel of the chair gives a clear sight of Bass Rock.

If I was David Huish, I'd pinch the starter's key, choose a dark and stormy *Treasure Island* night, shift all my stock into the hut and then bluntly refuse to budge. With the aid of a well-placed periscope and a loudhailer, I'm sure the starter could perform his duties from the underground pro's shop, without any loss of his present proficiency.

Unusually, a very close friend (whose disdain for the game of golf is only matched by that of Mark Twain) reluctantly accompanied me on my pre-emptive walk of the course. Experience had told me that wandering amongst golfers without a set of clubs can be a highly dangerous occupation. Not only do golf balls regularly whiz past your head but the whole time is spent avoiding suspicious glances and, on the odd occasion, nose-to-nose confrontation. My way around this problem has been solved by adopting 'appropriate wandering tactics'. This includes dressing like a golfer (spiked shoes; heavily embossed Callaway baseball cap) and flourishing the symbols of authority (a bright red notebook and course planner). Equipped in such a manner, I have found myself making far more friends than enemies.

Standing by the 1ˢᵗ tee, I engaged a member in conversation, opening our exchange with my usual incisive, piercing question.

'Playing?' I asked meekly.

'Caddying for my son.' He smiled cheerfully. 'Club competition.'

'Good player?' I enquired.

'Hits the ball a mile,' he responded.

The father was true to his word. His athletic, twenty-something son turned his shoulders further than I can twist a corkscrew. The crack of his driver almost shattered my sunglasses. The ball, as promised, flew a mile. Unfortunately, it was also in the wrong direction, his brand-new Titleist ProV1 sailing over the coastal path and into the murky waters of the Firth of Forth.

Whilst I had immense sympathy for his closely observed embarrassment, I was also overcome with delight. His costly wayward drive was an early confirmation that my memory was still in full working order. North Berwick is a figure- (or pieces?) of-eight pure links course with two fairly distinct loops. Of these holes, seven may result in cries of 'ball overboard!', seven are threatened by out-of-bounds and the remaining four give some respite (despite the occasional requirement to fire approach shots over dry-stone walls).

The 1st (and high on my list of favourite opening holes) gives you every indication of what's to come. Your drive is threatened by water, the starter's gaze and the pen of an occasional wandering, rancorous writer. Having stayed on dry land, a six iron should see you home. Unfortunately (but delightfully), the approach shot is played to a completely blind green, which teeters on the edge of the waiting beach. Should you be playing an early-morning round and still red eyed from the previous evening's excesses, I guarantee you'll be fully awake by the time you step onto the 2nd tee. North Berwick hits you hard and hits you early.

The 3rd (464 yards, par four, stroke index one) contains just about every hazard known to golfers and, though rarely talked about, is a magnificent hole. The drive must be carried over a burn (hazard 1), landed short of a dry-stone wall (hazard 2). For the second shot (a fairway wood for the average golfer), the ball must carry over the wall (hazard 3), avoid the deep greenside bunker (hazard 4), avoid the wall by the green (hazard 5), avoid the nearby sea (hazard 6) and land on a contoured green, which you'll be happy to two-putt (hazard 7). What more could a naturally masochistic links-golfer ask for?

Sauntering to the 'turn', my companion and I were immediately accosted by a husband and wife two-ball. It was the beginning of an informative and engaging five-hole relationship. Accompanying them up the 9th hole (a needle-threading drive and a long second shot to a raised green), they began to deliver the words common to all club members who are fortunate to play on popular seaside links.

'Two hours!' exclaimed the grizzled member. 'Two hours for nine holes!'

'Is it always like this?' I asked.

'Hardly ever,' he laughed. 'But a round of golf should never take more than three hours.'

Bemoaning slow play is, in my experience, the birthright of all golfers whose club's financial solvency depends on visitors. There's nothing I enjoy more than a curmudgeonly whinge when I see convoys of strange cars drawing into my own club's car park.

But it's an insoluble problem. When visitors come to play, and pay fairly high prices, they want to savour their day and squeeze every last penny (or dime) out of their ticket. I've always found putting out for a nine completely beyond the pale, but I can understand the sentiment. My new acquaintances didn't quite share such a benevolent attitude.

'We waited so long on the seventh' he groaned, 'I could have died, been resurrected and still had time to play my shot.'

With lines like that you don't miss your chance and we gladly accepted their offer to take the guided tour in their company. We were treated to a swallow's nest in the shelter at the back of the 11th tee; more stories of Robert Louis Stevenson on the 12th; a detailed description of the squawking bird life that comes into full view on the 14th green. And then came the 'Redan', one of Scotland's most famous and infamous par-three holes.

Named after a defensive position at the Siege of Sebastopol in 1854, I was informed that it is one of the most copied holes in the golfing world. Stand on this 15th tee and you can see how the Light Brigade felt before they charged into the Valley of Death. You are lulled into a false sense of optimism by being completely unaware of the green's defensive *redoubts* or *redans*. Hit short and you will have bunkers to the right of you, bunkers to the left of you (apologies to Lord Tennyson). Hit long and you'll face more rising and falling contours than a Sebastopol valley. Even if you hit the green, the fear of Russian gunfire and borrows that couldn't be read by a theodolite will almost guarantee a three putt. Like Lord Cardigan, and however much blood might be spilled on the way, I couldn't wait to take it on and lead my cavalry into battle.

We left our companions at this point, still happily grumbling about slow play and wishing he'd gone sailing for the day. But the look on his face betrayed the truth. As he delivered his words, his expression confirmed there was no place in the world he would rather be.

I took my reluctant friend for a beer in the bar overlooking the 18th green, a hole which could easily be mistaken for the finish of the Old Course at St Andrews.

'So, what do you think?' I asked.

'How much is a set of golf clubs?' he answered apologetically.

'What!' I exclaimed. 'I thought you hated the game?'

'This place could convert an atheist,' he smiled.

Aware of the stern test I would face in the morning, I drank very little that night. This was not a result of my strong-willed character, but thanks to a swish hotel bar that took forty-five minutes to respond to a simple request for a large single malt.

My enquiry as to whether the horse-drawn carriage had met with an accident on its way back from the Western Isles was greeted with a blank stare of incomprehension. Concerned that I was likely to be accused of animal cruelty if I ordered a second drink, I settled for an early night and dreams of how I would master the 'Redan'. Soon after waking, I ordered a substantial breakfast. Given the time it took to arrive, the porridge was clearly shipped in from Perthshire and the eggs from an organic chicken farm on the lower slopes of a Patagonian mountain. But finally, I was well fuelled and ready for that opening drive.

My luck was holding, and in more ways than one. There was no more than a light breeze as I approached the starter's hut and the high scurrying clouds were ringed with sunlight. I was only halfway through my golfing excursion around the edge of Britain and, so far, I had enjoyed the company of all the players who had volunteered to see me round their golf course. Given the law of averages, I felt certain that fate would soon deliver a pompous partner or an objectionable opponent. But I was beginning to realize that it is only non-golfers who make such play of the haughtiness of blazer-clad club members or the presumptuousness of captains and secretaries. By the time I arrived at North Berwick, I had played with nothing but gentle men of gentle nature. Within three handshakes and a brief introduction, I knew I had struck gold once more.

The three senior members gave me a warm welcome and, as so often happens, the honour of teeing off first. This is an occupational hazard that had seen me age ten years in three months. It must have been the Perthshire porridge that did the trick, as my drive (at first unseen to my astigmatic eyes) hit the middle of the fairway in exactly the right position to make the green.

We had decided to play a Stableford competition (points mean prizes) and, much to my surprise, I found myself well ahead of the field by the time we came to the turn. But as I should have guessed, you can't relax when competing with men who have successfully engineered their careers, distilled their professions and forged their vocations. (There's a clue to their identity somewhere in this cunning, Robert Louis Stevenson description, but I respect their privacy.) By the time we reached the exquisite and idiosyncratic walled green of the 13th, my resolve was weakening and my swing beginning to quicken. And the Redan was yet to be faced. Like a Russian soldier, I decided to 'dig in' and waited to repel the inevitable charge.

But if digging in was required, I clearly needed a much bigger shovel. One of my opponents, with a high handicap on his card and a low handicap in his swing, attacked as if trying to win a Crimean War medal. I wobbled on the 13th, nosedived on the 14th and knew I must take my last stand at the 'Redan'.

The tee revealed we were to play from a distance of 167 yards. As a man terrified by anything bigger than a six iron, I would have given anything to play a wood from the back tees. It wasn't an option. I was forced to grab my five iron and fire into the unknown dangers of the fortified green.

I would love to say that I executed the shot with panache, precision and precocious talent. Instead, I can only describe it as a paltry slap, which sailed through the air with the grace of a featherless ostrich, trundled through the rough, bumbled between bunkers and finally came to rest just below the green. A fortuitous three was still a distinct possibility and I read the first putt perfectly as a gentle strike up the slope with a big left-to-right break. The Redan had sprung its trap, the ball swinging from right to left and accelerating past the hole like an Olympic sprinter.

I stared hard at the green. The Redan stared back. Whoever first seeded the green on this naturally contoured land appeared to have taken a hand in constructing a surface that defies all known laws of geometry. Some might call it unfair. I took a four, and I still think it's an astounding hole. It's no wonder that all those golf clubs that have tried to reconstruct the Redan for their own pleasure have universally failed to mimic its subtle challenge. For those clubs who make future attempts to recreate the putting surface of the Redan, I have the perfect 'recipe' for success: *First, take a volcano, add an ice age and leave to rest for no less than a million years. Seed in warm weather.*

The finish at North Berwick is not for the faint-hearted. Together with the Redan, the 16th and 17th holes require absolute accuracy, and second shots into blind greens. The 18th, though flat and unbunkered, can be an equally daunting affair. Though a par four, the temptation to go for the green is almost irresistible, the only drawback in this strategy being the roadway along the right-hand side of the fairway. Slice a ball here and you could be facing not only embarrassment but also a large bill for a broken windscreen or a cracked skull.

Needless to say, now only one point ahead of my nearest challenger, I treated the hole with respect and played it with my own brand of conservatism. Removing my jumper (*à la* Jack Nicklaus during the Open Championship of 1970), I hurled myself at the ball with all the finesse of a crazed gorilla. Clearly terrified of failure, and possible litigation from owners of the line of waiting car windscreens, the ball obeyed all instructions, and my job was done.

Returning to the bar and a welcome pint of Belhaven Best, I began to reflect on my day. Had my fears of being reunited with an 'old friend' been realized? Had my memory been tainted by youthful illusion? Had the realities of my return blurred those rose-tinted images? My conclusions came quickly.

Though an Open Championship qualifying course and likely venue for the Curtis Cup, North Berwick may not always appeal to the 'purists' (by which I mean pedantic golfing bores). As already noted, the course challenges you with blind shots, deep-riveted bunkers, infuriating contoured greens and treacherous dry-stone walls. The clubhouse is small but functional; there's no practice ground of any note and the pro's shop is almost subterranean. A 'purist' might explode with pompous guffaws. For my own part, I can only sing its praises. North Berwick gives me all I want from a true links course. The coastline setting is almost unparalleled, the variety of holes incomparable and the diversity of required shots unrivalled. I had found my old friend in rude health and not, as I had feared, showing any hint of becoming creased and tired. It is a unique place of extraordinary quality, which could never fail to give me the ultimate golfing pleasure. Steal a map from a golfing pirate, follow the clues and uncover the buried treasure.

Recommended Alternatives

Glen: Destined to play second fiddle to the magnificent North Berwick but definitely worth visiting. Something of an oddity with many blind shots and craggy terrain. Delightful.

Luffness: A little featureless at times but fine greens and an absolute brute if the wind blows. A great venue to hone your links skills or reveal your weaknesses.

Longniddry: Even though a mixture of parkland and links, not to be missed. An Open qualifying course for Muirfield, fine views to the Firth of Forth and quality greens.

WESTERN GAILES
Irvine, Scotland

June

The last time I had seen the golf links of Western Gailes had been from a juddering railway carriage, transporting me to a very profitable day at Ayr racecourse. Even through a grime-smeared window, a racing golfer can spot a 'good thing' and I had sworn to return.

At the time, little did I know that I was replicating an historical event. Over a hundred years before, four businessmen from Glasgow had peered out of a similar window and noticed a thin strip of unused, barren land, bordering the Ayrshire course. As men of Victorian vision, they saw far more than a desolate, gorse-filled desert. By 1897, they had raised the necessary finance, built themselves a golf course and were charging the members 10 shillings (50p or less than a dollar) per annum for the privilege of playing the new-found links. Without my earlier train journey to Ayr racecourse, I may never have discovered Western Gailes.

And, without that railway, I would not have experienced such an extraordinary end to my visit.

Sadly, the new millennium has witnessed the demise of our old transport systems as the railways now appear to be run by an idiot management. They have successfully turned a once favoured mode of travel into a system of ludicrously expensive cattle trucks, whose passengers enjoy their journey as much as a herd of bullocks on their way to the abattoir. Needless to say, this time I flew to Glasgow with a *s*d my carbon footprint* attitude, paid half the price of a train ticket and arrived fresh and ready to do battle.

The short car journey from the airport to the coast does little to set the golfing juices flowing. Unlike the more northern Highlands, Scotland's south-western terrain is rather drab and surprisingly flat, the towns functional but dreary, the scenery rarely reaching beyond the unexceptional.

Though heading for Turnberry later in the week, I decided to make camp in an upmarket Travelodge in the nearby town of Irvine. It seemed to mirror my first impressions of Ayrshire, the red-brick façade and straight-line architecture mimicking the dullness of the surrounding countryside. It appeared to have less soul than a pair of worn-out shoes. As far as I could see, the place was packed with red-faced golfers, their expressions displaying the usual mixture of grief-stricken anguish and orgasmic pleasure. Showering quickly, I went in search of a welcoming ice-cold beer.

The weather was unusually warm, the air robbed of oxygen by the burning sun, and, stepping to the back of the hotel, I found a small veranda decked out with table, chairs and wide, shading umbrellas. And it wasn't the only thing I found. Facing me was a nine-hole, par-three golf course and beyond it the sweeping bays of an enormous driving range.

In terms of my visit to Western Gailes, these may seem

a use of inconsequential, if not irrelevant facts. Far from it. As any golfer will know, we are often afflicted by *Swingitus Nervosa*, a mental complaint that, when first self-diagnosed, is considered to be terminal. Symptoms include increased pulse rate, heavy perspiration, nagging self-doubt and constantly fidgeting hands, feet and buttocks. Arriving in Scotland with all the early manifestations of this chronic condition was not ideal timing. I was about to play two of the finest links courses in Britain, yet, during the previous three or four days, had suddenly developed a banana-like slice: my irons were producing the occasional, unmentionable shank, and I could only employ my putting stroke after staring at the ball for at least ten minutes. The sight of a driving range appeared to have been delivered by providence.

Like a visiting soothsayer, I began to search for more predictive signs of my golfing future. A cheer from the nearby garden soon delivered the runes of fate. A wedding party had gathered on the lawn and as the flash bulbs fired, the loving couple beamed in self-congratulation. The bride looked suitably delicious, her hourglass figure suggesting that a single grain of sand would have difficulty in passing through her narrow, wedding day waist. Beside me, an obese middle-aged couple looked on with growing disinterest, their conversation muted by time, their faces suggesting that they had long since forgotten how to smile.

My creeping pessimism was suddenly banished, renewed by the symbolism of the grinning bride and groom. Golf is undoubtedly like marriage, a journey of uncertainty in which the opening scene is no predictor of the final act. Step onto the 1st tee with confidence and tragedy may await. Your opening drive may be a good one but a broken marriage between brain and body may see your second shot disappear into the clinging rough. Slice your drive onto the beach and there may yet be pleasures in store. It's the perfect cure for *Swingitus Nervosa*. Just get out there and do it. You can never know what lies ahead.

The next morning, mentally renewed, I awoke to a power cut. But the moment I walked into the blackened, deserted breakfast room, the lights immediately returned. My entrance had coincided with the second coming of electrical power and for the next half hour, I was treated like a messianic saviour, my every wish responded to with an instantaneous response. It was clearly yet another portentous sign and I was soon heading for Western Gailes to begin my inspection with a bloated stomach and a sense of saintly optimism.

It was only a ten-minute journey, yet I seemed to have been presented with a fuming guard of honour, the streets lined with puffing outdoor smokers waiting to start their eight hours of hellish abstinence behind the factory doors. It seemed ironic that Scotland, a country notorious for annually consuming 80 per cent of the world's lard production, should have adopted such draconian health measures as the banning of smoking in all public places. By the time you visit Scotland, it is likely that all those in authoritative positions will be attired in official tartan kilts, in which images of plump matrons have been weaved into a suitably penitent, haircloth fabric.

Now ranting with indignation, I took the narrow turn towards the golf club, only to be stopped in my tracks by a small bank of flashing lights. Golfers will no doubt write to me in their droves (or is it drives?), but Western Gailes has a unique entrance. The approach road is bisected by the Strathclyde railway line, guarded by one of those half-barrier level-crossing gates that sends fear through your veins as you nervously edge your vehicle across the track.

With thoughts of marriage still lingering in my head, the clubhouse appeared, rather like Trevose, as something of a white, wedding cake affair. (The use of the words 'wedding' and 'affair' in the same sentence is clearly a deep Freudian reference.) This was cemented in my mind by the fact that every other vehicle that pulled into the car park seemed to disgorge a driver who appeared to be dressed for a nuptial service. My smart–casual attire stood out like a Campbell tartan at a MacDonalds' party and I approached the austere pillared entrance in nervous apprehension.

A gatekeeper's box defended the hallway and, as I was to discover later, was occupied by an equally smart caddy master.

'Do I need jacket and tie?' I asked meekly.

'Only members.' He smiled knowingly. 'Gentlemen members are required to arrive and leave the clubhouse in appropriate dress.'

'Really?'

'We don't enforce it.' He chuckled. 'It's just understood.'

'Right,' I muttered. 'Pro's shop?'

'Don't have one.'

'You don't have a pro's shop?'

'Afraid not. Can I help?'

By now, I was certain that I was about to drown in a pool of pomposity, a rule-governed club, high on formality and low on relaxation. Reaching down, I produced my golf shoes with a number of missing spikes. Clearly due to attending a wine tasting class the previous month, I had developed a hyperuricaemic condition (or a 'bout of gout', as it's more commonly known), and had to watch my podalic posture. I passed the treacherous shoe to the caddy master.

A small canvas sack was produced, its contents revealing everything needed by the discerning golfer. It was reminiscent of the old button bags common in every household in the more austere, post-war days. With a shuffle and a flick, the spikes were produced, his fingers working quickly and with the expertise of an old hand. As I watched, a small terrier shuffled out of the main hallway and sniffed my leg, turning away in disappointment as he caught the nervous aroma of an unsatisfactory handicap. He looked like he'd been around so long that he was only prepared to nuzzle up to a single-figure golfer.

But somehow, the dog's appearance began to alter my earlier opinion of Western Gailes. I was comforted by the fact that this sniffing canine had not been required to don jacket and tie and that it had clearly been given free access to all parts of the clubhouse. There was obviously a formal façade, but also an indication that things might be more liberal than I had first assumed.

My shoes now repaired, I searched out the changing rooms. Following the dog's example, I pushed open the unmarked, aged, high wooden doors and sniffed the air. I would recommend this activity to all who enter a club for the first time. There's nothing like the fragrance of history to tell you all you need to know about what's on offer. During my journey around Britain, I have found sanitized odours are normally a portent of unsatisfactory greenhorn courses and staked-tree golf. The smell of burnished leather and time-worn oak usually suggests you are about to enter an arena of authentic pleasures. Western Gailes did nothing to disprove my hypothesis and can easily be mentioned in the same breath as Royal West Norfolk.

The changing room is truly a thing of beauty: the high vaulted ceiling towering over the dark timbered interior; rows of splintered lockers standing sentry over lines of boot-scarred bench seats. But most startling of all is the elaborate Romanesque 'looking glass', which greets you as you make your entrance. It is cleverly placed at the far end of the parading lockers and if Lewis Carroll's Alice were admitted as a member, she would be in paradise. The whole corridor, leading through to the ornate bathroom, is punctuated by glassed reflections. It is a hall of mirrors without any hint of distortion. Are the men of Ayrshire prone to vanity? In truth, it's a universal male quality and the members of Western Gailes don't have a monopoly. As I wandered down the satisfyingly threadbare carpet, I glanced at myself in every mirror. It took me so long, I'll swear I was ten minutes older before I reached the end.

I decided to delay my course inspection until the entrants in a club medal had cleared the 1st tee. Wandering down the fairways in the middle of a competition tends not to endear you to the membership. But this small delay gave me a chance to do yet more sniffing. As the pollen count was now at Mach 10, this didn't prove much of a difficulty.

The bars and lounges of Western Gailes present a fine example of old-fashioned style. It possesses the sort of interior that can only be achieved through evolution rather than enforced, snappy modernism. Though some areas, such as the members' bar, had been recently refurbished, there was no evidence of wholesale slaughter. New, grandly embossed leather armchairs sit happily with retained Victorian fireplaces, whilst the cleverly designed, glass-topped tables act as horizontal display cabinets for the club's extensive memorabilia. Anything with the slightest hint of vulgarity had obviously been rejected out of hand. The maintenance of 'good taste' and 'understatement' are clearly the watchwords of Western Gailes. Yet as hard as I sniffed, I could locate no scent of snobbery or affectation. Even the four elderly, suited members (taking coffee and whisky at nine thirty in the morning) did nothing to raise my hackles. I found myself warming to Western Gailes. It was as if the old building was making the declaration that, *as soon as a visitor steps through my portals, you're one of us, and you must make yourself at home.*

I could delay no longer. It was a perfect sun-filled day with only a zephyr of a breeze disturbing the slumbering flags. Donning my fully spiked shoes, I wandered out onto the course. The clubhouse is unusually positioned for a classic links, as it lies in an almost central position with the holes fanning out along the north-to-south Ayrshire coastline. Set above the fairways, players must make their way down twenty steps of a railed stairway that gives the feeling of descending into an amphitheatre of golf.

Pause at the top of the stairs before making your grand entrance. From here you will get a real sense of what lies ahead. The course is possibly one of the narrowest in the country, wedged between the railway line and the not too distant shore. The many hands that have moulded the links into its present state must all have been members of the Magic Circle and had the ability to feed a family of four with fresh vegetables from nothing more than a window box. Yet, as I was to discover the next day, the tight landing areas for the drives can occasionally seem quite intimidating.

You are given early warning of this as you stand on the 1st tee, where you are challenged by a carry over heather and mounds to a barely distinguishable fairway. Even having negotiated the opening shot, the receiving green is small and undulating and needs the sort of precision that I only possess in my golfing dreams. And as I wandered through the course, it soon became apparent that this pattern of challenges is repeated, hole after hole. Western Gailes gives you little respite and demands that you maintain concentration on every shot. As someone with the attention span of a schoolboy banished to the back row of the classroom, I began to fear the worst.

What finally confirmed my trepidation was that, whilst taking scribbled notes on the course planner, I appeared to be scrawling the words 'Keep Left!' with great regularity. The term 'Left' and my untrustworthy golf swing only have the most tenuous of relationships – the ability to draw a ball from right to left has always remained one of life's great mysteries. If you are plagued with a chronic slice, Western Gailes could well rip your heart out and have you screaming for the comforting embrace of a plump Scottish matron.

In my own case, slicing the ball is no more than the occasional irritant but the course layout suggested that if the wind blew the next day, I could be in for a hard time. The 5th to the 13th run along the coast and whilst presenting continually stunning views of Arran and a distant Ailsa Craig, the drives become increasingly blind from the tees, and the fairways more tight and treacherous. If you're playing well, it's bliss. If you're playing badly . . . well, it's still bliss. Even walking the course, you will soon know that Western Gailes is a magnificent course in immaculate condition, which might draw your innards with the sensitivity of a rusty knife, but will give you all the self-destructive gratification demanded by any golfer who worships at the shrine of links golf.

The course turns southward at the 14th and away from the sea. But don't expect any cessation of hostilities. Instead of being threatened by the sea, you will have to contend with the nearby railway track. This final 'stretch' (as we've unfortunately learned to call it, in mid-Atlantic speak) demands more 'Left', 'Left' and 'Left' again. If you see anyone crying on the 18th green, you'll know they have a slicing problem.

Fuelled with a quick cup of tea on the delightful terrace overlooking the putting green, I headed back to my hotel and the salvation of the driving range. I had twelve hours to readjust my swing and fortunately found a bookstore in the local town of Irvine. Armed with my new copy of *Teach Yourself How to Draw*, I collected a large bucket of balls and began the planned transformation.

Two hours later, I had the ability to sketch a bowl of fruit but not the slightest idea how to draw a golf ball. I knew all the theory. Stand slightly closed, keep your shoulders square to your target, flatten the backswing, attack the ball from the inside and indulge in deep prayer at all times. Needless to say, all I ended up with was a pair of bleeding, blistered hands and a conviction that I had the golfing talent of a one-armed chimpanzee.

Driving ranges are strange places and usually populated by poor golfers. Every bay seems to contain a frustrated player who has just discovered the secret of golf in a magazine they happened to flick through in a dentist's waiting room. Watch them carefully. The first few balls fly straight and true, their swings rhythmical and unhurried. Within five minutes, this controlled practice has evolved into a frenzy of hitting aimed at getting through their bucket of range balls in the shortest possible time. What has invariably happened in the intervening period is that they have suddenly hit a poor shot. To a single-figure golfer this is of no importance. To a high handicapper it represents the end of their golfing life. The seed of doubt has been sown, the grip becomes tighter, the swing increasingly fast and erratic. They have reached the point of no return, where every shot is another arrow in their fragile golfing soul. Driving ranges, like cigarettes, alcohol and any of life's pleasures, should be given an immediate government health warning.

I slept badly that night; my confidence torn to shreds by what I hoped would be my salvation. But, like all junkies (and John Wayne), I was back on the range the next morning, searching for that one golden key that might lock the door on my uncertainty. It was a futile strategy, which had me planning my excuses well before I stepped onto the 1st tee.

'Game's on a bit of a wobble,' I mumbled, as I was introduced to my playing companions. 'Can't understand it. Been hitting the ball well all summer.'

The words made me cringe with embarrassment. There is nothing more pathetic than a player telling you how he was playing yesterday or last week. Golf is a *now* game, in which only the present has any consequence.

I had been joined by two ex-captains and the club secretary, all with lower handicaps than my own. As the game progressed, they proved to be good company, affable in nature and kind enough never to reveal any hint of criticism for my sometimes paltry efforts. But, as we approached the 1st tee, I had been stripped of any remaining remnants of confidence and stood over the ball oozing with self-doubt.

Even when competing against friends at your home club, all golfers will be familiar with 1st-tee nerves. Put yourself on that tee with three strangers and you can find yourself in a situation of abject terror. In this one opening shot, you can either establish your credit rating or make a public admission of golfing bankruptcy. All that follows may well depend on the success or failure of this initial drive. Hit it well and any later, poorly hit shots will be viewed as a minor glitch. Hit your first drive badly and any subsequent, well-hit shots will be seen as no more than good fortune. It is akin to walking into the office Christmas party and spilling a glass of red wine down the laced cleavage of the chairman's wife. Whatever you do to retrieve the situation is likely to be worthless. You are branded as a fool and will remain a fool for the rest of the evening.

Gripping the club with my blistered fingers and miserably

failing to ignore the flashing visions of driving range nightmares, I lurched into the ball with all the grace of a fifteen-stone ballerina with a broken ankle.

Unable to follow the ball's flight, I waited for the cries of derision and began to make a selection from my long list of well-rehearsed excuses.

'Shot,' said my partner, with a congratulatory nod of approval.

'Shot?' I queried, peering down the fairway.

'Perfect position.' He smiled.

The die was cast. I had transformed my playing partners' psyche from major misgivings to great expectations. My blisters became inconsequential, my panic-laden practice a thing of history. My confidence had been renewed in that one lumbering shot. Even more surprisingly, I dropped only two shots in those opening four holes and by the 5th tee, felt that I could take on the world. What I failed to appreciate was that Western Gailes had yet to unleash its true battalions. If it had been a game of chess, I would have realized that I had done no more than rebuff a minor skirmish from a few scouting pawns. The main offensive was yet to come.

Had I paid more attention to the course planner, it would have been obvious. Western Gailes has an unusual circular layout of four holes out, ten holes along the coast and four holes back to the clubhouse. Viewed from the air, it would mirror the battle lines of a Cromwellian army, a thin line of infantry bordering the railway track whilst the cavalry and artillery lie in wait on the shore, their southern and northern regiments poised to outflank the enemy. Standing on the 5th tee, I attempted to grasp the initiative and create havoc amongst Western Gailes' northern phalanx. They must have seen me coming.

I hit a decent drive into the heart of the fairway but as I

strode purposefully around the heathers and wild orchids, a small breeze disturbed my carefully coiffured locks. By the time I stood over my shot to the green, my hair was being torn out by its roots. Western Gailes had lived up to its name and sprung its cunning trap.

I wasn't complaining. Links golf without wind can be as unsatisfactory as rhubarb without custard. It's acceptable, but short of a vital ingredient. Unfortunately, when your swing is as fragile as bone china, it will shatter your game into fragments. Though my golfing credentials had happily been established during the opening holes, by the time I arrived at the 13th, I had been reduced to shattered rubble. And sadly, my inability to handle the wind began at the 6th, a par-five hole, which had caught my attention the day before and had been marked as possibly the best hole on the course. The tee gives you a clear view of Lappock Rock, the Isle of Arran and the sweeping horizon of the Firth of Clyde. The almost blind drive must be precise; the second shot weaved through a valley that would have an ambushing Apache war party hooting with pleasure. By the time I struggled onto the green, I had lost count and suspect that if I had finished the hole, I would have been fortunate to record a ten on the card.

As I had anticipated, there was to be no respite. The 7th (and first par three on the course) is a fine hole guarded by six bunkers and more humps than you'd see on a string of camels. Remarkably I struggled to a four, but for the rest of the shoreline holes, found myself restricted to the enjoyment of a scenic seaside walk and the misery of a golf swing lost on the wind.

Fortunately, my admirable partner (the club secretary) broadened his shoulders and carried me round to the 14th. Surprisingly only two down, we prepared to turn for home.

And it was here that I was told the tale of the town council's unusual plan to increase the local tourist trade.

More than twenty years before, the beaches of nearby Irvine had become underused and unkempt. As a result, the local hotels and shops were starved of trade and something had to be done. The solution was, to say the least, unusual in its remedy. Stripped of any alternative suggestions, the shore, which borders Western Gailes Golf Club, was declared as a naturist beach.

I'm told it was an immediate success, though surprised that so many Scottish skinny-dippers were keen to get their togs off in the often arctic Ayrshire summer. They must breed sturdy women and brave men in the shrinking cold of Irvine.

Unfortunately, the consequences of this strategy were not fully thought through. Sunday-morning four-balls suddenly found themselves attracting bigger crowds than the Open Championship at nearby Troon, though the fact that the spectators all seemed to be facing the beach aroused a great deal of suspicion. Overnight, the dunes between the 5th and 13th holes had become viewing areas for groups of people who were training their binoculars on far more than a flock of black-headed gulls. The members' liberal tolerance came to an abrupt end when, during a monthly medal, a brazen man and his wife (the latter clearly recognizable as a 'non-member') crossed the course, entered the clubhouse wearing no more than a smile and demanded a glass of water. The details are lost in time, but to the best of my informant's knowledge, giving the couple a good 'dressing down' was considered pointless and the embarrassed club secretary settled for a polite refusal.

I stood on the 14th tee fully clothed but stripped of golfing pride. Western Gailes stood on the verge of victory, my battalions lying blood soaked on the windswept shoreline.

With the strong breeze now at my back I delivered a rallying call to my most dependable troops (a trusty three wood and a rusty six iron). Two holes later we were all-square and it seemed that the day might yet be saved. As I prepared to drive at the 17th, my optimism had returned and I struck the ball with all the assurance of an inevitable victory. But, to my horror, the driving range fiasco came back to haunt me, the ball flying viciously off to the right and bound for the steel of the Strathclyde railway.

The next few moments can only be described as a slice of luck or perhaps more simply, as a lucky slice. The errant ball hit the track at precisely the right angle and shot back over the fence only to land in the middle of the fairway with a rusty six iron all that was required to make the waiting green. Whilst an interesting way to play this hole, it is not a method I would recommend. I would have more chance of repeating this shot as I would of winning the Open at St Andrews or being asked to make up a four-ball at Muirfield.

With another par on the final hole, we shook hands on a well-fought halved match and, in the end, a wonderful day on a fine links course. Without the railway, Western Gailes might never have existed. Without that steel rail on the Strathclyde track, I may have left a very unhappy man. But as things turned out, I felt it was time to celebrate.

'Think I'll buy a new sweater,' I exclaimed as we sipped port (what else?) in the cosy bar. 'I know you don't have a pro's shop,' I added, 'but do you have a display?'

'Only on visitors' days,' smiled the secretary. 'We put it away on club days. The members find it rather vulgar.'

At last I had discovered the true secret of Western Gailes. It's a magnificent, testing links course for members intent on retaining the old values. In many clubs, this would result in the enforcement of magisterial rules and encourage pretentious behaviour. Yet this golf course has enough confidence to apply its standards with a twinkle in its eye and to make those who step onto its immaculate fairways feel as if they are truly welcome. The caddy master had given me all the clues I needed when I first stepped into the ornate hallway. Good golf clubs, like good parents, never need to wield the stick. Instead, they imbue the family members with a sense of shared values, which can be enforced with no more than a wary glance. Western Gailes works, not simply because it is one of the finest links courses in Britain, but because its ethos is never imposed. It is simply understood.

Recommended Alternatives

The obvious choices would include Loch Lomond, Royal Troon and Prestwick. They are all magnificent, sumptuous, testing and enough to make any golfer dribble with delight. All of them are also ridiculously expensive to play and are perhaps better left to members and corporate high-rollers. Instead, try the following:

Kilmarnock (Barassie): Wonderful seaside links at a fraction of the price of its ritzy neighbours. Good value for an Open qualifier. Superb.

Glasgow Gailes: Somewhere amongst the glorious gorse and heathers is a fine links golf course. Definitely one for the masochist's notebook. Another reasonably priced Open qualifier.

Ardrossan Ferry: Not a golf course but a way to tempt you into a delightful day trip to the Western Isles and the glories of Shiskine or Machrihanish. Half the cost of Troon, etc., and twice the pleasure.

11

TURNBERRY
Ayrshire, Scotland

June

In the summer of 1977, I witnessed two extraordinary events. The first was to watch an English tennis player, Virginia Wade, win the Wimbledon ladies final with a small wooden racquet and wearing a pair of frilly knickers of such titillating attraction that it prompted me to join my local tennis club the very next morning. Only a few weeks later, with my top-spin forehand now having developed into a thing of ugly inconsistency, I sat down to watch the very first Open Championship played on the links of Turnberry. Within four hours, my tennis racquet had hit the bin and I had ordered my very first set of brand-new Letters golf clubs, forged by a skilled Scottish club maker. As fate would have it, that very same craftsman had accompanied me around his glorious home course of North Berwick only a few weeks earlier.

The events and effects of that Open Championship are etched on my memory. In the twenty-first century, it is remembered as the Duel in the Sun. At the time, and not possessing the lexicon of a tabloid sub-editor, I only recall referring to it as 'One Hell of a Golf Game'. However it might be known, the 1977 Open saw Turnberry hit gold. Tom Watson and Jack Nicklaus decimated the field and engaged in a four-day private battle, which went to the last shot, on the last day, on the last green. The only other Green slightly involved was called Hubert, a talented American who finished in third place behind the winner Tom Watson and only a mere eleven shots adrift.

Interviewed later, Hubert Green suggested (without the slightest hint of rancour) that he had, in fact, won the Open, as Watson and Nicklaus appeared to be playing in a completely different competition. As for myself, the impact was immediate. I fell in love with Turnberry, out of love with Virginia Wade and only ever picked up a tennis racquet if my golf swing had contracted a severe dose of the shanks. From the moment Watson's winning putt dropped into that hole, it was golf or nothing.

With my golfing history branded by such memories, I feared I would approach Turnberry in a state of reverence and humility, a set of literary tools unsuited to objective appraisal. As I drove down from Ayr, winding my way along the stunning coastal road to the nearby village of Maidens, I was already in an over-submissive mood. Two days previously, I had been forced to watch my (sometimes) recalcitrant student son stand in the dock of a magistrates' court and suffer the indignity of verbal sanction from his fellow man. Some months before, he had thought it a good wheeze to drive his highly powered car down an empty motorway at 105 mph. A snoozing policeman, clearly irritated to be woken by the car's throaty exhaust, had applied the blue flashing lights and written out a very polite ticket of disapproval.

As the trial date loomed, we worked frantically on

statements of mitigation and pleas for leniency. The final letter, peppered with Shakespearean references from *The Merchant of Venice*, rose to a climax with Portia's cross-dressed words:

> *But mercy is above this sceptred sway*
> *It is enthroned in the heart of kings,*
> *It is an attribute to God himself;*
> *And earthly power doth then show likest God's*
> *When mercy seasons justice.*

As this well-delivered speech wafted through the courtroom air, grown men in the public gallery began to sob uncontrollably; the chief prosecuting officer wept tears of sympathy, her tears dropping onto her papers, as gentle rain from heaven. Unfortunately, the chief magistrate (obviously averse to verse and her quality of mercy completely restrained) sat stony faced, donned her black cap, stamped the driving licence with six points and issued a heavy fine.

Despite having dressed myself up like a country land-owner and my son doing a good impression of a television evangelist, our reverential demeanours hadn't quite cut the mustard. Ignoring these lessons, I arrived at Turnberry clad in a new white shirt, trousers with creases that could have sliced bacon and a pair of shoes polished to such a degree that dancing a tango with a woman in a short skirt would have had some unexpected benefits. The last time I had dressed in such a manner, I had been a spotty teenager failing to capture the heart of an inaccessible young goddess. It's amazing what you'll do when you are in awe of beauty.

By sheer chance, I arrived at Turnberry in its centenary year. It felt like a romantic date I had been anticipating for at least a hundred years. But as hard as I tried, I was unable to shake off the feeling that I had come to pay homage. My only gnawing concern was that, like many adolescent liaisons, my harboured illusions were about to be shattered by reality.

But Turnberry is no shrinking violet. As the coastal road drops down towards the sea, the golf course announces its presence with all the timidity of a twenty-gun salute, every barrel exploding in unison. There is no gradual effect. You are faced with a barrage of affluence and style, built on the sort of confidence that only comes from self-belief. If visiting for the first time, don't expect a golf club. What you are being offered is the 'Turnberry Experience'.

Approach from the north and your eye is immediately drawn to the famous red-roofed monolith of the Turnberry Hotel. I couldn't resist. Instead of turning into the golf club, I turned left into the sweeping drive and through the manicured, banked lawns. Having parked my Renault Clio hire car out of sight, I strode into the pillared reception area. Though given a short, guided tour, you need go no further than the entrance hall. Glance at a new Rolls-Royce and you know what's in store. The interior is so sumptuous it treads dangerously on the verge of shameless decadence. I made the usual mutterings about 'considering a visit for a special occasion' but, at not far off a thousand pounds a night (golf and extras thrown in), my £65-per-night Travelodge bed and breakfast wasn't about to lose my custom. If I ever do stay at the Turnberry Hotel, I will follow the words once delivered by an infamous miserly uncle, who took me to one side, and whispered: *If you ever stay in an expensive hotel get your money's worth and eat two breakfasts.* Sound advice, I think.

The importance of the hotel cannot be underestimated. Like many of the Scottish west coast links courses, Turnberry owes its existence to the railway. Opened in 1906, the once Station Hotel offered the great and good of Britain's Industrial

Revolution a chance to spend a little of their enormous wealth in a manner befitting gentlemen in tweed suits, sporting gigantic moustaches the size of two ferrets mating over a stiff white collar. What is extraordinary is that Turnberry's railway proprietors were so far ahead of the holiday game. In many ways, now more than a hundred years ago, they offered the very first package tours, providing luxurious accommodation, spa baths, haute cuisine and unlimited golf for starchy gentlemen and crinolined ladies.

It's often said that the Scots hate the English. I'd be surprised if they didn't. If my ancestors had spent their short lives being hacked to death by successive English armies, I think I'd feel the same. But if that hostility still remains, they have found a very clever way to exact centuries of revenge. Cunningly, they know precisely how to give Sassenachs a good time whilst quietly bleeding their wallets dry. As a man who still feels guilty every time I cross the border, I say good luck to them. Given the hospitality I invariably receive, a savaged bank account seems a small price to pay for a history of English kings and queens who viewed the continuous slaughter of Scots as a worthwhile and enjoyable weekend hobby.

Cross the road to the golf course and you will experience a seamless thread of style and welcome. The grandeur of the nearby hotel is cleverly mirrored in the clubhouse, its white walls and red-tiled roof standing as an ornate, miniature reflection of its older sibling. If your pulse isn't racing by this point you're either a second-hand car salesman with the sensitivity of a brick or a magistrate whose poetic soul has been surgically removed. Step inside and even an estate agent would feel obliged to write sonnets. The words 'well appointed' would do the interior a severe injustice. You are met with a cavernous hallway, deep luxurious carpets, sweeping staircases and a gallery of photographs, paintings and golfing memorabilia. Golfing greats rub shoulders with royalty and American presidents, whilst amateur visitors peer at their heroes in hope of being sprinkled with the same stardust of achievement. Not that there's much dust in evidence. The whole area, both inside and out, looked as if it was probably hoovered every ten seconds.

Having eaten only one breakfast in my economy lodgings, I swept up the sweeping stairs and into the bar. I'm probably wrong, but I'd guess this is the largest golf club bar in Britain. Though gaining some suspicious glances, I paced the floor out, quickly coming to the conclusion that I would need a decently hit wedge shot to send a golf ball from one end of the room to the other. Carefully selecting a position that gave me a view of the 18th green, I waited (as required) to be served at my table. It was a hot summer's day and with the windows open, I could hear the musical trill of song thrushes and the exhausted buzz of worker bees, eking out their living amongst the fairway heathers. To my horror, I could also hear something else.

I can only describe it as a conspicuous cacophony of canned music. From every conceivable direction, I was assaulted by one of life's major irritants. The ring tone of a single mobile phone is capable of sending me into a frenzy of irritation. When their owners gather in groups (the collective noun being a 'mob of mobiles'), I become incandescent with rage. But when the recipients of those metallic ring tones answer their calls in a brash, *I don't care who I'm disturbing* voice, I have to ring my counsellor on her mobile and demand another course of anger management. I was at Turnberry. I was in heaven. Sadly, someone had left the door open to hell.

Only when I received the bill for my meagre lunch of cheeseburger and Coke did I begin to understand why such behaviour is tolerated. Turnberry is primarily designed for 'high-rollers' with high aspirations and high phone bills. Though it has a membership, it's essentially one of the world's most luxurious pay-and-play golf courses. For those of us who (like the majority) are more accustomed to private golf clubs that gain their revenues from the annual subscriptions, such a format comes as something of a shock. The Westin Turnberry Resort, as it is more formally and presently known, is unashamedly a profit-making business, offering a service to a competitive, affluent market place. Mobile phone users are part of that market and I guess you don't bite the hand that feeds you.

As I wandered back down the staircase to the magnificent changing rooms, I began to realize that I had approached Turnberry with a whole catalogue of misplaced attitudes. My reverence and humility had blurred my reason. I was not here to wallow in golfing history or to become dewy eyed about my youthful memories. I was here to assess a working business, to ask if it met its customers needs. In management speak: I was here to check out the product.

I had kindly been allocated a locker by the caddy master and as I retrieved my spiked shoes, an agitated figure threw his sports bag onto a nearby, carpeted bench and began to rummage through its contents. His hands ran quickly through every pocket, through his jacket, through his trousers and even through his shoes.

'Lost something?' I asked helpfully.

'Spare mobile,' he grunted.

'You have a *spare* mobile?' I exclaimed.

'Must be in the hotel,' he grumbled, ignoring my surprised expression.

'And your other mobile?'

'Lost it on the course,' he grumbled. 'Cost me a bloody big contract.'

'Gosh,' I responded simply.

My parting shot had been chosen carefully. It implied sympathy without committing myself to heartfelt compassion. In rough translation, the use of the interjection *Gosh* can be interpreted as: *I'm so terribly sorry*, or, in this particular case, *Serves you right, you ignorant b******, golf courses are for playing golf not making b***** telephone calls.*

With some relief, I finally made it onto the hallowed turf, stopping briefly to chat to the starter in his immaculate attire and equally immaculate white-walled cabin. You will not be surprised to discover that just as the clubhouse reflects the hotel, so the starter's cabin mirrors the clubhouse. I felt as if I was unwrapping a Russian doll with white skin and red-tiled hair, each newly exposed building being a miniature representation of the original.

As I was to find on my walk around the main Ailsa course, simple granite blocks are placed by the tee and marked with the name and yardage of the waiting hole. The 1st tee contains something a little different, a humbling message that strikes both fear and admiration into the hopeful golfers. Carved into the stone's surface are the names and remarkable scores of Tom Watson, Greg Norman and Nick Price, the three previous Open winners who have been announced onto the opening hole. With the hairs still rising on the back of my neck, I strode out with the feigned stride of a champion.

I'd heard it said that the first few holes of the Ailsa course are a bit of a disappointment. It's a claim I would refute in every respect and if the opening three holes constitute a letdown, I'm happy to suffer a lifetime of disappointment. The finest restaurants don't serve the main course first. They tease you with canapés and hors d'oeuvres, whetting your appetite for the treats in store. And if Turnberry were a restaurant, it would have three Michelin stars. The sheer beauty of the course is immediately apparent, the salty sea breeze rippling the heathers, wild briar roses colouring the trampled rough. Sound too poetic? Only by intention. If Wordsworth had been a golfer, his pen would have moved faster than a bee-stung greyhound.

Appropriately, the distant island of Ailsa Craig dominates the backdrop to this idyllic setting. It's a rock with a shape that must fill the dreams of every restaurant glutton. Imagine, if you will, the most perfectly formed, individual chocolate sponge pudding you have ever encountered. This is Ailsa Craig, and the gods must hover over it with giant spoons and brimming ladles of custard.

By the time you are standing on the 4th tee, the course explodes into its full glory. From this point you will be struck dumb with pleasure whilst your swing is tested to its limits. The next eight holes hug the shoreline, gradually drawing you towards the course's most northerly point and the rocky outcrop that supports the renowned Turnberry lighthouse. Its white-walled minaret design dominates the coastal skyline, its blinking eye offering praise and disapproval for the myriad talents who trudge beneath its shadow. With a light that has beamed since 1878, it must have witnessed over a century of the finest swings ever seen. No wonder it turns its light towards the golf course every fifteen seconds.

Ambling down the 7th fairway (a particular dogleg favourite), I was interrupted by a shout of 'Fore!' Inadvertently, I had wandered into the middle of a ladies' medal competition and, to avoid embarrassment, quickly scurried into the rough. A ball thudded into the deep grass only a few yards from my feet and, taking the opportunity to ingratiate myself with a potentially irate four-ball, I marked the mishit shot with a freshly laundered handkerchief.

The strategy worked to perfection, the owner of the 'lost' ball effusive with thanks as she approached.

'I doubt I'd have seen it again.' She smiled. 'Good job you were here.'

'Nae problem,' I answered, quickly adopting the local vernacular.

Spotting my red notebook, she pressed me with questions.

'What are you up to?'

'Just taking a few notes.'

'Caddying for a professional?'

'Writing a book.'

'Really?'

'Links courses, that sort of thing,' I replied vaguely.

'Well, I hope you write better than Peter Allis,' she said sharply. 'That man's made a fortune out of bletherin'.'

For those of you unfamiliar with the Scottish term 'blethering', it is a commonly used insult aimed at those who indulge in garrulous nonsense. By now, you may have come to the conclusion that I also deserve this descriptive epithet, though I thought her comment was a little hard on Peter Allis. He's an old-school, professional golfer and broadcaster, who mourns the past with a wry sense of humour that never fails to entertain.

The lighthouse marks the turn for home, a point where the course moves from idyllic scenery to spectacular drama. The championship tee at the 9th demands a 260-yard carry over the clifftop edge whilst the 10th has you flirting with the crumbling castle ruins of Robert the Bruce. There's not a golfer who wouldn't pay a king's ransom to play these two holes. Not only are they beautifully designed but you play each shot with a sense of history and a feeling that you are privileged to be alive. And just so you can savour the moment and collect your thoughts, a halfway house perches on the clifftop, a small veranda allowing you time to gaze out over the sea to Kintyre and think how lucky you have been to discover a corner of Elysian golf.

Though the course now heads inward, away from the shore, there is no lessening of its demands or of Turnberry's more recent history. The boundary between the Ailsa links and the stunning fairways of the more recent and alternative Kintyre course is marked by the landing strips built before the Second World War. Requisitioned by the government in the late 1930s, the Turnberry course was lucky to survive, but the retention of the airfield as parking for major championships acts as a constant reminder of heroic men and women who lost their lives during the dark days of war.

Still scribbling notes, I headed back to the clubhouse, surprisingly jotting down the words 'Best Hole' as I left the 16th green. In many ways it's a hole with limited views, only 380 yards off the white tees and demanding a fairly uncomplicated drive. The problem comes when you try to access the green. Its contoured, plateau surface is guarded by bunkers and a deep ravine burn, immediately below the landing area. If you are chasing a good score, the 16th will find the slightest glitch in your tiring swing. As I would find out the next day, it was a hole destined to play a major role in my own Turnberry experience.

My game on the Ailsa course was scheduled for 4 p.m. and I woke to the most perfect day I imagine the Ayrshire coast has witnessed in the last hundred years. Impatient to play, I found myself killing time around the Turnberry resort. There's plenty to keep you occupied, though spending seven hours sampling the various delights could see you move from solvency to bankruptcy before you stepped onto the course. Adopting a policy of window-shopping only, I took a tour around the well-stocked pro's shop, on to the Colin Montgomery Golf

Academy and blew the rest of my life savings on a sandwich and coffee in the Tappie Toorie Restaurant. The putting green beckoned, but, after surprisingly holing five six-footers in a row, my golfer's superstitious nature kicked in. Terrified of using up all my luck and with still three hours to go, I spent the next couple of hours in the gardens of nearby Culzean Castle, an extraordinary eighteenth-century clifftop stately home, overlooking the Isle of Arran. It was in these floral gardens that I formulated my game plan. No more reverence. No more humility. No more 'Mr Nice Guy'. Even playing off the white tees, the course didn't seem too threatening. Whatever the outcome, and just like Tom Watson and Jack Nicklaus, I was going to attack the Ailsa course and bring it to its knees.

As the clock struck four, and still suffering from delusions of grandeur, I sent my opening drive high into the Ayrshire sky, a small bounce to the right placing me in a perfect position to reach the green. Minutes later a five iron sent my ball towering towards the green, covering the pin as if guided by radar. My playing partner nodded his approval and I marched forward to begin my taming of Turnberry.

Unfortunately I never saw my sparkling new Titleist again, though I did find the small indentation it left in the green as it continued its journey into the back garden of a nearby bungalow. I had slapped Turnberry in the face with a soft leather glove and it had returned my foppish challenge with a sledgehammer. Standing on the 2nd tee, already one down, my earlier adrenalin-pumped confidence was beginning to diminish.

I had been joined in my game by George Brown, Turnberry's fabled and fêted golf course manager. We had first introduced ourselves on the practice putting green, and though I didn't mention it at the time, his face looked vaguely familiar. I had a sense that, at some point in my life, he had played a part in my own golfing history.

Having spent a great deal of my professional life theorizing about the interaction between strangers (that's enough information), I was fascinated by my first exchange with George. He was an amiable, humorous man with a gravelled Tommy Cooper voice, a relaxed attitude to golf and a no-nonsense approach to life. But what I sensed more than anything was an aura of competitiveness. If I was going to beat this man, I would need to concentrate harder than a tightrope-walker who's just dropped his pole.

Despite my misfortune on the 1st hole, I slowly began to claw my way back into the game. Apart from my ugly swing, I can only attribute this success to the fact that I was receiving eight shots and that my opponent's right knee was beginning to grate like a piece of chalk on a blackboard. He was there for the taking. He was wounded. He was hobbling. To paraphrase W. C. Fields, I adopted the attitude of 'never give a limping golfer an even break'. By the time we were at the turn, I was two up, merciless and contented.

Stopping at the halfway house, we sat for a few moments with a well-earned drink. The sun was beginning to drop over the ocean; Ailsa Craig was shadowed in soft evening light, whilst flashing swallows danced on the warm southerly breeze. It was a moment when all seemed right with the world. Glancing towards the nearby lighthouse, we fell into conversation.

'It's still in use?' I asked.

'The lighthouse?'

'Yes.'

'Only at night,' chuckled George.

As he spoke, the sun caught his face and kicked my memory into action.

'I knew I'd seen you before,' I exclaimed.

'Really?'

'With the President,' I answered.

'Oh, that.' He smiled quietly.

It was a typically dismissive and understated response. I doubt whether my companion would have mentioned it had I not raised the subject first. Some years before, George Brown had joined President Bill Clinton in a round of golf on the Ailsa course and their picture had been all over the golfing press. Naturally, I pressed him with sharp investigative questions.

'Enjoy it?'

'Only after I started calling him Bill,' he laughed.

'You called him Bill!'

'There's only so many times you can say, "Good shot, Mr President,"' chortled George. 'It starts to sound a bit silly after a while.'

'He didn't mind?'

'Not a bit.' He smiled. 'His security guards didn't seem too happy. But I'm sure he preferred it. Nice chap.'

As he spoke, George played his joker. Pulling a canister from his bag, he began to spray his injured knee with some unidentifiable remedy. Like the prosecutor at my son's recent trial, I became aware of the worm of mercy burrowing into my soul. The will to win at all costs was beginning to crumble. My concentration was in ruins.

I'm not sure what was in that knee spray, but George's tee shot seared down the middle of the 10th fairway, his iron at the short 11th peppered the pin. By the time we reached the 16th tee, I was two down with three to play and about to be counted out. History was repeating itself. I found myself involved in a personal 'Duel in the Sun' and was determined, just like Jack Nicklaus, to take my opponent to the last shot, on the last green.

Two good drives saw us both well placed and, a little shorter off the tee than my opponent, I had to play first. My second shot flew high over the waiting burn and only 10 feet from the flag. George offered a generous word of congratulation, settled over his ball and struck it with the sort of purity you'd only find behind a convent wall. With a sharp check on the green, the ball came to rest no more than 6 feet below the hole. I missed. He holed his putt for a birdie. I was a broken golfer. And on reflection, it had nothing to do with my sympathy for his injured knee. The admirable George Brown simply raised his game when needed and played me like a Scottish salmon, caught on the hook of an irresistible fly.

The last two holes were played in a series of lost balls and hacking mayhem, my mind and body unwilling to respond to pleas for clemency. But it had been an extraordinary game and I left the 18th green swatting away the growing clouds of blood-hungry midges, satisfied that I had at last gained the true feel of the Turnberry links. Yes, it's expensive. Yes, it's teeming with corporate 'high-rollers' carrying mobile phones. Yes, it's a business rather than a golf club. But forget all that. Turnberry is a golfer's paradise where the greens are true, the scenery unparalleled and the holes sublime.

There are things in life we should do at least once. Amongst these I would suggest walking the Great Wall of China, watching a sunset from the Mull of Kintyre and eating a Cheddar cheese and blackcurrant jam sandwich, made with heavily buttered, fresh granary bread. Since playing my own Duel in the Sun, Turnberry has now been added to the list. The Ailsa course *is* a jewel in the sun. It would be a jewel on a wet November morning. You *must* play it – even if it's only once.

Recommended Alternatives

See suggestions at end of Western Gailes chapter (page 160) – especially my advice to catch the ferry at Ardrossan. Don't miss this opportunity.

12

CASTLETOWN
Isle of Man

July

Perhaps if I'd said an early prayer to the Norse god Odin, things would have worked out differently. Maybe I should have landed in a longboat, instead of stuttering over the Irish Sea in a small reluctant prop plane. Whatever the case, I think the islanders had spotted my Danish ancestry and decided to repel the invader with their finest troops. I was well into my journey around the golfing edge of Britain and suddenly realized that two names had dominated my experience. Wherever I landed, I seem to have been preceded by either the Viking hordes or Oliver Cromwell's New Model Army. The Isle of Man was to prove no exception.

Things didn't start too well. A delightful oriental lady, across the aisle from my own cramped seat, was clearly not one of the world's greatest fliers. Having survived our take-off with a shriek of terror, she spent the next hour depositing her noodle-filled breakfast into a large paper bag.

Though I had visited the island before, I was now taking

my first ever step onto the Isle of Man's terrain. The reason for this apparent contradiction is that I had last come to the island as a babe in arms, when being sick on someone else's shoulder was considered socially acceptable. Because of my proximity to the vomiting Oriental, I approached the taxi rank as if history was about to be repeated. Fortunately, a sun-filled sea breeze soon revived my spirits and, despite my feeling a little queasy, the cab driver's shirt remained in pristine condition.

Castletown Golf Club proved to be only a ten-minute journey by car. After eight minutes, the rather grand white tower of the nearby hotel dominated the skyline as the narrow bay road edged its way along the shoreline. The taxi came to an abrupt halt.

'Problem?' I asked, seeing no other car in sight.

'They're on the fifth tee,' mumbled the driver, without any further explanation.

'What?'

'Not played here before?' he asked.

'No.'

'Always best to stop till they've all driven off. I guarantee one of them will hit the road.'

Ten seconds later, a ball bit into the tarmac no more than thirty feet in front of our waiting car and bounced onto the stony beach.

'See what I mean?' laughed the cabby. 'Never fails.'

'The fifth you say?'

'The Road Hole. Even Greg Norman nearly hit a car. And he still made a four.'

'I'll make a note,' I responded nervously.

As I was to discover, the course and hotel stand on Langness Peninsula with three sides of its boundary marked by the dark waters of the Irish Sea. As is becoming increasingly common, the golf course is integral to the hotel, the members' 'clubhouse' situated in a dark basement area near to the indoor pool and obligatory saunas, which no one ever seems to use. I have always found that the naturally conservative British prefer to sweat on buses and trains rather than in the confines of pine-clad ovens.

But the hotel (due for a complete redevelopment at some indeterminate time) should not be missed. The white exterior, which has had numerous facelifts over the last hundred years, is now reminiscent of a 1920s seaside retreat. The entrance hall alone is worth the reasonably priced tariff, a sweeping wooden staircase meeting your eyes as you are propelled through the heavy revolving doors. Within a few moments, I was convinced I had entered the set of an Agatha Christie murder mystery. Approaching the reception desk, I assumed that the mysteries of Castletown would be revealed once Hercule Poirot had bumbled down the stairway in his black tie and tails. Waiting for my room key, in no more than a golf shirt and an old pair of chinos, I felt singularly under dressed.

'*Je suis desolé*,' I whispered with a slight Belgian inflection.

Wondering if I could manage to grow a waxed moustache in under three days, I toured the facilities.

The hotel looked physically worn, slightly tired in spirit and ragged at its ancient edges. There was a feeling that the whole place had come to a halt, trapped in a time warp of gentler days. It was a delight and I couldn't have asked for more. The bedroom mirrored this pining for history, the wall-mounted trouser press an anachronism in the crumpled twenty-first century. Like saunas, I doubt they ever come into service – unless you have a sudden desire to toast a threatening wasp.

Pushing the window fully open, I leaned forward. Directly in front lay St Michael's Island, a small promontory now joined to the peninsula by a narrow causeway bridge. At the furthest point a thirteenth-century fort looked out to sea, its guns protecting the nearby bay of Derby Haven, now dotted with nothing more threatening than a few bobbing yachts. Pushing my head further through the open window, I glanced to the right and caught sight of a small slice of my own war zone.

The 18th green sits at the most easterly end of the course, almost encircled by water. It is built on its own mini peninsula, the jagged cliffs dropping sharply to the sea below. The entrance to the green is narrowed to the left by two bunkers and to the right by the wounding gash of a deep rocky gully that eats into the fairway and restricts the approach to little more than 20 yards. It was love at first sight and, like pubescent attraction, it was built on no more than a gut feeling that pleasure was in store. I was eager to throw down my challenge.

But it was to be another thirty-six hours before I could test my judgement. Casting my well-prepared plans to one side, I decided to walk the course in the evening sun, leaving me free to inspect the island on the next day. I felt sure that playing the golf course should be more than the Castletown experience; it needed to be an Isle of Man adventure.

With the sun already dipping in the wide western sky, I soon realized that it's an ideal time to assess a golf course. Long twilight shadows seem to give a much clearer definition of humps, hollows and contours, each hole given a 3D image of the terrain, which is sometimes lost in the glaring flat light of a midday sun. In some respects, Castletown has a 'Turnberry feel'. My saunter around the course revealed that, apart from the 4th, 9th and 18th, there are very few blind tee shots. The rest of the holes present a clear visual challenge and you are left in little doubt about the line that needs to be taken. But what will strike you most of all is that the sea is clearly visible from every tee box. Castletown may not be unique in this respect, but what makes it so distinctive is that the course weaves its way around three well-defined spurs of land, all of which are flanked by the shoreline on both sides. (The fine Ross-shire links of Fortrose & Rosemarkie is, I think, the only other British course capable of sharing this accolade.)

Castletown, like all good courses and gifts, unwraps its pleasures in a gradual rather than dramatic manner, initially teasing you with four steady, but well-designed holes. But if your game isn't in full swing by the time you reach the 5th, then you will receive a very sharp wake-up call. The Road Hole (a term not unfamiliar to those who have played the Old Course at St Andrews) is a thing of terror and beauty. Stand on the tee and you'll know why my taxi driver had the sense to delay my arrival at the hotel. Not only are you faced with impenetrable gorse along the whole left side of the fairway, but also with a road to the right, which borders the out-of-bounds sweeping shoreline. On flat terrain, this might not prove too difficult. Unfortunately (but blissfully), the needle-thin fairway also possesses a left-to-right slope of Alpine proportions. In the winter, I imagine you might just hold the ball on the tight links turf. But when this has been summer baked and has the sponge-like quality of hardened concrete, the only option appeared to be aim at the gorse bushes, pray that you don't hit the drive too well and then watch your ball bounce back into the middle. It is the golfing equivalent of playing a pinball machine that has two legs shorter than the others. And even if you manage to keep your ball in play, the second shot demands a long iron to a tight green, which nestles up to the road and waiting sea. Only a links junkie could enjoy such madness. Needless to say, I would happily give it a five-star rating.

Obviously, I can have no idea what 'turns you on' and given some of the strange people I've met on golf courses over the years, it's probably best I don't know. But for my own part, golf has two distinct qualities. Firstly, it is possibly the finest and most demanding sport ever invented whilst also being the most infuriating game you can play. We may try to repeat our swings but we can never repeat the experience of each individual round. But the sport's second great asset is that we enjoy our regular eighteen holes as a contest with opponents, as a self-examination of our temperament and as a battle with the sights, sounds and vagaries of nature.

Castletown, though one of the least well known of coastal links courses visited, brings these qualities into stark relief. The sea, which laps and sometimes rages onto the surrounding shoreline, plays a major yet minor role. Its peninsular position means that the wind can shift in seconds, deceive your early optimism with a millpond calm and within three holes see you bending into a gale.

Though you'll encounter the odd miniature palm, thankfully, there is only one real tree on the course – a sapling oak presented to the club to celebrate the PGA centenary in 2001 and reared from seed from Oak Hill, New York. The rest of the course is hard links terrain, flanked by high gorse and low, unforgiving rough. Cast your eyes north and a fully preserved medieval castle looms in the distance, whilst to the west a nineteenth-century herring tower dominates the skyline. It's from this giant structure that local boatmen would look over the water and shout highly technical fishing terms such as *I can see a big shoal of herrings!* or *Anyone fancy a fish supper?* Stand near this monolith, and if your golfing concentration isn't completely shattered, glance out to sea and watch basking sharks and dolphins rise and fall as they gasp for breath in the constant swell. You wouldn't find that on a tennis court or in a tenpin bowling alley. If you're ever accused of wasting your time on a tedious sport played by fat men in check trousers and earnest women in silly visors, buy them a ticket to Castletown and watch the conversion begin.

If anything, the 6th and 7th holes provide the only hint of mundanity. But they are tempered by the shadowed hills sweeping down towards the distant Port Errin and planes from the nearby airport struggling into the air and banking low over the 7th green as they head for the English mainland. And from this point, the course begins to tighten its grip, forcing you along hog-back fairways, heavily bunkered greens and long par fours. By the time you reach the 16th tee, you will be aware that Castletown is building towards a crescendo, a climax of three holes that I would count as one of the best finishes in British golf. The par-three 16th warms you to the task ahead. Though it first appears to be a rather innocuous hole, it is beautifully designed. A single bunker guards the green at the front and only the most precise iron shot will give you any chance of holding on the ridged surface. Move onto the 17th and the course explodes into everything you could wish for when you play golf 'on the edge'. From the white boxes, you must carry your drive at least 250 yards to gain a decent position to reach the green in two. What makes this even more intimidating, however, is that your drive must first negotiate a deep ravine with the Irish Sea crashing onto the rocks below. With the tee raised high above the visually distant fairway, I doubt this hole has an equal on any other links course. In the true sense of the word, the 17th is magnificent, presenting you with the ultimate golfing challenge and the sort of ocean views that could turn a dispassionate stoic into a lyrical artist.

Whether the 18th is better or worse than the hole that precedes it can only be a matter of personal choice. Like the 16th, and despite a blind tee shot, this final hole seems to offer little challenge. But having hung out of my hotel bedroom window, I already knew the difficulties that lay ahead. As I began to tire, I slipped into the hotel bar, grabbed a large Scotch and sat by the 18th fairway to watch a few players finish their rounds. Of the three four-balls who passed by and glanced with envy at my ice-packed aperitif, only one player managed to hold the green in two. And they were no rabbits, all but one hitting long, accurate tee shots, well within range. One by one, their balls disappeared into the watery grave of the rocky gully, bounced into the guarding bunkers or sailed through into the tight clinging rough. By now I had more scribbled notes on the 18th green than you'd find in a Mozart sonata.

The following morning and with a day to spare before my game, I adopted Plan B for my visit to Castletown. Sadly, I also decided to walk to the airport to collect my hire car.

'About ten minutes,' assured the hotel receptionist.

Forty minutes later I was still circling the airfield like a jumbo lost in dense fog and at one point was very close to chancing my arm with a dash across the runway. Slightly deterred by the screaming engines of a small Boeing jet heading in my direction, I stuck to the road and arrived breathless and sweating at the hire car desk. Within ten minutes, I began my grand tour of the island in a luxury vehicle that seemed to have been converted from an empty sardine can. Undeterred, and with my foot flat to the floor, I headed slowly north.

The town of Douglas would not be the greatest introduction to the Isle of Man and came as something of a shock after spending twenty-four hours on the isolated peninsula of Langness. The high, towering and starkly white rows of apartments are a little too Costa del Sol for my liking and whilst the surrounding cliffs and wide beaches give it a certain attraction, I gave the place no more than two minutes of my time. Instead, I motored on to the pretty village of Laxey, following the tracks of the electric railway, which runs up to Ramsey. But I had another railway in mind and a chance to satisfy a childhood ambition.

I spent much of my formative years peering out to sea from the north-west coast of England. It wasn't the most exciting upbringing but I had been told that, with a little patience and perfect visibility, I might, one day, catch a glimpse of the Isle of Man. It became an obsession, matched only by my intention to make a hole in one at some time during my golfing career. (I had to wait until 4 June 2005 and suffer a bar bill of £175. Does anyone know a golfer who turns down a free drink?)

However, my childhood desire to see the Isle of Man from the Lancashire coast went unfulfilled. My parents, clearly distressed to see their son spending every day alone on the beach, decided that mendacity was the only possible remedy. Cleverly choosing a particularly clear day, my father joined me as I stared out to sea.

'There it is,' he said, pointing vaguely towards the ocean.

'You can *see* it?' I exclaimed.

'Snaefell. Look. You can just see it above the horizon. The highest mountain on the Isle of Man.'

I knew he was lying, but I wanted to believe. I had to believe.

'Yes! Yes! I can see it now,' I shouted, content with my self-deception. 'I'll climb it one day.'

'Why not?' smiled my father.

And so, many years later, I found myself at Laxey and at the base of Snaefell. Sadly, I also found I had only an hour to spare and a chronic attack of premature gout in my right foot. Climbing was not an option. The mountain railway came to my rescue.

It's a charming, rickety affair where the driver manoeuvres the one-carriage train up the steep gradients whilst reading a tabloid newspaper and consuming vast quantities of chocolate biscuits. I had been joined by my future – a delightful group of beige-clad pensioners who made me feel as young as the schoolboy who had once dreamt of this moment. It was a carriage full of wrinkled skin and witches' chins, thin discoloured legs hanging limply from youthful hiking shorts. Yet they shared my anticipation, the promised view from the summit, the hazy coastlines of England, Scotland, Ireland and Wales, clinging onto the edge of the world.

At 2,000 feet a mist began to swirl across the track. At 2,050 feet we found ourselves immersed in cloud. Fidgeting figures donned sweaters and jackets as the temperature dropped by 20 degrees. We shuddered to a halt in the eerie light, the collection of weak bladders grateful to see the mountaintop and the lavatorial relief. An elderly couple were perched on the wooden bench directly in front of my own. The woman, clearly aware of her impending mortality, leaned over to her husband.

'I wonder if heaven's like this?' she whispered.

'What?' he laughed. 'You mean a bloody disappoint-ment?'

'Hope not,' she answered tenderly.

With a tear in my eye, I peered out of the window. I

could see nothing more than the base of a bean-stalk radio mast climbing into the billowing cloud. I imagined a small, dispirited child on a distant beach, staring across the Irish Sea, his face masked in sadness. It was all too much.

'At least I had a hole in one,' I mused, as the train grated its way back down to the sun-drenched village of Laxey.

Within an hour I was standing by a lighthouse and contentedly looking across the water to the Scottish coast. The Point of Ayr is the most northerly part of the island, a desolate place ideal for casting out demons of the past. Quickly renewed in spirit, I headed south, winding my way through narrow country lanes and tight blind bends. Every time I manoeuvred round a corner, I was faced with a wall of sand bags, strapped to walls, gates and telegraph posts. As I was still high above the coastline, there seemed to be little chance of flooding and no apparent reason for this strange decoration. Assuming it was no more than a Manx tradition, perhaps a local fertility symbol, I pressed on towards the seaside town of Peel.

Expecting a quiet haven and a wander around the historic castle, I was instead met with a town full of waving national flags and Viking warriors. The beach itself had been submerged under a giant scaffolded arena and a recently constructed Nordic stockade. THE LARGEST VIKING INVASION SINCE 798AD, announced the fluttering posters and, after a few brief enquiries, I discovered that I had happened upon a Viking festival. Given my newly acquired knowledge of the island's bloody history, this seemed about as appropriate as the Israeli government introducing an annual holiday in celebration of Palestinian freedom fighters.

Unwilling to pay the entry fee or buy a ticket for the cunningly hired ABBA tribute band, I peered through the small gaps in the stockade wall. Whilst the collection of huts and armour looked authentic, the Viking marauders failed to convince. Clad in a variety of sackcloth, they flicked their ashes onto the burning sand as they chain-smoked through their boredom. Maybe the ancient Danes were far more advanced than I thought, but I'll swear those Vikings invaded the Isle of Man without a packet of Marlboro in their back pockets.

Forced, yet again, to disguise my Danish heritage, I sped off to seek the refuge of the Langness Peninsula and prepare for my own imminent battle. I was beginning to form a mixed impression of the Isle of Man. I had reached the summit of a mountain that had no view and become aware of a strange predilection to strap sandbags to stone walls. I had also discovered that the national flag bore the symbol of three legs festooned in medieval armour and bearing the Latin motto *Quocunque Jeceris Stabit*, or *Whichever way you throw it, it will stand*. Whilst this symbol bears an unnerving resemblance to a Nazi swastika, it is apparently derived from a more appropriate Nordic sun symbol. Why the Vikings thought the sun had three legs is beyond me, though I suppose if you've just sacked a few villages and drunk eight pints of 70 per cent proof Danish mead, everything looks like a tripod.

But it proved an appropriate symbol for the morning of my Castletown 'challenge'. I awoke to a clear blue sky and a furnace sun. Preparations took longer than usual, the liberally applied factor 30 cream refusing to be absorbed into my delicate artistic skin. Quickly checking the darkened mirror, to make sure I had covered every exposed piece of skin, I engaged in three minutes' deep breathing and then reached for my (legal) golfing aid. For some time now (due to years of youthful backflips performed as a party piece), I have taken to wearing a back support. Friends often refer to this accoutrement either as a girlie corset or, more unkindly, as a dubious sexual aid. Whatever the case, it does its job and turns my slightly drooping physique into a thing of Adonis-like beauty. And when I strap it on, I know it's time to go to work.

Stepping onto the 1ˢᵗ tee, I was joined by an Englishman, an Irishman and a Scotsman. Having already received notice of their golfing prowess, I knew this wasn't going to be a music-hall joke and once more decided to resist giving any information of my Danish heritage or my sneaking admiration for Oliver Cromwell. Unnervingly, my three companions comprised two professional golfers and an eminent local businessman, all kind enough to make no comment on my strangely erect body or sun-creamed, death-mask face. I shuffled towards them with a nervous greeting. Two minutes later, and with great relief, my opening drive sailed down the middle of the fairway.

'If there's anything you need to know, just ask,' said one of the professionals as we sauntered towards the green.

'Just one question,' I responded.

'Go ahead.'

'Have you declared war on Ireland?'

'What?'

'All those sandbags – on the walls and bridges. It looks like you're preparing for an invasion.'

'Oh those,' laughed the professional. 'It's for the motor-bikes. You know. The TT Races.'

'Right.'

'We put them on all the bends,' he added. 'Just in case they crash.'

'Does it save them?' I asked.

'No. But it makes death less painful,' smiled the Irishman.

I was suddenly more relaxed than I would have been in

an underused sauna. It was the completion of my mental journey through childhood, when motorbiking heroes flashed past my front door on their way to the ferry and the mystical Isle of Man. Leather-clad, godlike riders decorated my room. Pictures of Masetti, Surtees and Duke, hunched over the gleaming frames of their Nortons and Gileras, sent me to sleep with the imaginary whiff of burning two-stroke oil. Though I was now on a golf course, it had been transformed into my spiritual home.

In such a state of euphoria, even the infamous Road Hole seemed to offer little danger. Hovering over the ball, it crossed my mind that Castletown should consider flying a flag on the 5th tee bearing a three-legged golf ball with the Latin motto *Quo vos ledo mihi ego mos vado versus profundum*, or, in golf speak, *Wherever you hit me I will go towards the sea.*

Employing my carefully honed plan, I struck the drive towards the gorse bushes high on the left and with the intended poor swing. Sure enough, it fell short of the menacing scrub and trickled back across the fairway only 2 feet from the road. My professional opponent fired his own ball some 300 yards onto the only minuscule piece of flat land on the fairway, wedged to the green and sank the putt. It was his third birdie in the opening five holes and though I was playing well, I was beginning to feel like a rabbit, with an all-consuming desire to nibble carrots. I dug into my personal mental burrow and tried to match the professional's skills.

It proved a futile gesture, my game suddenly becoming littered with snap hooks and fat irons. Whilst the Irishman began to sink putts from obscene distances, and entertain us with his jigs of delight, my partner and I were sinking faster than my ill-advised stock market investments.

Five down and five to play, I finally prayed to Odin. It must have been his rest day, visiting a Danish bacon factory or having a fitting at his horned-helmet maker. My prayers went unanswered and we shook hands on the 14th green as the professional's sixth birdie dropped into the hole.

'Any tips?' I asked, my head bowed in defeat.

'You're a tilter,' came the friendly and sympathetic reply.

'Tilter?'

'Turn. Don't tilt,' he smiled.

He must have seen it the moment I hit my drive on the 1st tee. Girlie corsets might give a chap a trim figure, but trying to make a full turn with a boa constrictor choking your waist isn't exactly a piece of cake. Excusing myself with the false claim that I needed a 'comfort break', I slipped into the gorse, unwound the stifling contraption, ripped away the Velcro fastenings and concealed the offending girdle in my golf bag. I intended to finish with a flourish.

On the 15th my drive disappeared into the heathery rough never to be seen again but, on the short 16th, my newly released body responded to my urgings and, with a turn and a swish, sent the iron shot firing towards the green. I was ready to take on the 17th.

'Anyone fancy the championship tee?' laughed the Irishman.

'Love to,' I answered with false bravado.

If you ever play Castletown (and you should) don't miss this opportunity. From the blue championship tee, the 17th fairway looks as if it's in another country, requires a passport and a 280-yard drive to give you any chance of reaching the green in two or of avoiding the waiting, watery ravine.

With a comfortable par under my belt, I strode onto the 18th with a smile that didn't leave me for two days. Despite my highly detailed notes, the final hole was played in a flurry of mishit shots. Yet I left the course in a state of glowing euphoria. Checking my card, and despite being given the sort of thrashing that would have had revengeful, three-legged Manxmen cooing with delight, I had played two shots below my handicap.

The next morning, waiting patiently in the airport lounge and tapping my fingers in anticipation of the flight home, I opened the local free newspaper. Scanning the sports section I spotted the professional's familiar name in small but distinct type. Not only had he come third in the recent Pro/Am Manx Classic but he had also failed, by one measly shot, to make the final qualifying rounds for the forthcoming Open Championship. Little did I know I had been in such exalted company.

'I'll never tilt again,' I murmured as my flight was called.

As the plane and my fellow nine passengers climbed into the high wispy clouds, I pressed my face against the scratched perspex window and glanced once more over the giant retirement home of the Isle of Man. Directly below, the Castletown links came into view. There was something vaguely familiar about the course, as though it was trying to leave me with a final startling memory. And just as the wings began to shudder in the cold air, it came to me, the image so stark in its message that I was startled by my ignorance. The peninsulas of land that support this wonderful golf course were clearly laid out in the shape of the island's national symbol, the three spurs bending like armoured legs, washed by the breaking ocean waves. I had played at Turnberry only a few weeks before but I couldn't choose between them. Need I say more?

Well, perhaps I do. As the plane took off, I began to feel queasy. I had noticed a few rumblings as I showered that morning but had dismissed it with a large breakfast. Sadly, a quarter of an hour into the flight, I was forced to reach forward and grip a large paper bag. It had been exactly three days since I had been in close proximity with someone else in a similar predicament. Whoever she was, that oriental woman (and her regurgitated noodles) had come on board with far more than a fear of flying. Thanks a lot.

Recommended Alternatives

Mount Murray: Long on yardage, long on pleasure. Great views and very exposed to the quickly changing weather.

King Edward Bay: Stunning scenery if you can see over the gorse. Fairly short, but a good test of golf.

Rowany: More fine scenic views of the Irish Sea and a tricky course to negotiate. You can even arrive by steam train from nearby Douglas.

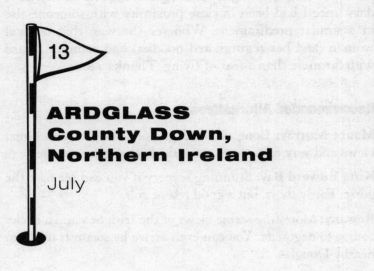

ARDGLASS
County Down,
Northern Ireland
July

Unlike Tennessee Williams, I've never really developed any affection for the Deep South. Through the unexpected twists and turns of life, I had set up home in the southern county of Buckinghamshire. Though the rolling hills hardly bristle with sugar canes and tobacco plantations, I had been forced to endure a long, humid and wearying summer. The prospect of heading north, to the damp green swathes of Irish turf, had filled me with impatience for cooler climes.

Already three-quarters of my way around the selected seaside links of the UK, my progress had become a matter of constant monitoring by my weekly golfing companions.

'Where next?' they would ask.

On most occasions, my response would be met with nods of approval, only rarely with tutting reservations. Days before my trip to the Emerald Isle, I was asked the same question.

'Ardglass,' I replied.

There was a universal reaction.

'Where?'

'Never heard of it.'

'Is it a links?'

'Is it in the UK?'

'How did you find *that* one?'

If, two months earlier, I had not taken a London tube journey from Victoria Station to South Kensington, I would have reacted to the name Ardglass in a similar manner. Engaged in my habitual eavesdropping on fellow passengers, I chanced upon a brief exchange between two Canadian golfers, their nationality revealed by the maple leaf badges carefully sewn onto their travel-battered golf bags.

'Great holiday.'

'Great.'

'Best course?'

'Got to be Turnberry. You?'

'Close call. Maybe Turnberry. But I had the most fun at Ardglass.'

'Me too.'

I had my notebook out faster than a tabloid hack and, within seconds of reaching my office appointment, had borrowed a computer and was typing the letters ARDGLASS GOLF CLUB into the Google box. Five minutes after viewing the website, I had booked my flight. Ardglass, like Chicago, looked like my kind of town. What drove me to such an instantaneous response was not only the obvious eccentricity of the golf course but also the fact that I was about to fulfil another ambition. Belfast had been on my list of 'must do' cities for many years, my intentions only postponed by the small matter of daily shootings, car bomb mayhem and the city streets crawling with heavily armed soldiers. Thankfully, 'The Troubles', as they are euphemistically known, have now abated. The use of such epithets is an interesting modern phenomenon, which pastes over the realities and reduces our fear. Golfers are no strangers to this kind of self-deception.

Two weeks before boarding my flight to Belfast, I had a noticeable attack of the 'wobbles', a 'bit of a bug in the swing', a hint of the 'J. Arthur Ranks'. Despite my fairly high handicap, I had enjoyed a long period of settled play and rising confidence. But as any golfer knows, such optimism is as brittle as an empty eggshell. I was developing a problem. 'The Troubles' were looming on my golfing horizon.

With rising panic I hunted frantically through every page of my extensive golfing library and snatched at the straws of salvation.

'Got it!' I murmured. 'Back inside. Turn those wrists over. Get onto the front foot. Cured.'

The local driving range witnessed my recovery; the hunched, distraught figure gradually rising from the ashes of despair as the ball began to soar towards my chosen targets. Ardglass was at my mercy.

Still dreaming of cool Irish air, I walked down the aircraft steps into the sort of searing heat that must have tempted local farmers to transform their emerald arable land into Deep South cotton fields. Thankfully, it was only an hour's drive to the coast and though I pulled into the golf club car park in a lather of perspiration, the welcome sea breeze soon revived my spirits and dried my ugly, sweat-patched shirt. Curiously, a Canadian flag fluttered in the wind, high above the 18th green. Having made my brief introductions, I sat in the comfortable bar with a pint of Guinness (what else?) and surveyed the course through the arched church windows.

I doubt any other course has made such an immediate impact. The 1st tee of the opening par four nestles against the ruins of a fourteenth-century castle and stands no more than

10 feet from the rocky edge of the Irish Sea. (I was to discover that in the windy, high-tide winter, your drive must be timed to avoid the spray from the crashing waves.) From here the land rises sharply to a steep sloping fairway that runs directly along a shoreline riddled with deep gulleys and craggy cliffs. The long narrow green is barely visible, set on a natural plateau between heathery knolls and the deep rough of the clifftop edge. Sipping the clerical collar of my dark beer, I sensed a quiver of fear surge through my veins. Would my 'cured' swing hold up to such an assault? Would the gremlins of doubt return?

Unwilling to face my demons, I turned away from the ecclesiastical window and decided to run my eye over the facilities. The clubhouse (reputed to be the oldest in the world) is a remarkable and pleasantly shambolic affair. Forming part of a medieval castle, the ground floor is a maze of narrow corridors, some of the passageways only accessible by bending low under original stone archways. A small, simple restaurant greets you to the left of the main entrance whilst to the right, the equally basic changing rooms act as a delightful symbol of the Ardglass philosophy. To call these modest rooms unpretentious would be to overstate their opulence.

The clutter of discarded shoes, broken trolleys and forsaken clubs may not sound like a recommendation, but somehow it sends out a comforting message to its first-time visitors. At many clubs, such disorder would represent a badge of dishonour. At Ardglass, you immediately feel that you are being instructed into a way of life, into a club that is determined to relax its guests and to reject the pomposity so often found in the golfing world. It suggested that Ardglass viewed its sport as a game to be enjoyed rather than feared, and that it was only a part of, rather than the purpose of, life itself. As I changed into my spiked shoes and prepared to walk the course, my opinion was confirmed. Sitting on the splintered bench, below the lines of age-worn lockers, something caught my eye. Two long, tapered, black metal tubes protruded from the nearby wall. Pulling them gently forward, I exposed their purpose. It was a unique discovery, never encountered in any other golf club I had visited. The sea fishing rods sat comfortably in my hands, the reels turning with the ease of equipment that was clearly in regular use. They seemed like an emblem of Irish wisdom, and a confirmation that the Ardglass members clearly shared my sense of values.

Soothing my burning skin with heavy layers of suncream, I strode out to discover the course and, within minutes, realized that the opening hole is no more than a taster of future dramas. The 2nd hole (an undemanding par three) requires a long iron with a 170-yard carry over a cavernous gorge containing a raging sea. The distant, minuscule green is only identifiable by the top of a fluttering flag. You'll already have spotted the irony. This 2nd hole is about as undemanding as a mistress with a sexual addiction and needs to be handled with similar discretion and complete attention to detail.

And so it continues, the first five holes weaving their way along the coastal edge, your concentration endangered by glittering seas, screeching wildlife and the views of the shadowed Isle of Man, perched on the sun-hazed horizon. It is a truly picturesque opening and has, I would claim, no equal on any other seaside links in the UK.

Briefly engaging a passing player in conversation, I was informed of the secret to playing this dangerous stretch of holes: 'Never forget, keep right. You have the whole of Ireland to hit at. Go left and you might as well go home.'

Jotting these words of wisdom in my notebook, I headed towards the 6th.

From this point the course cuts inland and strangely, with a lessening of hazards, the greens become bigger. But, after such a dramatic opening, and despite their beautiful layout and tough approaches to well-guarded, silky greens, the next four holes seem a little disappointing. On their own, they are superb, only suffering in comparison to the testing drama of the earlier holes. They are, however, nothing more than a brief punctuation. At the furthest point from the clubhouse, the course turns yet again towards the sea and continues its golfing narrative with the three stunning holes that border the bay of Coney Island. From here you are given a roller-coaster ride down a dramatic par three towards the shore; a par five of indescribable beauty (which I *will* attempt to describe later, as it proved to be such a contentious hole); followed by another immaculate par three played from a high tee down to a barely visible beachside green. To add to their drama, the distant Mountains of Mourne loom high on the horizon and bring a tear to even an Englishman's eye. They were holes of dramatic charm and terrifying threat, which, if my gremlins returned, would undoubtedly rip the heart out of my golfer's body. If I could hold my score through this chamber of idyllic horrors, I might be able to come home on a full sail. It seemed more likely, however, that I would emerge onto the 13th tee with a broken mast and a rudderless tiller.

And, in relative terms, the final six holes seem quite benign as they gradually fall back towards the clubhouse and finish on a tricky 18th, a hole that could wreck a card at the very moment you feel victory in your grasp. Yet I felt well prepared and itching to take it on. The next day, my newly repaired swing would put it to the test.

Returning to the changing rooms, I caught sight of my lobster-skinned features in the mirror, the sea breeze having turned my face into something that could have found employment as a human barbecue. Searching through sunburnt, swollen eyelids, I went to find my shoes. Oddly, they had been moved from their original position and had been placed carefully on top of someone's bag, their heels resting against the two fishing rods I discovered earlier. Now appropriately dressed, I climbed the stairs to the bar to renew my acquaintance with the Guinness nectar.

The small landing reflects the cluttered feel of the ground-floor areas. Papers and boxes are scattered liberally against the walls, whilst a computer, used to record players' scores, wobbles precariously on a makeshift stand. It is an agreeable disorder, which appears to both accept and reject modernity in the same breath. As someone who adheres to the dictum that a home should be a home and not a museum, I can only praise the 'Ardglass way'. Too many clubs throughout Britain have imposed such austerity on their surroundings that members and visitors feel they hardly dare use the toilet facilities without making a formal application to the secretary's office.

The bar had recently been refurbished yet remained relaxed and friendly. And as I made a small tour of the room, Ardglass revealed yet another unique feature. As if the seascape panorama from the front were not enough, the opposite wall contains a large bay window that looks directly over the harbour, a line of fishing smacks bobbing into view on the rising tide.

'Eating with us?' asked the barmaid.

'Well, er, not . . .' I stuttered.

'Curran's,' whispered another voice at my side.

'Sorry?'

'Curran's at Chapeltown. Only two minutes down the road. Best chowder in Ireland.'

'Food no good here?' I asked.

'Superb,' answered the grizzled face. 'But if you're only here for a few days, you shouldn't miss Curran's.'

'Thanks.'

A quick shower later, I pulled into the pub car park and viewed the recommendation. Curran's didn't appear to be anything special, a long single-storey building, uniformly painted in a startling shade of ochre that could frighten a dog from twenty paces. The interior presented a different face and unless they send me a voucher that supplies me with free food for life, I will say no more than it was very wooden, welcoming and wonderful in every respect. Whether the chowder was really as good as its billing, I have no idea, apart from reporting that by the time I consumed the final spoonful my taste buds had entered a state of euphoric delirium.

Advertising Curran's is not, however, the object of this digression. As I entered, I was immediately drawn into a conversation with a man at the bar. Given the size of his over-hanging stomach, he was clearly a customer who regarded Curran's as his second home. He was also, it transpired, a member of Ardglass Golf Club. And as any good investigative scribbler would do, I plied him with drink and loosened his tongue.

'So, you haven't played it yet?' he asked.

'No. Just walked it. Looks great.'

'What did you think of the eleventh?'

'Eleventh?'

'New par five. Along Coney Bay.'

'Oh, that one. Loved it.'

'Members hate it,' he slurred.

'What? All of them?'

'Well . . .'

His voice submerged into his beer as he considered my

challenge. And when his throat was oiled, his words quivered with emotion.

'It's just too hard, too damned hard. You can't keep the ball on the fairway.'

'Really?'

'Invited three friends over a few months ago. We lost nineteen balls between us. All on that bloody hole.'

'Nineteen! On one hole?'

'We weren't going to let the friggin' thing beat us.'

'You lost nineteen balls? You're serious?'

'Too right I am. Buy you a beer?'

I accepted gracefully and he began to present his grand theory on the perils of the now infamous 11th hole. Though his lucidity was dropping with every gulp, his account was so detailed that I offer his analysis in a more palatable note form.

The tee shot is virtually blind and must carry a dry-stone wall, the sea and thick gorse, by at least 200 yards.

Hit the fairway in the middle and it will still roll into the sea from a steeply sloping fairway.

Hit too far to the left and your ball will disappear into either deep rough or thick gorse.

If you are a visitor, you will see it as a challenge, enjoy the experience and be so ignorant of the dangers that you will approach it without fear.

If you are a member, with a medal card in your hand, you will have been worrying about the 11th during the first ten holes and will approach it with such a growing sense of imminent doom that disaster is guaranteed.

'Not easy then?' I offered, as an inadequate response.

'You'll see.' He smiled. 'You'll see.'

*   *   *

I was already worrying about the 11th hole as I headed back to my bed and breakfast retreat. I slept fitfully that night, tossing and turning as if my Ardglass purity had been defiled by just a little too much information. I could sense that 'The Troubles' were about to return.

Remarkably, the following day saw my opening drive sail down the middle, leaving the tight opening green at my mercy. Walking to the 2nd tee with a surprised look on my face and a double bogey six on my card, it suggested that I had been slightly overoptimistic. Unfortunately, one member of our proposed group had been forced to withdraw at the last minute and it was agreed that we play a 'skins game' for ten pence per hole. Despite the threat of financial ruin, I accepted the challenge with the sort of valiant bravado only enjoyed by idiots.

The secretary and the president (both men with non-threatening handicaps, and equally non-threatening characters) had joined me for the game. They were true Ardglass men who played our high-stakes contest in the relaxed and friendly manner I had anticipated. As an added bonus, they were both fine storytellers who peppered their conversations with local tales and enough archival facts to furnish me with sufficient knowledge to complete a successful treatise on Irish history. But before I had time to probe their knowledge of 'The Troubles', my own troubles returned. Despite focusing hard on my new-found 'cure', I developed a slice of such proportions that any banana republic would happily have selected me for their national team. As hard as my inner voice repeated the diagnostic mantra, *back inside; turn those wrists over; get on the front foot*, my limbs refused to obey even the smallest demand. I had no recollection of my spinal cord having been severed during my fretful sleep, but whatever occurred, it had resulted in a complete disconnection between brain and body.

By the time we approached the turn, I found myself in a game in which the term 'skins' was becoming far too literal. And then I started to think about the 11th, a hole which, had I not spent the previous evening in Curran's bar, would have held no fear. Now, laden with knowledge, I approached the tee like a member, convinced that I was about to face my nemesis.

My drive was hit straight and true but sadly in the wrong direction, the sea swallowing the apparently suicidal ball with a satisfied splash of pleasure. Refusing to submit, I played another, which happily found the middle of the fairway and surprisingly held its ground. Determined to make the green with my second (but officially fourth) shot, I reached for my trusty three wood. Unfortunately, my inebriated bar companion had failed to mention the difficulty of the second shot and the Irish Sea claimed yet another naive victim.

I was broken, defeated and declared that I was 'resting'. Another ten pence went into the president's pocket as I tore up my 'cure all' crib notes and commanded my brain to form some sort of tenuous relationship with my forlorn body. And while I waited to trudge up the hill to the high tee of the 12th, I had time to reflect on my experience. I finally had the answer to the two questions that had plagued me since my evening in Curran's bar. Could the course at Ardglass *really* be categorized as a true links? Was the 11th *really* such a barbaric hole?

The more fastidious members of the golfing cognoscenti would no doubt chew over these contentious bones until their teeth were worn down to the gums. Let me save them from extortionate dental bills. Ardglass *is* a links course. OK, I'll admit that the majority of the land is above the shoreline and that not all the fairways have a truly sand base and therefore might be considered as 'coastal downs'. But such an analysis misses the central point. Ardglass is completely links in *nature*, and in the required variety of shots it demands of its players. In addition, it is totally treeless, the arable land marinated in the salted air of the Irish Sea. The sometimes unpopular 11th only confirms this claim. Yes, it's tough. Yes, it might call on golfing skills you don't possess. But barbaric it isn't. What the 11th offers are all the challenges that links lovers desire, a total gratification of their universal, self-destructive wishes. For those Ardglass members who have misgivings about the 11th, I have only one message: come out of the closet. Admit your passion for links golf. Admit you enjoy the pain – and remember the old adage, that 'we only hurt the ones we love' – which is invariably ourselves.

I was in such a frame of mind as I turned for home. Suddenly my 'Troubles' dissipated, my swing relaxed into its former rhythm and I began to claw back my financial losses. And though I took a miserable eight on the final par four (in full view of the members peering out of the clubhouse window), I completed my round with a sense that I had been on a voyage of self-discovery. My score may have depressed me, but I was elated by the exhilarating misery, which only a true links golfer could really understand.

Back in the locker room, I changed quickly. Or as quickly as I could. Once again my shoes had gone missing and, following a hurried search, were located in the middle of the adjacent floor. Oddly, as if arranged in some demonic symbol, they had been carefully placed toe to toe, the untied laces placed neatly inside the body of the shoe. Thinking no more of it, I raced upstairs.

Joined by my playing companions, we dined in the clubhouse. The food was as good as Curran's but the conversation far superior. One of the group (and it wasn't me) proved to have a memory with a sharper response time than a Yahoo search engine. Unsurprisingly, he turned out to have once been a finalist on the BBC's *Mastermind* contest. His specialist subject was the Punic Wars, a brief two-hundred-year skirmish that took place long before Jesus dropped in and muddied the Roman waters. As my historical scholarship is limited to knowing Napoleon Bonaparte's first name, I pressed him for more local knowledge.

Within ten minutes my notebook was laden with dates, names and tales of Protestant/Catholic divisions, and how the tentacles of civil war had sometimes gripped even the small village of Ardglass. Though I would have liked to press him further, he suddenly turned his attention to the history of the castle clubhouse.

'We have a ghost, you know,' he said casually.

'A ghost?'

'Woman in a blue dress. There's a few people have seen her. We think she's searching for a child.'

'A child?'

'We found the body buried in the walls when we did some restoration work. It must have been there for centuries. Gave the workmen quite a shock.'

'Does she do anything else?' I asked.

'Such as?'

'Like moving shoes around the locker room?'

'Not as far as I know.' He smiled. 'But you can never be sure.'

My feet felt strangely cold as I bid my farewells and gave genuine thanks for their good company. It was time to pack my bags and prepare to fulfil my next ambition.

Belfast is an odd city, especially when viewed from an open-topped, double-decker bus. Something makes me very uneasy about voyeurism and the fact that still-remembered anguish can so quickly be transformed into a tourist attraction. History isn't buried in the rubble, it pervades the air and leaves its traces in the expressions of those who remain. And this Northern Ireland city still has stark reminders of its troubled days. The high metal 'Peace Gates' of curfew are still in operation, the strings of Republican and Unionist flags continue to flutter their challenge across the Falls and Shankill Roads. Urban museums of warlike wall murals, painted by peaceful artistic hands, still scream at you from tired terraced houses.

But turn towards the banks of the River Lagan and you know that peace has come. Close to the bridge, the city has erected a 50-foot modernistic statue of a wired abstract figure, holding a circle of steel high above its featureless face. To celebrate the coming of less troubled days, the sculptor had entitled his piece *Ring of Thanksgiving*. Speak to any Belfast man or woman and they'll tell you it's more commonly known as, *The Thing With the Ring*. Like 'The Troubles', it's an epithet that calms the waters and tells you that Belfast has begun to reclaim its humour and its once prosperous, peaceful past.

I had become so immersed in the city's history that I almost missed my flight to the equally troubled mainland of England. But with only minutes to spare, I strapped myself in and listened to the engines roar their farewell. And by chance, my plane climbed into the Irish sky and banked high over the emerald fields of County Down. I could just make out the landmarks around the familiar coastline and began to recall and reassess my visit. Ardglass is a memorable golf course in every sense of the word. The greens had proved fast and true; the sea had been visible from every fairway; each hole had presented a different challenge to even the finest players. But, should you ever visit, the memory of that 1st tee will never be erased. I can think of no other venue where my erratic swing would be accompanied by the steady beat of waves on the rocky shore; where I could steady my nerves with the calming sight of fishing boats hauling lobster creels onto their splintered decks; where I could glance towards the horizon and watch the shadows race across the glowering Mountains of Mourne. It's little wonder that Ireland produced the literary figures of Joyce, Yeats and Wilde. Like the country and its writers, Ardglass seems to possess a language of its own. You may not feel inspired to put pen to paper but I guarantee that it will ignite your golfing soul.

Recommended Alternatives

Rather like the top courses of the Ayrshire coast, the prime clubs of Northern Ireland can be a little expensive. If you're feeling 'flush', Royal County Down and Royal Portrush are must-play courses – both breathtaking, exquisite and of the finest quality. There are numerous other choices but I would suggest:

Ballyliffin: Stunning, challenging and as though you are challenging nature itself. It will test all your golfing skills.

Donegal: One of the longest, newest and yet traditional links courses in the UK. Exposed, beautiful and brutish. Heavenly course, heavenly location.

Portsalon: Extraordinary setting as the course runs along the dramatic Ballymastoker Bay and is ringed by the nearby mountains of Knockalla. A wonderful links course, though you may leave with either tears of pleasure or tears of pain.

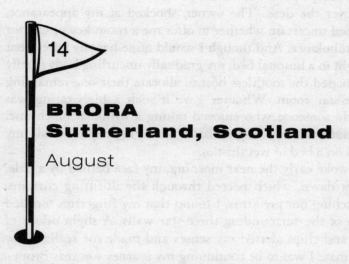

BRORA
Sutherland, Scotland
August

Whatever future mental state awaits me, I doubt that I will ever forget Brora Golf Club. It left me with a miscellany of memories; of country tales imbued with ancient crofters, ruminating cattle, wild horses, evangelical Christians, electric tripwires, Old Pulteney whisky and, strangest of all, three large bags of dog biscuits. They're not the sorts of thing that escape easily from the dungeons of recollection.

This was my most northerly destination, a golf course on the desolate east coast of the Scottish Highlands and more than a 600-mile drive from the comfort of my rural English home. As I crossed the Forth Road Bridge, with still 200 miles to go, my body was whimpering in discomfort. By the time I arrived in Pitlochry, every muscle was screaming with pain and demanding to be released from the torturous cockpit of my equally exhausted Volkswagen. Waving the white flag of submission, I pulled to a halt.

Levering myself out of the driver's seat, I approached the

hotel reception in such a contorted state that I could hardly see over the desk. The owner, shocked at my appearance, seemed uncertain whether to offer me a room key or call for an ambulance. And though I would quite happily have spent a night in a hospital bed, my gradually uncurling body finally persuaded the toothless host to allocate their one remaining three-star room. Whoever gave it such a high rating was clearly someone who enjoyed taking a drink at lunchtime. But such was my fatigue that I would happily have laid my head on a bed of wet thistles.

I woke early the next morning, my face bathed by a pale, sunlit dawn, which peered through the ill-fitting curtains. Stretching out my arms, I found that my fingertips touched both of the surrounding three-star walls. A slight odour of fish and chips alerted my senses and made me realize how fortunate I was to be continuing my journey towards Brora.

The previous evening, in desperate need of victuals, and despite my need for sleep, I had wandered through the gift-shop streets of Pitlochry. As now accustomed to, I had been forced to fight my way through the cigarette-littered pavement dwellings of *Fumersaurus Macs*, the latest Scottish form of their wheezing species. The distinctive aroma of battered food soon alerted my nostrils to a more pleasurable, salty feast.

'Fish and chips, please,' I asked with a visitor's politeness.

'Fish supper?' came the reply.

'No. Fish and chips,' I responded. 'Slice of bread. Cup of tea. Mushy peas.'*

---

*For those unfamiliar with the term 'mushy peas', this is a British delicacy concocted from Marrowfat peas; clearly boiled for a minimum of eight hours, pulped by bare feet and then dyed bright green with the sort of food colouring that could make you hyperactive for the next six months. It goes without saying that it is a dish irresistible to any discerning palate.

'Fish supper then,' came an irritated voice.

'If you say so.'

As I waited, an elderly gentleman at the nearest table was apparently choking to death, his staccato breathing punctuated by spluttered cries, his lips tinged with the blue pallor of imminent extinction. Having not been introduced, I left him to his fate and began to worry about my own mortality.

I sat outside on a rain-soaked plastic seat and began the nervous consumption. My hesitancy paid dividends within seconds. The piece of battered cod proved to contain more bones than a Victorian corset, the fine, sharp slithers piercing my gums and cheeks the moment I took my first bite. As an unretrieved bone bit back and lodged itself into the soft flesh of my throat, I began to choke. As I was alone, and had not enjoyed one single introduction to my fellow gourmets, no one came to my aid. I did what any man would do. Praying silently, I shovelled chips, mushy peas and bread into my mouth and swallowed hard. It did the trick. As I left, I peered through the misted windows of the plastic restaurant. The elderly man appeared to be sucking in his last breath, whilst a number of other diners began to risk their lives with every greasy morsel. I ignored them all and hurried back to my three-star cell.

I swallowed continually up the stunningly scenic A9 road towards Inverness. There's always that element of doubt in the mind that the fish bone still lingers, that it is quietly preparing to remount its sharp attack. But all proved well and within three hours I entered the small seaside hamlet of Brora. And to be honest, it had seen better days; a fact verified by picking up a leaflet in the local store where the appearance of a 'stranger' must provide a week's barroom conversation. The pamphlet, entitled BRORA. *Industrial Capital of the*

Highlands, informed me of the village's golden era of coal mining, woollen mills and whisky distilleries. Oddly, a whole section is devoted to the Brora Lemonade Factory, which saw its end in the 1920s influenza epidemic. That'll teach them not to share straws rather than adopt the modern trend of drinking straight out of the bottle top.

A wise old mentor once told me that a paint-peeled front door can never give you any indication of the joy or misery that lies beyond. It's an adage that has often given me comfort as I stare bleary eyed into the shaving mirror on a wet February morning. But driving into the club car park, I feared the worst. The clubhouse is a strange affair, reminiscent of a giant Second World War, flat-roofed pillbox, with its guns trained out to sea.

A quick inspection of the interior gave me no grounds for hope. The echoing stairs to the top floor were dreary, the long corridor to the bar unkempt, with an electronic games machine tucked into a small alcove. Even the bar failed to raise my spirits, the cavernous room laid out with leatherette bench seats, the dining area a collection of basic chairs and tables surprisingly surrounding a small tiled dance floor. In the far corner, a small kitchen blared out the sort of rock music that would have sent a Muirfield member into a frenzy of anger.

Retreating to the toilets, I glanced in the mirror and stared hard at my paint-peeled face.

'You're missing the point,' I mumbled.

'Really?' I answered.

'Of course you are!' I exclaimed. 'You're seven hundred miles from London. You're in the Scottish Highlands. This isn't Wentworth or Sunningdale. What the hell did you expect?'

'Well, I—'

'You all right?' came a voice at my side.

I turned quickly, startled by the intrusion into my private debate.

'Fine,' I stuttered.

'Beautiful day,' he said cheerily. 'Playing?'

'Tomorrow,' I replied.

'Forecast's good.'

'Great.'

Flushing away my pessimism, I returned to the bar and crossed to the large panoramic windows.

Brora exploded into a scene of joy, the humps and hollows of the course stretching away to the left, the windswept waters of the Dornoch Firth battling with the heavy swells of the North Sea, the whole picture framed by the arching colours of a full, iridescent rainbow. It was a moment of revelation, a realization that my old mentor's words contained a wheat field of truth. And in many ways, it reminded me why I have such a love of links golf and why so many parkland courses hide their mediocrity behind the opulence of their over-elaborate clubhouses. Golf was never meant to be played in a power-shower dressing room, a crystal-filled dining room or a deep-carpeted bar. The heart of a golf club is out on the course, battling the elements, challenging fairways and greens supplied by nature, rather than the bulldozed landscapes favoured by modern course designers.

Brora Golf Club was beginning to reveal its true colours and I was finally coming to my senses. I ordered lunch from the Rock Café. It was delicious. I ordered a drink from the bar. The reception was unreservedly friendly. The secretary greeted me in a similarly relaxed and welcoming manner. I mentioned the rainbow.

'We get them all the time.' He smiled.

'Really?'

'We once thought of calling it the Rainbow Golf Club,' he laughed, 'but we thought it had too many dodgy connotations.'

'Right.'

'You should have been here this morning. We had a square one.'

'A square rainbow?'

'Well, rectangular.'

'You're joking.'

'No. Honestly.'

Making a note that the secretary was clearly demented, I challenged his claim to have seen a rectangular rainbow with my child's encyclopedic knowledge of physics. Despite introducing him to the basic theories of light refraction in prisms, I received not a hint of secretarial rectangular retraction. But however fantastical his memory might have been, he was clearly a very bright and astute individual. Having spent much of his life looking out over a Heathrow Airport car park, he had ditched his office-bound accountancy and now earned his living from a room overlooking the North Sea, the 1st tee and the distant Cairngorm Mountains. If pleasure is a relative value, he had more relatives than Adam and Eve. It was time to walk the course.

A quick glance through the detailed course planner suggested that the affability of the clubhouse follows you onto the course. The description of the opening hole ends with the words, *Pin placement can be arranged to ensure three putts*. For the 8th hole it is suggested that *It takes three good shots to reach the green in two*. It seems that Brora, like the secretary, has a good sense of values and an equally wry sense of humour. You might wish to come attired in your best check pants and heavily logo-emblazoned golf shirt; you might even wish to compete as if your life depended on the outcome. But above all, you gain the sense that Brora's philosophy is that you should simply enjoy the experience of (what was about to be revealed as) their glorious links golf course.

The 1ˢᵗ hole confirms that this really is 'Golf on the Edge' territory. The tee sits on the brink of the beach and ocean, the constant wind biting into your face as you steady yourself for the inevitably nervous opening drive. And what you notice immediately is that you are about to play on a course of entirely natural contours, which has refused to compromise with the demands for target golf. Every hole you confront has been simply laid out, following the twists and turns of the land, using the natural terrain of hummocks, hollows and sometimes long saddleback humps, to present a different option on every shot. Even the immaculate greens make no concession to modernity, their shape and contours being determined only by the indigenous landscape. By the time I reached the 10ᵗʰ hole, I was convinced that Brora represented one of the truest links courses I had encountered on my journey around Britain. The layout is truly classical, the first nine holes running out to the north-east and then returning to the south-west. And the mundanity of the clubhouse is soon forgotten. The tees are immaculate, the bunkers beautifully riveted, the greens booby-trapped with electric wires.

I should explain.

Brora Golf Club has had an historic running battle (perhaps discussion) with local crofters. For those unfamiliar with these small agricultural families, they are remnants of nineteenth-century folk who were 'cleared' off their land by various members of the Scottish aristocracy. Persuasion was often violent and irresistible though often began with the diplomatic words: *'Right, you lot. I've a fancy to grow turnips and 'tatties in large quantities. I'll give you a small strip of land for your trouble but if you don't accept you can all bugger off to*

New Zealand or Canada. To be honest, I don't care where you go. Just clear off!'

Though this is a slight reconstruction of history, it contains a kernel of truth, and those who remained were allowed grazing rights on much of the coastal land – including the developing Brora Golf Club.

Wild horses and cattle therefore accompanied me on my walk around the course, though their willingness to pose for the odd photograph suggested that they were teetering on the edge of domesticity. But, because of their constant presence, the club has been forced to protect its greens with electrified wire. It is an inconvenience that I doubt bothers many of the members, but for the first-time visitor, a casual uniform of shorts and slightly damp legs is not recommended. Having said that, I'm sure it's a far more attractive remedy than the one adopted in 1964 when the club bought 30lbs of garlic powder and sprinkled it around every green. The effect on the offending horses and cattle was minimal, though the people of Brora were reported to have suddenly shown a very keen interest in French cuisine.

My scarred, electrified legs carried me all the way round the course and I can think of no single highlight. Brora is one continuous highlight. Every hole has something different to offer (one of the tests of a good golf course), and members must never tire of taking it on. Flat tees give way to raised platforms; open fairways contrast to mountainous hummocks; carpets of fast-breaking, sloping hollows follow virtually level greens. And despite the course turning inland at the 10th, the sea is rarely out of sight and the wind an ever present.

Unusually, the links are laid out on a fairly flat plain, the nearby hills towards Killin Rock and Loch Brora too far away to offer any protection. The course is fully exposed to even the slightest change in weather and it would be no surprise to find the wind in your face both on the way out and on the way back. The only guarantee is that you will probably find one of the par threes easier to play than the others. Uniquely (I think), each one of these short holes faces a different point of the compass and every one demands a precise, crisply hit shot to well-guarded greens. While the short 18th is considered a feature hole finish, I would choose the very short 13th as something of exceptional beauty and design. In the space of only 125 yards you are required to cross the burn twice, carry over three deep bunkers and hold your ball on a green with heavy banking on every side. Of the longer holes, my walk round the course produced 'star ratings' for the 11th, 16th and 17th. But 'window shopping' is never quite the same as buying the goods and I would put them to the test on the following day. Now it was time for a quick drink, a stroll back to my hotel and a quiet night with my latest Sebastian Faulks novel.

If only things had turned out so simply.

During my course inspection I had come across two elderly men engaged in their own private Ryder Cup tussle. It transpired that they had once been colleagues in the whisky industry and since retiring had annually alternated their game between Brora and Chicago. Both the American and the Scot were affable men but revealed that they had almost missed their game after having been blocked into their hotel car park by a large white van.

'That one,' said the American, pointing to the side of the clubhouse.

'Aye,' said the Scot. 'They even followed us here. Lovely, isn't it?'

The word 'lovely' was delivered with heavy irony. The vehicle might have started its life as a white van but it was now emblazoned with more bright colours than you would find on a square Brora rainbow. Bidding farewell to these two contented men at the 18th, I grabbed a quick cup of tea and sauntered back to my hotel.

It was already early evening and, once showered and changed, I slipped into the bar to continue my in-depth study of Scottish single malts. Taking advice from the two Ryder Cup combatants, I ordered an Old Pulteney.

'Twelve year or seventeen year?' asked the barmaid.

'What's best?' I asked.

'Seventeen.'

'And more expensive,' I smiled.

'Well . . .'

'OK.'

Handing over a week's wages, I sipped the liquid gold with the care of a miser.

'Old Pulteney, eh?' came a voice at my side.

'Er, yes,' I responded, surprised by the stranger's bustling entry.

'Twelve or seventeen?'

'Er, seventeen.'

'Don't you read the papers?' he asked, handing me a folded sheet of pink newsprint.

'Not the *Financial Times*,' I laughed.

'Try page fifteen.'

Following instructions has always been my forte and I unfolded the pink broadsheet without further protest. The headline, *Old Pulteney raises spirits at Inver House*, immediately sprang off the page, as did the fact that the distilling company had recently been acquired by a Thai entrepreneur by the name of Charoen Sirivadhanabhakdi. Thankfully there was no mention of plans to name a whisky after the owner. The thought of a drunken whisky drinker trying to order two large Sirivadhanabhakdis in a crowded pub was almost too much to contemplate. But worse was to follow. Deep in the article, I was informed that the twelve-year matured Old Pulteney (rather than the seventeen) had recently won the gold medal in the International Wine & Spirit Competition.

'Golfing?' asked the man as I sipped and slipped into depression.

'Sort of,' I answered. 'You?'

'Sales trip.' He smiled. 'Not seen the van?'

'The van?'

The collection of unconnected events suddenly snapped together like the pieces of an unsolvable jigsaw.

'White?'

'Yes.'

'Decorated in coloured signs?'

'Yes.'

'I have some friends who'd like to meet you,' I murmured.

What followed next was not part of my evening's plans. The young, tall and ebullient Englishman revealed himself to possess a cut-glass accent and the timidity of a testosterone-fuelled gorilla. A member of his sales team, an equally vibrant Glaswegian woman with a broken-glass Scottish brogue, soon joined him. The night was young and so were they. I feared the worst.

We dined together. We drank together. And by the time a game of snooker was suggested there appeared to be 250 balls on the table. I have no idea what time we finally made it to our separate beds, but my early-morning pulsating head suggested that my return to the bedroom probably coincided with the dawn chorus.

Though I normally stay in cheap hotels or breakfast-whispering boarding houses, I had unusually booked into a rather swish hotel only a few minutes' stroll from the golf course. Surprisingly, access to a luxurious health spa came with my price-negotiated deal and the bubbling Jacuzzi proved to be my lifeline. Slumped in the foaming waters, I began to recall the events of the previous evening.

My companions had proved good company, their constant tales made up of a series of revelatory stories and strange, detailed conversations about Oakley, my trusty boxer dog. It transpired that the notorious white van belonged to a pet food company who had engineered a sales plan to advertise their products by driving the logo-festooned vehicle between Land's End and John o'Groats. Brora had been the final stop before reaching their destination. The generous and effusive sales manager had also revealed the fact that he was a non-proselytizing, born-again Christian with a penchant for fine malt whiskies. At least we shared one thing in common.

My head now clearing, I was joined in the restorative waters by what I think was a female figure. (Without my glasses, any Jacuzzi companion is non-gender specific.) Whatever sex it was, it left quickly. I was at my most friendly and approachable self, but the unique bouquet of Old Pulteney whisky bubbling into the air may have been slightly off-putting.

Having confirmed that my body still had a pulse, I dried off, dressed hurriedly and went in search of food. The breakfast room was already quite full, but I found a table quickly.

'Mr Cartmell?' asked the waitress.

'Yes?'

'Table four,' she demanded.

'This'll do,' I responded.

'Table four,' she insisted.

'I have to?' I complained.

'Table four,' she repeated sternly.

Tiring of the verbal tennis, I submitted to her authority

and was guided into an adjacent room, which proved to be a hubbub of breakfast chatter. The moment I entered, the conversation dropped from *molto forte* to *sotto voce* and all the heads turned in my direction.

Table four looked unusual. Very unusual. The white starched linen cloth had been laid with three round dishes and in each stood a box of dog biscuits, carrying the colours I had last seen on the side of the garish white van. The central box carried a small note:

> *Had to leave early. John o'Groats here we come! Your dog will love these! God bless. Henry & Sam.*

'Can I get you anything else?' smiled the once frightening waitress.

'Just a bowl of water,' I barked. 'I'll have it on the floor. I'm not allowed on the furniture.'

Two hours later, I hovered over my opening drive, the steely-eyed expressions of my opponents suggesting that they were ready to bring me to heel. I had been joined by the ex-secretary, the treasurer and a random visitor with a bad back, who was staying on the small caravan park that borders the 12th hole. Still troubled with my 'late summer bad patch', I hurled my fragile swing at the ball, grateful to see it climb skywards and leave me no more than an eight iron onto the waiting green. Immediately tripping over the electric wires (thankfully with long trousers and dry legs), I made my first three-putt of the day. By contrast, my partner (the treasurer) made the first of his many one-putts, and put our damp noses in front with an admirable birdie. Brora was living up to my expectations, every shot giving me at least three options to fly the ball high, bump and run to the green or even resort to

50-foot putts out of the light rough. A fresh northerly breeze had blown up, clearing the misty air to reveal the silhouetted mountains of Easter Ross to the west and, to the south, the distant Moray coastline of Spey Bay. With the whole golf course now bathed in sunshine, and the North Sea raging against the nearby shoreline, I was quite happy to play second fiddle to my partner. He was having the sort of day when a winning lottery ticket would be an expectation rather than a surprise. Yet despite his efforts, we were only one up at the turn and the caravaner's back appeared to have benefited from some form of miracle cure, his drives sailing some 80 yards beyond my own. Fortunately, this new-found agility was also accompanied by his putter developing a mind of its own, in which its main objective seemed to be a desire to mimic a full-blooded three wood.

It proved to be a tense encounter, but wandering down the 15th fairway, the ex-secretary drew me to one side.

'See the lines?' he said, pointing to his right.

'Railway lines?' I queried.

'Beyond those. See. There.' He gestured. 'The long strips of land.'

I peered through the now murky light. A small herd of cattle grazed by the green, showing their usual disinterest in our hard-fought game. Beyond them, I could just make out the roughly formed divisions between the crofters' sparse lines of ground, their small cottages framed against the hills towards Killin Rock.

It was as though I had been transported back in time; as though, for a moment, history had held its breath to reveal its feudal days.

'They still farm the land?' I enquired.

'Things change slowly in Brora,' he replied with a confirming smile.

'How far to the green?' I asked, settling over my shot.

'This is real links golf,' he answered kindly. 'Trust your eyes. That's what the old pros used to do. It's a game of feel, not yardage.'

Though having played reasonably well, I had contributed very little to the game and I approached the 16th tee with a realization that my partner would have to see us home to victory. Whilst my playing partners took the more advisable line to the left, my own drive was pushed well to the right. Reduced to a completely blind shot to a plateau green, I watched my seven iron cut through the rough and my ball disappear from view.

Arriving at the green, I was shocked to find my ball only 7 feet from the pin, whilst my companions were either in the surrounding rough or sitting on the fringes of the green, some 20 feet away. And after much toing and froing, none of them succeeded in getting down in two. Lagging my putt to the side of the hole, I offered my hand in victory.

'Three and two,' I smiled. 'Great game.'

'I thought that was halved in fives,' said the startled ex-secretary.

'Just the four, I'm afraid.'

'Well done,' he answered graciously. 'We all missed your second shot.'

'So did I,' I laughed, with a hint of apology. 'Must have had a good bounce.'

I had crept up like a thief in the night and picked the pockets of the unwary travellers.

'I'll buy the drinks,' I offered.

'Just the one for me,' came the chorus of replies. 'Mustn't be too late.'

Two hours later, another line of whiskies were placed on the barroom counter. We had begun to exchange golfing stories. And, in truth, with no more than a cup of tea in hand, golfers' tales can be tedious in the extreme. But, after two pints of Guinness, chased home by a few single malts, it can make for a wonderful evening. As a precautionary measure, I slipped away for a few minutes and booked a space in the Jacuzzi for the following morning.

Finally making my exit, I reflected on my visit to Brora. Was I looking at it through rose-tinted glasses, which convinced me that square rainbows really existed? Would I have had the same reaction if my golfing companions hadn't been such good company? Would I have viewed it with such favour if I hadn't encountered electric tripwires, wild horses and Old Pulteney whisky? Had dog biscuits for breakfast robbed me of my objective faculties? The answer was clear. I sensed I would enjoy Brora on a wet February morning. But, returning home a few weeks later, I was still concerned about my starry-eyed view. For some reason, I couldn't quite put my finger on the reasons for such a positive response.

One morning, flicking through my disorganized notes and memorabilia, I chanced upon a history of the James Braid Golfing Society, founded to commemorate the work of the famed Scottish course designer. To my astonishment, it revealed that Brora was the headquarters of this august body and its president was no less than Peter Thomson CBE, the five-times winner of the Open Championship. After further rummaging, I uncovered his opinion of Brora Golf Club, which he still plays on a regular basis.

It's magical in my view, he begins. *The holes that James Braid laid out there are wonderful. It's a bit wild, not perfect. But it's how golf was played . . . a long time ago.*

How much convincing do you need? If Peter Thomson couldn't spot a fine links course when he saw one, then who could?

Recommended Alternatives

Golspie: Only part links but a great setting by the sea and well worth a visit. I received one of the warmest welcomes I've ever had at a golf course.

Tain: Dornoch junkies can easily miss this one. Don't. A course to concentrate the mind, as you negotiate the tight fairways, heather and gorse.

Wick: A bit of a trek – but at least you can say you have played the most northerly links course on the British mainland. Madness in parts but fun to play.

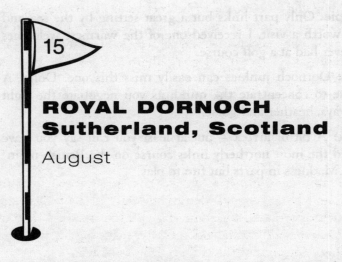

ROYAL DORNOCH
Sutherland, Scotland
August

I have an admission to make. There have been a number of (infrequent) occasions when I have been accused of being overjudgemental. Ironically, those who have found me guilty of such a heinous crime are, of course, guilty of the very thing on which I stood indicted. Even stranger is that in a former life I was employed to introduce aspiring counsellors to the tender skills needed to save broken marriages. At the heart of this technique is the simple strategy of only answering a question with a question and on no occasion offering a solution. Can you think of anything more infuriating?

Yet my time at Royal Dornoch was to prove one of mental excavation when these long-buried skills became suddenly re-employed. I had driven south from the glories of Brora and, though I pride myself on objectivity, I knew that comparisons would be hard to avoid. To make matters worse, I dropped in to have a quick glance at Golspie on the East Sutherland coast. With the air already filled with heavy rain, I went in search of a new waterproof top. I approached the pro's shop of this delightful course to be met by a charming, elderly woman, whose total stock of golfing equipment amounted to eight golf balls, four shirts and six woolly jumpers.

'Poor day,' I offered as I glanced around the tiny shack of an office.

'God's tap needs a new washer,' she replied.

'Quite.' I smiled in agreement.

'He suffers just like us.'

'Suffers?'

'Can't find a plumber when he needs one.'

Making an immediate note to play Golspie one day (if only for the secretary's damp humour), I continued my journey, negotiating the route through the frenzied swirl of hyperactive windscreen blades, finally splashing my way into the main entrance of Royal Dornoch Golf Club.

I use the term 'entrance' loosely. In many ways, your expectations will be raised well before the links come into sight. The isolated village of Dornoch immediately sets the scene. The sandstone edifices of the exquisite thirteenth-century cathedral and bishop's palace give the small hamlet a sense of stylish austerity, whilst the wide, light-filled square seems inviting, even on the coldest morning.

It was certainly a little warmer in 1727. Just off the main square is the site of the Witch's Stone, where a certain Janet Horne was painted with tar and became the last supposed Scottish 'witch' to be burned at the stake. Employing good eighteenth-century logic, she was accused and found guilty of turning her daughter into a horse. Given the shortage of tractors in eighteenth-century Scotland, this seems a reasonable activity. But it also appears to make about as much sense as accusing me of being a scratch golfer or measuring a piece of cloth with a large brick. The village of Dornoch clearly has a history of bizarre practices. Inside the churchyard is the Plaiden Ell, a stone used by cloth merchants, to make sure they weren't being duped by local weavers. The question *'Can I borrow your tape measure?'* was clearly only used by large kilted men with magnificent bulging muscles.

Despite these early distractions, I went in search of the course. This proved far harder than anticipated. It took two abortive attempts before I finally spotted the minuscule sign that led me down two narrow streets and, inadvertently, into the members only car park. Chancing my arm, I quickly jumped ship, grabbed my notebook, hurried into the clubhouse and bumped straight into golfing history.

By an odd quirk of fate, I had arrived at Dornoch on the semi-finals day of the club's most famous tournament. The Carnegie Shield has been contested since 1901 and is said to be one of the most beautiful golf trophies in the world. As I haven't seen all the others, I can only take their word for it, though there's little doubt that it lives up to its star billing. The giant round shield is so ornate that the silversmith must have devoted his life to its making, and any winner would need the spinach-enhanced forearms of Popeye to lift it victoriously above his head. All amateurs who get the Carnegie Shield on their CV will undoubtedly have the respect of their fellow players. Presented by the Scottish industrialist and philanthropist, Andrew Carnegie, the trophy sits in a glass-fronted cabinet, close to the main bar. Taking up the game in later life, this immensely wealthy benefactor (only shaded into second place on the rich list by John D. Rockefeller) probably bought the shield out of his loose change. Having given more than $350 million to various charities before his sixty-fifth birthday, he was clearly the one-man lottery of the nineteenth century.

But should you visit Dornoch, don't miss this trophy

cabinet. The pleasure is not in the Carnegie Shield but in the detail that surrounds it. It would be futile to try and describe the numerous golfing mementoes but two particular exhibits scream at you through the sparkling window. First is a picture of J. S. Miller, a man with a wonderful pair of sideboards (and probably a lovely fitted kitchen), who won the Carnegie Shield on no less than ten occasions. What was even more remarkable is that he was a member of Brora, a course I had played only forty-eight hours before. Now that must have really got up the noses of the Dornoch members.

But finest of all is a small, faded, sepia photograph of two tweed-clad men, sporting moustaches the size of a pair of sewer rats. Between them stands a reluctant woman obviously not amused by their close attentions. The inscription informs the onlookers that they are viewing *The club captain A. J. Ryle, and secretary John Sutherland, escorting a suffragette off the course for* molesting *Mr Asquith, Prime Minister, while playing golf in 1913.* She was not an unattractive suffragette and if I had been Mr Asquith, I would have counted it as my lucky day and asked the political strumpet if she fancied a bite of dinner. Whatever the case, it was apparent that Royal Dornoch didn't seem to tolerate any sort of misbehaviour. Checking my attire for any hint of sartorial indiscretion, I headed for the course.

Royal Dornoch doesn't announce itself quietly. The 1st tee is the biggest I've ever encountered and could probably double as a decently sized football pitch. Perhaps reflecting their Carnegie connections, two fluttering Scottish flags are kept company by their American and Canadian equivalents, whilst a modest wooden starter's hut stands guard over the immaculate turf. And though I was only about to walk the course, my pulse was already starting to quicken. Looking out towards the first fairway and the distant raised green, I immediately came to an (apparently characteristic) judgemental conclusion.

'Oh God!' I mumbled. 'It's a monster!'

In terms of measurement, one quick glance at the scorecard showed this to be a false assumption. At only 6,552 off the white tees, it is barely a 100 or so yards longer than the 'premier' links of Turnberry or Nairn, and shorter than either Kingsbarns or Western Gailes. But Dornoch's visual threat is constantly more imposing. Wherever the eye turns, gorse sprouts like angry clumps of giant prickly broccoli, whilst banks, humps and hollows of bent-grasses prepare to swallow any ill-directed ball. From a distance, its landscape of potential misery is intimidating and seems to beckon you to disaster. It is also stunningly beautiful. The eastern edge is carved out along the shores of the North Sea, whilst the westerly holes rise high onto a rugged plateau of land, in which two long par fours have been etched into the dark tangled whins. I already knew that if the wind were to blow, my meagre, fragile swing would shatter in submission and the Goliath of Dornoch would have nothing to fear from my diminutive challenge.

Apart from a few twists and turns, Dornoch (like nearby Brora) is a classic 'nine holes out', 'nine holes in' true links course. The opening hole (a short par four) could easily lull you into a false sense of optimism as the 2nd hole (par three) is a stunning but brutish affair with a raised green offering more slopes than a Swiss ski resort. And even after such a short time, my exploratory walk had begun to reveal Dornoch's admirable attention to detail. The riveted bunkers can only be described as works of art, their design even mirrored on some of the arced banking surrounding the tees (particularly on the 3rd). It was already proving to be the most immaculate course I had visited, its presentation startling in every respect.

My admiration was growing by the second, with each hole unique in design and quality. I drew another judgemental conclusion.

'It's a golfer's course,' I whispered into the strengthening breeze.

Though this may sound like a statement of the obvious (who else would you build a golf course for, other than a golfer?), there is a distinction to be made. Anyone with a handicap between 0 and 5 is a golfer; anyone with a handicap between 6 and 10 can aspire to be a golfer. But anyone with a handicap between 10 and 24 is not a golfer, they are someone who simply 'plays golf'.

Having now depressed over 99 per cent of my readership, I am happy to admit that I belong to your majority. My own handicap is, however, low enough still to provide me with infrequent moments of intense pleasure though enough knowledge to confirm that I am not 'a golfer' but someone who 'plays the game'. If I had a handicap between 0 and 5, or had completely lost all of my mental faculties, I would certainly enjoy playing a medal at Dornoch. But if my only object in life was to try and retain my present handicap, I would limit my medal competitions to a flat, municipal parkland course in Essex or Lincolnshire.

Yes. Of course I'm indulging in mendacity. But stand on the wonderful 5th tee and you will be left in no doubt that Royal Dornoch is as tough a course as you'll find on the British shoreline. From here you can see almost 60 per cent of the course's panorama and as I surveyed the unfolding fairways, my eye caught sight of a small crowd of spectators, making their way along the adjacent 12th. Small ripples of applause competed with squawking gulls as the two Carnegie Shield semi-finalists strode out across the tight sandy turf. Leaving my lofty perch, I moved closer to the action.

'Two iron?' asked one of the competitors.

'Two iron,' affirmed the caddy with appropriate confidence.

Seconds later, the ball soared through the air and nestled gently on the waiting green.

This may sound like no more than a tale of everyday amateur golfers. But what left me in a state of wracked despair is that the 557-yard, slightly doglegged, par-five 12th had been reduced to no more than a drive and a long iron. It is a game with which I am not familiar, a game that I can never hope to attain, yet a sporting pastime that, despite my inadequacies, I will always savour.

Returning to my walk, the short 6th hove into view. It's a magnificent par three, which it is best not to contemplate for more than a few seconds. Any greater time than this will probably result in such nervous tremors that your swing will resemble a broken windmill in a force-eight gale. The major visual problem is that the green appears to be hanging from a cliff edge with impenetrable gorse to the left and steep banks and deep bunkers to the right. Anything but a perfectly hit iron will see you happy to record a five on your card.

And if you've had a bad experience on the 6th, the steep path to the next hole will feel like a lung-burning mountain trek. The 7th provides one of the course's few disappointments. As you would expect, it is still an immaculate par four but you sense that because of its position on a high plateau of land, it is something of an appendage to the main dish of pleasures. But it is a minor punctuation. The 8th fairway sees you bowling down a valley back to the green on the water's edge and turning for home along the coastline of the Dornoch Firth, until finally cutting back inland for the final two holes.

This 'back nine' (at least to the eye) is perhaps a little more forgiving than the first half of the course. Despite the inclusion of 'Foxy' (the infamous 14th with one of the most difficult greens in world golf), the terrain opens out and seems to offer slightly less threat than the outward holes. But sadly, the course rather fizzles out towards the end, instead of climaxing in the anticipated crescendo. The 17th, though spectacular in design, has a rather parkland feel, whilst the 18th is the longest and least scenic par four on the whole course, the green isolated some distance from the clubhouse and lacking any sense of theatrical dénouement. Whether this would prove the case with a set of golf clubs on my shoulder would have to wait. I had, for the moment, far more important issues on my mind.

Unusually, the pause between inspecting and playing had been extended to seven days. Now I had to turn my attention to the Nairn Open Week and a clash of giants in Inverness.

For those unfamiliar with Scottish football, it has become unjustly labelled as a second-class citizen with (apart from Rangers and Celtic – 'The Old Firm') small crowds, small stadiums, even smaller media coverage but big passion. I had been driving past the wonderfully named Inverness Caledonian Thistle's ground for many years and was transfixed by its stunning setting on the banks of the Moray Firth. I grabbed my opportunity and treated my tired body to a few hours' rest whilst 'Inverness Cally' took on the might of Edinburgh's Hibernian. Sadly, the game proved to be a mind-numbingly dull 0–0 draw, in which the woman in front of me spent the whole of the second half reading an academic book on Bronze Age Britain. I became so entranced by this mighty tome that I sidled out of the ground with not only a sense of disappointment but also a detailed knowledge of how to make a bronze arrowhead and a basic understanding of how to gut a dead deer. But it wasn't all bad. Where else in Britain could you enjoy your half-time cup of tea whilst leaning over the back of the main stand to watch fishing smacks sailing out to sea and dolphins enjoying their watery gymnastics?

A week later, I found myself passing the ground once more and heading back to Dornoch. My pathetic attempts to win the Nairn Open had again foundered on the rocks of inability and a second medal round played in torrential rain. My hopes had been raised briefly with a nice par on the opening hole but quickly dashed by a hard-fought eleven on the second. As is usually the case at Nairn, my enjoyment had been tempered by having my golfing soul ripped out by a course whose severity invariably outweighs my limited talents. It was not the best preparation for what lay ahead.

The journey, however, soon raised my spirits. If you fly to Inverness and happen to have extremely wealthy friends, ignore all offers of a helicopter ride to Royal Dornoch. From the south, the road to the course is worth every penny of the hefty green fee you are about to pay. Not only are you treated to the craggy Highland scenery but you also have to traverse three wide stretches of glittering water. The crossing to the Black Isle is followed by a long causeway over the Cromarty Firth, and a further bridge across the Dornoch Firth. By the time you see the small signs for Dornoch, you begin to realize why this golf course is considered to be one of the remotest links in Britain.

There was already rain in the air as I made myself known in the surprisingly small professional's shop.

'Who's joining me?' I asked cheerily.

My words were offered with the false bravado of someone who felt sure that his luck had run out. I feared I was about to play with two potentially starchy members.

'Sorry,' came the assistant's reply, 'couldn't find any volunteers. Fixed you up with a couple of visitors.'

'Visitors?' I exclaimed. 'You're sure they don't mind?'

'Don't think so.' He smiled. 'In fact, they looked really pleased when I told them.'

I was becoming wary. If I fix up a two-ball with a chum, I don't welcome the intrusion of a complete stranger with an unknown handicap.

'Not scratch golfers, are they?' I asked nervously.

'No worries,' laughed the assistant. 'You'll have to give them both a shot or two.'

With some relief, I changed quickly and went in search of my opponents. Hovering at the side of the 1st tee, two rain-suited figures soon appeared and I was kindly given the honour of striking the first blow.

Midway through my well-rehearsed Ben Hogan waggle, the starter suddenly asked me to step away. Thinking that I had broken some ancient club rule, I bowed to his authority.

'We get a lot of this on a Saturday,' he explained quickly.

'What?'

My question went unanswered as a flurry of flashlights illuminated the rain-filled skies. As I turned, a full wedding party came into view, the dampened but traditionally radiant bride trailing her virginal dress along the rough muddied track that runs in front of the 1st tee. I could have sworn it was the same bride I had seen at Western Gailes only a few months earlier but put such mad meanderings down to pre-match nerves.

'Where on earth are they going?' I asked, avoiding the temptation to accuse the woman in white of brass-necked bigamy.

'Down to the beach. They always go there for the wedding shots.'

'In *this* weather?'

'You don't feel the rain on your wedding day,' the starter smiled kindly.

Despite the surprising longevity of my own marriage, I usually find weddings unsettling. On this occasion, and with a brief re-enactment of my former waggle, my drive sailed down the middle of the fairway.

'Perfect,' said the starter. 'Enjoy your game.'

My companions were equally well placed and though we all took five down the opening hole there was a general air of contentment as we stepped onto the 2nd tee and began to add some detail to our earlier, hurried introductions.

'Hope you don't mind me joining you,' I began.

'I'm pleased to see you,' said one.

'Me too,' said the other.

'That's what they said in the pro's shop.' I smiled. 'Why so pleased?'

'You know what fathers and sons are like,' said the younger.

'Bloody competitive,' said the elder.

'You're father and son?'

'That's right. And we need someone to keep us apart.'

'Me?'

'Yes.'

'Because you're competitive?'

'Yes.'

'Why's that?'

And so it continued, my every questioning response sticking rigidly to the subtle techniques of counselling. I offered no judgements or solutions, no opinion on their competitive instincts, no remedy for their deep-seated golfing rivalry. I must have been the most annoying man on the planet. But old habits die hard.

For reasons that will quickly become obvious, I will keep our match report brief. The weather began to close in and, as it did so, my swing disintegrated like a paper tissue in the rain. By the turn, my golf bag was five balls lighter and my spirit was broken. But despite my ill fortune and the torrents of water running down my chilled spine, the humour remained as dry as a Chablis La Calombe. My two Glaswegian companions were excellent company, full of golfing tales and reverential opinions of Royal Dornoch. Their rooted competitive nature masked a true father and son friendship, which thankfully soon made my conciliatory skills completely redundant.

'Foxy!' exclaimed the son as we stepped onto the 14th tee.

As I soon learned, his first trip to Dornoch was a birthday gift from his wife and he was wringing every drop of pleasure out of the sodden course.

'You know it?' I asked.

'Foxy?' he enthused. 'Read about it for years. Always wanted to play it. I've been thinking about it since we stood on the first tee.'

My exploratory walk had led me to underestimate the hole's severity. What makes it so remarkable is that there isn't a bunker to be seen and all that's required is a good drive and a medium iron. That's the easy bit. The drive must be coaxed through a tight corridor of gorse and rough towards a fairway that would have no understanding of the word 'flat'. Natural humps and hollows lie at every point and the centre of the fairway is dominated by two immense hillocks. But even if these are successfully negotiated, the shot to the highly elevated, heavily banked, rectangular green looks virtually impossible.

Whilst I fluffed the next two pitch shots and the father hacked out of the rough, the birthday son had clearly planned this moment. With a cry of delight, his short final putt hit the hole for the par he had dreamed of for so many years. His day was made.

'What a golf course!' he spluttered through rain-drenched lips. 'What a *fantastic* golf course!'

And despite my torrid experience, he was plainly right. Royal Dornoch deserves its claims to rank so high amongst the finest links courses in the world. Whilst being consistently tough and demanding, it is exceptional in every golfing respect. No two holes are the same, no shot you will face is predictable. You will find yourself playing against an ingenious design and the vagaries of nature set in a landscape of sublime beauty. If a golfer ever tired of playing Dornoch he would tire of life itself.

With my objectivity still intact, we finished our game and dragged our damp bodies into the clubhouse for a hard-earned beer. And as we sat steaming gently by the bar, I suddenly became aware of yet another strange marriage, which might well benefit from my supposed judgemental character. It was something that had been playing on my mind since I had first visited the club more than a week before. There seemed to have been an inexplicable union, in which the clubhouse groom had married a golf course bride, well above his station. To paraphrase an old song:

> Course and clubhouse,
> Course and clubhouse,
> Go together like a cat and dormouse.

In the case of Royal Dornoch Golf Club, it would have been better to *have one without the other.* A course of such unquestionable quality deserves far better than an untidy rabbit warren clubhouse, an inadequate professional's shop, a minuscule changing room and a dress code that is so liberal that visiting guests feel uncomfortable amongst the apparently acceptable T-shirts, trainers and cut-off jeans.

I can hear the cries of derision as I write, especially as the club authorities stress that they *Welcome golfers and their friends in an informal style. Jackets and ties are not required, smart casual is all we ask.* If smart casual is what I witnessed, then I must dress like Oscar Wilde on a particularly foppish day. And I must stress that I have a complete hatred of stuffy golf clubs, but I also understand that welcoming golfers in an informal style, without jackets and ties, need not be interpreted as an acceptance of slovenliness.

I have no time to engage in the tender words of counselling, no time to avoid offering remedies. For once in my life I'm going to admit to the charge of being judgemental and provide a solution. Tighten up your dress code and give in to your suicidal tendencies, Royal Dornoch. Self-destruct. Hire a large bulldozer. Knock the clubhouse down and give your extraordinary golf course a companion who will make a worthy marriage partner.

But, to repeat the words of my Glaswegian golfing partner, 'What a golf course! What a *fantastic* golf course!' I couldn't agree with him more.

PS By the time you read this piece, a new clubhouse might have been built and I may well have egg on my face. No apologies. You can't make omelettes without . . .

Recommended Alternatives

See end of Brora chapter . . . or . . . play Dornoch three times. If there is even the slightest change in the weather, it will seem as if you are playing three completely different golf courses.

16

CRUDEN BAY
Aberdeenshire,
Scotland

August

I arrived at this Aberdeenshire golf course looking like a cling-film-wrapped chicken. Any hope I had of swinging a golf club to the required 90 degree angle had been abandoned well before I drew into the sizeable car park.

Having been on the road for almost three weeks, my original travelling wardrobe had seen me around the golfing delights of Brora, Royal Dornoch and Nairn. But, by the time I began to head south towards Cruden Bay, I had reached a point of soiled sartorial crisis and, with a little time to spare, wandered the outskirts of Dundee in search of a laundry. Fortune was on my side.

Spotting a shop sign displaying a *Two-Hour Washing Service*, it seemed that my problems were over. Unfortunately, the woman behind the counter appeared to have great difficulty understanding the words 'Could you wash this bag of clothes please?'

Instead, she responded with a detailed account of the laundry industry from 1850 to the present day, which included a fascinating analysis of the historical development of the industrial tumble dryer and their dire effects on modern fabrics.

Three hours later, I was climbing the stairs of my Cruden Bay hotel with an empty suitcase in one hand and a bulging black plastic bag in the other. Reaching inside the shiny container, I pulled out my welcome, freshly laundered golf shirt. It wasn't quite what I had expected. The last time I had seen a garment this size was when, many years before, I had won a prize in a children's golfing competition. Quickly checking the rest of the contents, I appeared to have collected a bag of washing that had been laundered by the Lilliput Cleaning Services. Forcing the shirt over my shoulders, I glanced in the mirror to admire a body that had been transformed into a rippling mass of bulging muscle, delightfully enhanced by a heavily constrained, one-pack stomach. For one nervous second, I feared that I might be in the later stages of pregnancy.

It was in such an expectant state that I first arrived at Cruden Bay Golf Club, making my way through the small, featureless housing estate towards the main entrance. And, at this point, I had no interest in the course, the clubhouse or its inhabitants. I had only one thing on my mind.

'Pro's shop?' I asked a wary passer-by, clearly startled by my pre-packed appearance.

Following his pointing finger, I shuffled furtively through the professional's door and began to rummage through his shelves.

'Nothing without a logo on the front?' I enquired.

'Not in *your* size,' he smiled knowingly.

I have a thing about logo-emblazoned shirts. I've always found them a little too 'in your face' for my liking and they invite the possibility of leaving a chap open to scornful derision. There's no point in standing on a 1st tee with *Turnberry, Kingsbarns* or *St Andrews* plastered across your chest and then slicing your ball 120 yards into the rough. Logos from high-class golf courses leave you as no more than a hostage to ill fortune. But having no choice, I made my purchase, changed quickly, and headed, logo resplendent, into the main clubhouse.

Having heard some good reports of Cruden Bay, I had arranged for a caddy to be flown in from London and having picked up my *aide de bag* from Inverness airport, we wandered into the entrance with a sense of anticipation. It was far from what we expected from a club that can be dated as far back as 1791. Instead of being greeted by cobwebbed old retainers and a dusty honesty box, you are immediately faced by an official reception desk, which smacks of twenty-first-century efficiency. The clubhouse is modern in every respect, the grand entrance quickly leading you through to an open-plan bar and restaurant.

In some ways, this inaugural scene felt disappointingly incongruous, as if Cruden Bay had deposited its history in a local landfill site and taken a giant step into modernity. How wrong could I be?

Even from the entrance, history beckons you on, the distant panoramic windows taunting you with nothing more than the sight of a vacant sky. But take a few steps forward and the curtain is raised on one of the most enthralling stages in British golf. I gasped in pleasure. And, most strangely of all, so did my poorly paid caddy.

You'll not be surprised to hear that golfers of my own mediocre standard tend not to fly employees into Scotland for one round of golf. There were two reasons for this apparent show of affluence. Firstly, my wife had grown tired of receiving weekly reports from luxurious, paint-peeling bed and breakfasts with dripping taps and greasy breakfasts. (It would make anybody jealous.) Secondly, my trip to Cruden Bay happened to coincide with the Edinburgh Festival of arts, theatre, music and fine eating. Carrying my bag around Cruden Bay was, therefore, no more than a trade-off hors d'oeuvre to the main cerebral feast.

If ever you sit in a bar and hear a whimpering man declare, *My wife doesn't understand me*, this can invariably be translated as, *My wife doesn't understand why I spend so much time on the golf course.* And I can whimper with the best of them. My artistically inclined Dutch wife has little concept of the agonies involved in missing a 3-foot putt and considers the only thing in life worth competing for is the last piece of raw herring left on a dinner table.

But (apart from the first time she spotted me across a crowded room) she knows beauty when she sees it. Cruden Bay hit her like a delicious wet fish and I hadn't been so excited since a sherbet flying saucer first burst onto my tongue. (If you haven't experienced one of these exotic, chemically enhanced childhood sweets, you haven't lived.)

The majority of golf courses initially present you with barely a hint of what lies in store, the 1st tee often snaking off into the woods and giving you no clue as to what lies beyond. From Cruden Bay's upper windows, this course brushes its pleasures onto the eyes with the power of a misty Turner landscape. With the North Sea as its backdrop, almost the whole of this superb links is laid out before you, the holes set out in a sandy, moonscape arena that will have you quivering with delight. The ground rises and falls with the indiscriminate contours that only nature can supply, whilst the treeless landscape is peppered with snaking lines of gorse and needle-pointed bent-grasses.

Directly below the window lies the old but now disused professional's shop. It's a fine wooden structure and a thing of such old-fashioned delight that it should be left in position. Any ambitious 'new-broom' who demands its removal should be shown the door immediately. At its side, the immaculate 1st tee points north towards the small harbour of Port Erroll, its steep-banked sides running down to an adjacent practice putting green. As we glanced down, a small family group were engaged in friendly competition, their two wire-haired terriers scampering across the tightly mown turf to collect the succession of missed putts and return them to their owners. And though this may appear to be an inconsequential vignette, it seemed to enhance the feel of the whole golf course and confirm the welcoming atmosphere of the entire venue.

'Lunch?' asked my reluctant caddy.

'Walk,' I replied with uncharacteristic assertiveness. 'I can't wait to get out there.'

The otherwise excellent course planner, full of yardage information, pro's tips and clubbing advice, sadly does not include an overall course map. But as I was to discover, the layout, for such a traditional links course, is highly unusual. Presented as a figure of eight, the holes are constructed in two distinct loops, the first nine circling the delightful nine-hole St Olaf's course, originally built, in less politically correct days, for use by lady members. In contrast, the second nine takes you on a switchback of high ground, starting on the raised headland plateau of Hawklaw and then dropping dramatically down towards the shore from the 10th tee.

The opening nine holes will undoubtedly prove to be a test of all your golfing skills whilst the back nine will quickly reveal your emotional fragility. The views from this section of the course will fill you with indecision, unsure whether to select your five iron, or forget the golf and reach for a camera. It is startling in every respect, the wide sweep of Cruden Bay's golden beach squeezing the links into a narrow strip of land, criss-crossed by running burns whose waters search for the freedom of the open sea. For a man with my notoriously brittle concentration and sensitive poetic nature, it's a setting that is not conducive to competent golf.

The start, however, is a different animal and until I had completed the first loop of my exploratory walk, I was becoming nervous.

'What do you think?' asked my caddy, as we clambered up onto the 4th tee.

'Superb,' I answered. 'Just superb. I'm just a bit worried that it doesn't quite fit my criteria.'

'Criteria?'

'You know. The sea coming into play. Views over the ocean.'

'Doesn't that count?' she asked, pointing to a small rivulet of a river.

And in a way she was right. This long par three, described by some as one of Scotland's greatest short holes, borders the soft sands of Cruden Bay and gives you the first taste of the salty air. To the left, a quaint, wooden, pedestrian bridge spans the river to the pretty terraced cottages of Port Erroll fishing harbour, nestling below the high cliff face of the crumbling Slains Castle. Yet, as soon as you leave the 4th green, the course cuts back once more, away from the shore and heads back to the intersection of the two loops. It was as though Cruden Bay was goading me with a brief glimpse of the sea before it began its grand finale.

The compensation is, however, worth every moment of frustration. All the holes on this front nine are exquisite, protected from criticism by their layout, variety and presentation.

Not once can you relax into the comfort of predictability. At one moment you are firing onto raised greens; at another you must bump and run your approach to a bunker-surrounded basin, or chip carefully over a threatening burn. Such are the options of shot that, if the rules of golf allowed it, I would be demanding that my caddy must struggle onto the 1st tee with twenty-five clubs in the bag.

The feeling that the course is about to reveal another side of its character begins at the 6th or, as it's known, the *Bluidy Burn*. This is not a reference to golfers who find themselves knee deep in water and cursing it with the words *You Bloody Burn!* but to the historical events that give Cruden Bay its name. Folklore has it, that in AD 1012, the fearsome Scots finally gave the horned-helmeted, hairy Danes a jolly good hiding. The battle resulted in the burn that now crosses the 6th fairway running with Viking blood for over seven hours. Some ancient bard then gave it the name of Croch-Dane Burn, which, I'm informed, roughly translates to 'Slaughter of the Danes'. There are various other explanations but, as they're not half as much fun, these have deliberately been omitted.

Whatever the correct interpretation, it's from the wonderful 6th hole that Cruden Bay begins to really introduce what my local garden centre would describe as its 'water features'. But unlike a garden designer's imagination, which rarely goes beyond *Yeah, stick a pond there, pop in a fountain and throw in a couple of expensive Japanese coy,* the featured water at Cruden Bay is only provided by the great architect Himself. For a great deal of the back nine, if you're not hitting over water, you're looking at it. Stand on the 10th tee and you'll find yourself entering a corner of paradise – or at least how I'd like it to be, once I'm finally queuing outside the Pearly Gates with a golf bag over my shoulder. The holes are blissful, changing suddenly from high mountainous tees looking down onto wide sweeping fairways, only to be followed by subtle par threes and deceptively tricky short par fours.

My walk down the 13th, 14th and 15th had me scribbling the words 'Blind Alley' in my tattered notebook. Though they have some strong competition, I felt this triad of holes exemplified the true nature of the golf course. The shot to the green on each of these holes is either virtually or totally blind. Whilst this might not appeal to the golfing purists, you have to trust my judgement that they will provide as much fun as you could hope to find on a golf course of any nature. The sublime, snaking burn on the par-five 13th is truly one of nature's great gifts; the hidden basin green of the par-four 14th a thing of beauty, whilst the par-three 15th is unadulterated madness – but all the better for its demented construction. Quite literally, the 15th is 'round the bend' and the only blind, dogleg par three in the British Isles. (See Shiskine 'report', page 269.) To hit the green in one requires the imagination of an idiot, as the marker post is set high on a heathery bank, and seemingly 30 degrees away from what you would guess is the necessary line. And whilst you manoeuvre your ball through this fun-filled labyrinth, the North Sea laps onto the nearby shore with not one care for the pains or pleasures you may encounter.

I've heard it said that the closing holes of Cruden Bay can be a bit of a disappointment. As I'm not prone to sitting on fences, I reject this entirely. By the time you prepare to take your drive at the 17th (and if you haven't played like a demented rabbit) you will be exhausted by a constant stream of euphoria. The last two holes, though by no means easy, allow you, like all true athletes, to engage in a necessary period of warming down and indulge yourself in psychologically beneficial, quiet reflection.

As always, I was impatient to take it on.

The following morning, and with a few hours before my tee-off time, I went in search of a large black bat. This isn't the sort of thing that normally forms part of my pre-match preparation. But the previous evening I had heard some dark stories being whispered in the hotel bar.

With my caddy still in tow, we wandered back to the harbour of Port Erroll and then up to the fields above the rugged cliffs. Striding ahead quickly, we came in sight of the menacing, silhouetted ruins of the Earl of Erroll's abandoned ancestral home. The mist-shrouded towers of Slains Castle lay before us, our faces pinched by a strange chilling wind that seemed to cut through the warm morning air. And as the castle walls began to cast their shadows across our steps, we rested on a ring of jagged rocks, to peer up the high sheer battlements that seemed to emerge from the raging sea below.

'Did they have golfing umbrellas in 1895?' I asked my shivering caddy.

'Maybe,' she replied.

'Black ones?'

'Suppose so.'

'That's it then,' I answered triumphantly.

'That's what?'

'The explanation.' I smiled.

'How many whiskies did you have last night?' she asked.

Having spent a great deal of my professional life attempting to prove or disprove questionable hypotheses, I was in familiar territory. At the end of the nineteenth century, a certain Bram Stoker had sat on these very same rocks and been consumed by the satanic aura surrounding the now derelict Castle of Slains. It is said that he saw a man emerge from one of the high windows and begin to crawl, head first, down the castle wall. His slithering descent took him towards the abyss of the dark sea, his black cloak spread out like leathery wings. And in that moment, the tale of a blood-sucking Count Dracula was given its devilish birth.

But history is there to be challenged and all my deductive instincts suggested a far simpler explanation. It was quite obvious that a visiting castle guest had returned to their room with a damp umbrella, flapped it violently out of his window and then hung it on the creeping ivy. The emergence of Count Dracula into the literary canon is clearly thanks to no more than a wet Aberdeenshire morning and the evolution of the golfing umbrella.

Having offered my reluctant caddy a fascinating and highly detailed account of my questionable theories, I suggested it was time to go.

'*Please*,' she pleaded, a small tear of desperation trickling down her cheek.

'Practice ground?'

'Anywhere, anywhere,' she sobbed.

To be honest, I rarely practise before a game and, like many amateurs, remain convinced that you can drive into your club car park at 7.58 a.m. and smack a drive down the middle at 8.05. It's nonsense, of course, but most of us continue to justify such lunacy with the words *It's only a game* or *I don't want to use up all my good shots in the nets*. On this occasion, I decided to become a reformed character.

Cruden Bay is highly unusual in possessing an immaculate, ten-bay driving range, which runs along the edge of the 17th and 18th fairways. Even my caddy (a woman who has never hit a golf ball in her life) was tempted to 'have a go'. But once she began to hit my seven iron straight past the 125-yard marker, I was forced to demand its immediate return. As you'll understand, any golfer preparing for a match doesn't want to step onto the course with a huge inferiority complex.

Waiting by the 1st tee, my opponent emerged from the clubhouse and descended the steep path. He looked vaguely familiar.

'Isn't that . . . ?' I choked.

'Yes,' replied my caddy. 'Can't believe it.'

The previous day's studious course inspection had been interrupted by the more juvenile activities of taking snapshots of the views from the 10th tee; of pulling the warning bell (just for the hell of it) at the 15th; of using the toilet facilities at the 16th and dipping our toes into the healing waters of St Olaf's Well at the 17th. (Come on – we've all done it.) Unknown to us, a lone man on a golfing buggy had witnessed these sometimes childish, but always respectful, activities.

'Can I help you?' he had asked politely.

'Just doing some research . . .' I had stuttered.

We had been accosted by the course ranger, the very same man who now approached me on the 1st tee.

Shaking his hand with the vigour of a long-lost friend, we exchanged handicaps. To my horror, I was obliged to give him five shots on a course I had never played and one that my opponent probably knew better than his own reflection. What made matters even worse was that by the time we stepped onto the glorious 4th, I knew I had a battle on my hands.

I reached this conclusion, not because of his admirable golfing skills, but because he was turning out to be one of the most affable opponents I had ever played. Not only was I being treated to his good company but also to his encyclopedic knowledge of Cruden Bay's history. The desire to dispatch this man with a flurry of pars and birdies was weakening with every shot I played and with every story I was told. With my caddy puffing behind me, my shoulders unburdened by golf clubs, I was just having too much fun to summon my competitive spirits.

Yet, despite this weak-backboned approach, I arrived at the 14th with the game in my grasp, confirming my superiority with a searing drive into the heart of the fairway. A well-struck six iron put the final nail into the coffin.

'Shot,' said the ranger graciously. 'Bit right. But good swing.'

My self-satisfied smile (hopefully like my future obituary) proved to be somewhat premature. The description of my ball being *a bit right* was clearly a sobriquet for *you've just hit it onto the beach*, and after five more attempts to hack my way out of the sand dunes, I was forced to concede the hole. With the eccentric 15th halved in fours and the tricky 16th halved in threes, I was still one up with two to play. And just to make sure I won the day, I engaged in a spot of acceptable cheating.

Walking down the 17th after a rather scrubby drive into the left rough, I spotted my guarantor of victory. The moment my opponent's back was turned, I slipped quietly to one side and dipped my five iron into the restorative waters of St Olaf's Well, an eleventh-century spring that had supposedly saved Cruden Bay from pest and plague. I assumed that if it was that powerful, it could surely see me home to my ultimate triumph.

St Olaf must have been on holiday. My intended shot to the green veered wildly to the right (I daren't use the word shank), my ball burying deep into nearby gorse. We were all-square with only the last to play and, in an act of petulance, I wiped the remaining droplets of saintly water from my disobedient iron.

'I can see the words in your book already,' laughed my

companion. *'The hardened, tenacious Scot refused to be beaten.'*

'I can't use a cliché like that.' I smiled.

'I suppose not,' he chuckled.

The hardened, tenacious Scot refused to be beaten, and as my putt rimmed the final hole, I was forced to offer my hand in defeat. The caddy remained head bowed and silent as she added a record of my submission to her long list of notes headed, *Reasons for an Immediate Divorce.*

After an enjoyable meal in the clubhouse, where the chef tried to kill us with buttery kindness, we made our way back into the village to have a last look at what it had to offer. Discovering a small, dilapidated post office near to our hotel, we stopped briefly to sample its delights. It appeared to sell everything from penny sweets to a thousand items of dusty bric-a-brac, for which we could establish no human use. But as we left, a small notice in the window drew my attention.

Seeking The Promised Land? it stated. *A Pilgrimage to Israel, Palestine & Jordan with the Revd Roger Nickson.*

'The man's an idiot,' I muttered to my now retired caddy. 'If I was seeking the Promised Land, I'd start here. Fancy the beach?'

Crossing the white wooden bridge to the edge of the 4th green, we circled round to the sweeping sands of Cruden Bay to re-engage with our childhood. Slipping off our shoes, we skipped through the shallow breaking waves as the evening light began to dip its own feet into the darkening horizon.

'He's wrong, you know,' I gasped, as the freezing waters drenched my rolled-up trousers.

'Who is?'

'The professional. He reckons a great golf course should have six hard holes, six easy ones and six full of fun. He thinks that's what Cruden Bay has to offer.'

'Well he's right, isn't he?'

'Not quite. The holes are all hard if you play them badly. All easy if you play them well. But however you play, they're *all* full of fun. I don't care what your handicap is. I can't think of anyone who wouldn't get a thrill out of it.'

Five days later, I walked into the bar of my own golf club. Breaking my golden rule of always wearing understated clothing, I purposely sported my newly acquired Cruden Bay golf shirt, with the distinctive heraldic logo emblazoned on my chest. An old friend leaned forward to examine the detail.

'Cruden Bay?' he asked. 'Where's that?'

'Scotland. Peterhead,' I replied. 'Not far from Aberdeen.'

'What's it like?' he added.

'How long have you got?' I smiled contentedly. 'How long have you got?'

Recommended Alternatives

Royal Aberdeen: Is this the finest links course in Britain? It would be hard to find its equal and if I receive any criticisms for omissions, this may well come top of the list. My wallet, mind and body were hung, drawn and quartered by this golf course, but unlike William Wallace, I revelled in the experience. It's said that it's tougher than Carnoustie, more terrifying than Dornoch, as demanding as Royal County Down. This could be an underestimation. It's a links barbarian with the silky charms of an Italian gigolo and easily good enough to host an Open Championship. Save up your pennies or dimes and give yourself a day to remember.

Murcar: Superb views, elevated tees, punishing heathery rough, slick greens and if you're heading for Royal

Aberdeen, a fine place to test your shredded nerves. Slightly overshadowed by Cruden Bay and Royal Aberdeen but not far off their equal.

Newburgh-on-Ythan: Despite a name that sounds as if it should be in Wales, this Aberdeenshire course has all the Scottish elements of good links golf. Tough and uncompromising, you'll need to think your way round. Well worth a visit and reasonably priced.

17

SOUTHERNESS
Dumfries, Scotland
September

As someone who prefers to live in the present rather than the past, I have only a passing interest in genealogy. What sense is there in exhuming the murky lives of ancestors, if they prove to consume you with genetic guilt for their criminal actions or reveal themselves to have been so successful that you live your own life with a sense of abject inferiority? If, however, I am ever tempted into such an ill-advised pursuit of my biological antecedents, I would be very surprised if the name Captain Richard Pearson doesn't emerge from the genetic gloom. As my visit to Southerness was to prove, we shared so much in common that he must form part of my heritage.

The journey to this most southerly Scottish links course immediately had me thinking of Birmingham (England, not Alabama). Both these locations tend to be places you pass through on your way to somewhere else, a transit camp in which you might pause in your travels, in order to refuel and press on to greater things. For golfers, the Dumfriesshire coastline is normally regarded as an alternative route to the bright lights of Turnberry, Prestwick and Troon. Mention the word Southerness to the average player and you are likely to be greeted with the words: 'Southerness? Heard of it. No idea where it is. Any good?'

The simple answer is that it is well worth the detour from the more familiar golfing tour. Turn south from the town of Dumfries and head for the Solway Firth, a strip of Scottish coastline that glares across the water to its English counterpart. By the time you slip through the delightful hamlet of New Abbey, you will enter a forgotten world that would have had the writer Edgar Rice Burroughs reaching for his ancient typewriter. And it's here, within this desolate landscape, that a certain Major Richard Oswald spotted the potential and a way to satisfy his golfing passion.

'Look at it,' he might have said. 'Featureless, barren, windswept, salt-poisoned ground. Perfect. I'm tired of the military life. I think I'll build a golf course.'

It proved to be a good decision, which is more than can be said for one of Major Oswald's eighteenth-century ancestors who seemed convinced that the coastline of Southerness was clearly brimming with profitable unmined coal. On no more evidence than picking up a black stone on the nearby beach, he proceeded to build a village for the workers and a lighthouse for the anticipated fleets of ships that would inevitably turn the area into a hub of the Industrial Revolution.

I've always enjoyed the company of optimists but remain wary of their hare-brained schemes. Those who invested in Oswald's adventure must have had their fingers burned on the one single fire that was successfully mined out of the coal-barren land. The legacy was, however, worth their delusional endeavour. The peat surface of the land only proves that they were men ahead of their time and had only misjudged their coal-mining ambitions by about five million years.

I had originally planned to inspect the course on the following day, but due to an appalling weather forecast, decided to step out in the evening sunlight. A single golfer stood waiting on the 1st tee.

'Mind if I join you?' I asked. 'Just walking the course. Won't get in the way.'

'Of course not. Knee problems?'

'What?'

He had obviously seen me approaching and for some strange reason was more fascinated by my limping gait than my bright red notebook. After a 350-mile road trip, it tends to take me at least half an hour to persuade both my legs to go in the same direction.

'Cartilage?' he enquired once more.

'Medial ligaments,' I answered limply. 'Old rugby wound.'

'Ah! Medial ligaments!'

Oddly, he seemed as excited as a man who holes in one during a monthly medal, his reaction only becoming explainable when he introduced himself as a junior doctor from the local hospital.

'Going into orthopedics?' I asked.

'How did you guess?' he replied.

Fortunately, as well as possessing a fine medical knowledge, he was also well versed in the club's history and the challenges that would soon confront my erratic swing. In the short time we spent together, I learned that Southerness first opened in 1947 (it looks at least 150 years old), and that its configuration had seen some drastic changes.

'Used to be nine out and nine back, but since they built the new clubhouse in 1975, it's now more of a figure of eight.'

'Right.'

'The fourteenth is now the first and has been since they moved out of the Paul Jones Hotel.'

'They moved out of a hotel?'

'Yes. Well, two rooms in the hotel.'

'And who's Paul Jones?'

'You know. After John Paul Jones. The pirate. Not been to his museum?'

'Just arrived.'

'Worth a look. Interesting man.'

And with these final words he took his stance and nailed a 280-yard drive, hitting the centre of the fairway with a beautifully controlled draw. He was clearly a man in the wrong profession.

'What's your handicap?' I asked.

'Don't have one.' He laughed. 'Far too busy.'

Depressed by his admission, I strolled after him towards the waiting links.

From the 1st tee, it is impossible to know what lies ahead. As Major Oswald noticed, it's a bleak flat landscape, which gives you little impression of the terrain. Instead, you are presented with a panorama of gorse and heathers that seem to stretch, uninterrupted, towards the distant horizon. It seems that every hole is separately wrapped in startling shades of bright yellow petals and sombre purple flowers. Any sense that man has made an attempt to interfere with nature is completely absent, the wide generous fairways winding their way through the links land as if ingrained by a far greater power than a course architect. Within a few holes, I became convinced that Southerness is golf in the raw and should become part of a links golfer's pilgrimage. I made my thoughts known to my companion.

'You know what J. H. Arthur said?' asked my medical companion.

'Who?'

'One of the great links specialists. Did a lot of work at Southerness. He reckoned all greenkeepers should ask a farmer for advice and then do exactly the opposite. You know. Let nature do the work and get rid of all the fertilizers. Jim Arthur was convinced that the odd passing seagull and a few sheep droppings could do a much better job. It became the Southerness philosophy. Still is.'

I had only been on the course for half an hour but already felt that I had gained a true understanding of my surroundings. Ironically, Southerness appears determined to be remembered for being the land that time forgot, to have created the uncreated and serve a dish of purely organic fare. And, as I was to learn later, they had rejected the modern notion that a green is not a green unless it is green. Gobbledegook? Not really. The wisdom of sticking to fundamentals is apparent on every immaculate fairway and green (whatever its colour), and has resulted in a links course so true in nature that it is possibly only matched by the Old Course at St Andrews or the barren landscape of Royal North Devon.

The Southerness doctrine is confirmed early by the course's setting. The opening fairway is flanked by pastureland on either side. Sheep and cattle graze happily, oblivious to the constant thwack of clubs and shouts of disapproval as the ball cuts away from its intended line and submerges into the waiting gorse. To the distant left, the Solway Firth shimmers its welcome whilst to the right, the rugged slopes of Criffel Fell loom over the course. But, by the time you turn towards the sea at the 6th, there is only one dominant sensation. Unlike any other course I had played, you become startlingly aware of the remoteness of this bleak yet beautiful links. The horizon views, at every quarter, leave you with an overpowering sense of isolation, your eyes constantly drawn back to the sand-banked coastline and, some thirty miles across the water, the hazy forms of giant Cumbrian mountains.

Leaving my medical informer at the turn, I strode out quickly to beat the fading light, stopping briefly for a 'comfort break' at an irresistible contraption placed at the side of the 8th green. Shrewdly emblazoned with the sign *W.C. in Fields*, I doubted it would be welcoming to children or dogs and stepped inside, grateful that I had at least cast off my youth and left my dog in kennels.

In many ways, it's from this point that Southerness begins to build towards its organic dénouement. The front nine is smattered with tough par fours but now the test really begins, as the holes increase in length and in difficulty. The 10th should give you a clue of what is to come. This delightful (though short) par three is guarded by no less than seven bunkers and will require all your golfing skills. And once negotiated, burns now start to cut across the fairways, the par fours become longer and the wind begins to whip off the Solway Firth. The five holes along the shoreline are possibly the best part of the course, though the 12th hole is probably worth the trip, just on its own.

As a right-hand dogleg, the drive needs to be hit accurately to allow access to a green that is guarded by a high mound and pond to the left, bunkers to the right and the out-of-bounds beach only a few yards behind a sloping green. From here, the wide expanse of treacherous sands stretch out into the bay, accentuating the sense of isolation.

The lighthouse folly (adopted as the club's emblem) now becomes your guiding light, as it provides the perfect line for your tee shots along the coastal stretch, before turning back to the clubhouse at the 14th.

It's at this hole that I encountered two semi-naked golfers.

Or so it seemed. Drawing closer, I was confronted by two young men wearing no more than baggy tracksuit bottoms and heavily scuffed trainers. Carrying one bag between them, they were trying to hit their separate balls with clubs that must have been made when Ben Hogan was a child prodigy.

'Are you members?' I asked with suitable gravitas.

'Er . . .'

'Don't you realize,' I continued, 'that this is one of the finest links courses in Scotland?'

'Er . . .'

'Let me give you a word of advice.'

'Er . . .'

'Strengthen the grip of your left hand and don't get too close to the ball.'

'Er . . . Thanks, mister.'

Leaving them to hack up clumps of fairway, I completed my tour of inspection. The quality of greens and fairways continues all the way back to the clubhouse, the course, unusually, finishing with a long par three and a challenging par five.

I mentioned my encounter with the two partially clad youths as soon as I entered the bar.

'They'll be off the caravan park,' answered one member.

'You don't chase them off?' I asked.

'Well . . .'

If it had been Wentworth, Sunningdale or Muirfield I suspect such an occurrence would have sparked an Extraordinary General Meeting. At Southerness it was met with no more than a resigned shrug of the shoulders, as if, in line with their philosophy, intruders from the nearby caravan park are just part of nature. It's a response that could only endear me to this remote outpost of Scottish golf.

Returning to my hotel and in desperate need of sleep, I ate hurriedly and retired to my bed. Sadly, I appeared to have booked into a room with paper-thin walls and found myself trapped between one set of guests with the sexual appetite of two mating baboons and a couple who were clearly on a snoring tour of Britain. By 6 a.m. I abandoned all hope of sleep and began to replan my day. For once the weather forecasters had earned their wages. Rain was beating on my window whilst a gale-force wind was doing its best to remove my flimsy curtains from their equally flimsy rails. Despite my exhaustion, the name of John Paul Jones quickly came to mind and within half an hour I was on the road to the museum.

The curator greeted me like a man who had been in solitary confinement for ten years.

'First visitor in two days,' he announced, as I stepped into the cottage. 'Like a cup of tea?'

We sat together for almost half an hour, the lonely guardian savouring my every question with the appetite of a starving prisoner. By the time I left, I had become an authority on a man who had briefly terrorized the coastline of Southerness. Often revered as the father of the American Navy, John Paul (as he was first known) earned a dubious living in the slave trade and then embarked on a career as a gentleman pirate. By way of disguise, he later changed his name to John Paul Jones, which seems about as clever as Tiger Woods booking into a restaurant under the name of Tiger Woodchip and hoping for a quiet night. But whatever your thoughts on this Southerness pirate, one of his great claims to fame was the capture of HMS *Serapis* in 1779. This pride of the British fleet was commanded by (my genetic forebear?) Captain Richard Pearson and had so much firepower that it must have seemed like an encounter between a bow and arrow and a nuclear bomb. Maybe Captain Pearson was just having a bad day, but he was finally forced into submission and had to watch as John Paul Jones sailed off in his gun-bristling ship – without one word of thanks.

The weather was improving as I stepped out of the museum and there were definite signs of hope in the breaking clouds. The members of Southerness were enjoying their monthly medal and I was forced to look elsewhere to prepare for my match on the following day. I asked my final question of the grateful curator.

'Anywhere nearby?'

'Try Colvend,' he answered. 'It's only a few minutes from here.'

As usual, I had arrived at Southerness with an untrustworthy golf swing but also certain that I had found the solution. My confidence of easy repair was based on no more than a flick through a golf magazine at a motorway petrol station. Like many mid-handicap golfers, if there's a straw to be clutched, I'll grab it with both hands. The latest cure-all remedy involved the simple technique of turning my right hip away on the backswing in order to achieve a fully coiled turn. And, sadly, it worked. The scenic parkland course of Colvend succumbed to my new-found talents and by the time I putted out on the final green, I had managed to negotiate the eighteen holes with only five dropped shots. The fact that this had been achieved by imitating a rheumatic contortionist didn't really seem to matter. I was ready for Southerness, ready to take on anything it might throw at me. Like Captain Richard Pearson, I would stand on that 1st tee with firepower far superior to that of any of my opponents.

As I drove away from the course, I whispered those words that no average golfer should dare to speak: 'Got it! The secret of golf is mine!'

With my discovery of the fool's swing, I had become the self-delusional golfing alchemist.

Following yet another disturbed night of adjacent sexual romps and apnoeic snoring, I arrived in the hotel dining room exhausted but still brimming with quiet confidence. During my frequent visits to the breakfast bar, I wasted no opportunity to flex my right hip, forcing some muscle memory into a previously underused joint. As I was to discover, this is not an advisable practice when carrying a bowl of milk-swimming cornflakes in a shallow bowl and, much to my fellow guests' amusement, I left the room with its floor etched in a trail of dairy products.

The weather had relented and a warm westerly breeze was all that remained of the previous day's storm. I went in search of my prey.

'Apologies,' said the secretary. 'Long John couldn't make it.'

'Silver?' I answered, maintaining my new obsession with alchemy and pirates.

'What?' answered the bemused official.

'Sorry. Silly joke. Who will I be playing with?'

'Just the two of us I'm afraid. Hope that's OK?'

'Fine.'

We exchanged handicaps.

'So I get six shots?' I asked.

'Sounds about right. See you on the tee.'

My opponent's single-figure handicap indicated that he was a far more talented golfer than myself. Yet I approached the 1st tee with a sense of pity for the man I was about to sink with my superior firepower. It seemed unkind to admit that during the last twenty-four hours I had discovered the secret of golf and I hovered over my opening drive ready to unveil the transformation of my former base metal swing. With a contorted right hip, the ball bit into the air and landed safely in the middle of the fairway.

Ten holes later I shook my opponent's hand warmly and congratulated him on his nine-and-eight victory. It was the heaviest loss I had ever suffered in singles match play and only ever surpassed by Captain Richard Pearson's humbling loss of his ship to John Paul Jones.

'I thought there was only one famous pirate in Southerness,' I mumbled.

'Caught me on a good day,' answered my companion amiably.

'You should wear an eyepatch,' I suggested.

'And a wooden leg?' he laughed.

'At least it would have given me some hope.'

The game over, we relaxed into the final eight holes and it was during this time that I learned of the club's peculiar history and the maintenance of its nature-based ideology. And, despite my depressing defeat, it turned out to be one of the most enjoyable mornings I have spent on a golf course, the secretary proving himself to be not only a talented golfer but a man of great humour and knowledge. Not least amongst his many stories was the 'fact' that some of the popularity of Southerness (particularly the somewhat suspicious caravan park), had grown out of the former Troubles of Northern Ireland. During these dark days, those seeking a brief escape from the riots and bombings could make it to the Dumfries coastline on one tank of petrol and a homemade packed lunch.

Driving sombrely back to my hotel, I stopped briefly at the small village of Rockcliffe, only a few miles down the coast. A vacant bench overlooking the sunlit bay allowed me time to reflect on my shattered confidence. Notebook in hand, I began to jot down my deepest, soul-searching thoughts:

The next time you feel you have discovered the secret of the golf swing, book in for a two-hour session with a psychiatrist. Listen carefully and double the suggested dosage of any prescribed medicine.

Understand the psychology of your thought processes when you are having a 'bad day at the office'.

1 down after 1 – no problem

2 down after 2 – slight problem

3 down after 3 – tricky problem

4 down after 4 – real problem

5 down after 5 – big problem – tighten grip

6 down after 6 – major problem – grip even tighter, hit ball harder

7 down after 7 – crisis – tighten all muscles (including face), begin to indulge in prayer

8 down after 8 – catastrophe – relax muscles to a state of rigor mortis, use mobile phone to join bizarre religious sect

Halve the 9th to remain 8 down with 9 to play – allow all fantasies of a late comeback to invade your thoughts, there is obviously still hope of ultimate victory

Take a 7 on the 10th and lose the match 9 & 8 – cancel membership of bizarre religious sect and search for high cliffs. Alternatively, rummage through golf bag for a sharp knife, write a brief note of apology to your family and ask your opponent if he wouldn't mind posting it with a first-class stamp. Apply sharp knife to jugular vein.

Whenever you are having a nightmare on the golf course and are feeling completely suicidal, I think these words of advice will prove invaluable.

Moments after completing these scribblings, I looked out over the beach, only to see a man running into the cold waters of the Solway Firth.

'Golfer?' I shouted. 'I can help you!'

In response to my call, he turned briefly but then disappeared into the dark swell of the open sea. Whether he ever made it back to shore, I shall never know as, submerged in my own ocean of despair, I resumed my journey and prepared for my next golfing adventure to the Western Isles.

The following morning, as I headed north into the Galloway hills, I was able to indulge in a far more objective assessment of Southerness Golf Club. There's an old adage that *Good golf courses are those you've played well.* There's no doubt that there is always a danger of letting your own performance colour your judgement. And it's true that Southerness shared my hotel experience of having caravan neighbours who disturb its sleepy setting; that the clubhouse suffers from the shameful architects who plied their unimaginative trade in the 1970s; and that it has the disadvantage of being off the golfers' beaten track. But the course is sublime, uniquely natural in design and condition, and well worth breaking your journey towards the better known links of the Ayrshire coast. Southerness will test the ability of any golfer, whatever their level of skill, and shouldn't be missed. Unlike the defeated Captain Richard Pearson, I will have a second chance to engage the enemy in battle. It's a challenge that can't come soon enough.

Recommended Alternatives

Silloth-on-Solway: If you're heading north, and really on the grand tour, this is a must. Set on the northernmost coastline of the Lake District it is the equal of Southerness.

An exposed and natural arena with fine views. This is top-class links golf at a reasonable price and you will not regret the extra mileage. If it wasn't so remote it could easily take its place amongst Britain's Top Twenty. Superb.

Portpatrick: Yes, it's a long way from anywhere but if you fancy wending your way up to Turnberry along the coastal roads of Dumfries and Galloway, it's worth a stop. Clifftop holes, traditional in nature and it won't break the bank.

Stranraer: Parkland (but we all need a break). Wonderful setting looking over Loch Ryan and sea views to the west. James Braid had a hand in its design – a recommendation in itself.

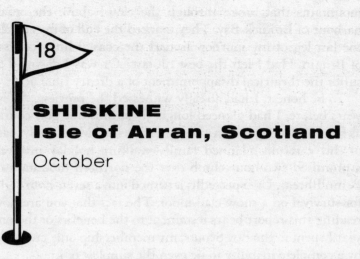

SHISKINE
Isle of Arran, Scotland
October

To make any sense of Shiskine's story, I must begin with the end of my visit. At 7 a.m. on a cold blustery October morning, I stood on a glistening damp slipway, searching the murky horizon for the approaching ferry and contemplating my return to the mainland. It was a quiet, reflective moment when the dull knot of depression weighed heavily on my stomach. The thought of being thrown back into the hurly-burly of buzzing motorways and frenetic careworn cities was erasing my former high spirits. And, to make matters worse, I had become plagued by a single word, confused by the relevance of a name, which, at the time, had received no more than a cursory glance. As the ship finally left the shores of Arran and the waves began to play with their familiar toy, the word was cast to and fro in my mind. That word was *Drumadoon*. Yet, within half an hour and in calmer waters, I finally had my answer.

Three days before, I had arrived on the Isle of Arran under

clearing skies and fully aware of the symbolic nature of the mountains that broke through the cloud above the small harbour of Brodick Bay. They marked the end of my travels, the last leg of my journey around the coastal links courses of Britain. Had I left the best till last? Or was I destined to suffer the theatrical disappointment of a dreary final act?

To be honest, I had already witnessed the preview. A few years before, I had glanced longingly at Shiskine golf course as I trekked along Arran's western shoreline. Memorably, part of this carefully planned family walking holiday involved a promised two-hour climb over the northern mountain of Beinn Bhreac. Unexpectedly, it turned into a seven-hour fight for survival on a snow-clad moor. The fact that you are now reading this report bears testament to the benefits of the one year I spent in the Boy Scouts, my membership only curtailed by a complete inability to tie even the simplest of knots.

But, during this previous and life-threatening first visit, I had seen enough of Shiskine to know that it would make my final list of links courses. The venue's title does, however, disguise its geographic position. If you stop at the village of Shiskine you won't find a golf course in sight and you must continue towards the tiny coastal hamlet of Blackwaterfoot.

I doubt you will ever experience a more grandiose approach to any golf course in the world. The road from Brodick harbour immediately casts you west into the wilds of Arran, the narrow lane winding its way precariously along a deep valley floor with the heights of Glen Easbuig and Ard Bheinn looming on either side. If, by some freak of fortune, I was ever invited to play at the Augusta National (I've more chance of winning the British Amateur Championship), I doubt it would raise as much anticipation as that thirty-minute journey to the coastal waters that lie between the western beaches of Arran and the distant hills of the Mull of Kintyre.

Such was my excitement that I forsook my usual strategy of walking the course first and, instead, grabbed my clubs and stepped onto a virtually empty course. Having driven up from Dumfries and the heavy drubbing I had suffered at Southerness, my swing was in need of therapy. I had drifted into a state with which all golfers will be familiar. Following a reasonably successful summer, my body now felt as if it had been constructed from a collection of second-hand prosthetic limbs that refused to respond to any of my mental demands. All attempts to turn my shoulders or hips were rejected with such a stiff response that any self-respecting Shiskine doctor would happily have declared me dead on arrival.

Employing the deceit of a desperate golfer, I introduced myself to the golfing gods as a distant relative of Lazarus and prayed for salvation. Such was my wretchedness that, as I stood alone on that 1st tee, I would happily have made a pact with the devil and worried about the consequences later.

It's worth mentioning at this point that your opening drive at Shiskine will never be easy. Despite the sea providing a threatening out-of-bounds along the whole length of the fairway, this is only a minor problem. The major difficulty is that the window of the starter's small pavilion is no more than 15 feet from the tee and looks directly over your right shoulder. As I would discover over the next three days, it is guaranteed that at least one pair of eyes will be judging your swing, to see if it equates, in any way, with your declared handicap.

My drive sailed down the middle, the ball cutting through the air with a surgeon's nerveless precision.

'Thank you,' I murmured, glancing towards the heavens.

There was a small nod of approval as I glanced back to the starter's window and then turned quickly away to throw down the gauntlet to Shiskine.

I will resist the temptation to bore you with the tedious

details of my round but as I left the final green, I felt that rather than having smacked Shiskine's face with a leather golf glove, I had delivered my challenge with an iron fist to the jaw. After marking a final three on the card, I quickly totted up my gross score. It amounted to no more than forty-seven shots.

'Scoundrel!' I can hear you shout. 'The man should be horsewhipped. He's a downright liar and a blackguard! I won't read another word of this fantasy.'

Thank you. I'm glad you persevered. The reason for my sudden transmutation from itinerant hacker to majestic ball striker is that I finished on the 12th green. And the reason I completed my round on this 12th hole is that there was nowhere else to go. Shiskine, unique amongst its deserved membership of the world's top one hundred golf courses, is a twelve-hole links, which contains seven par threes, four par fours and one par five. The next time you hear some pompous twit regaling his audience with a boastful story of shooting a gross sixty-two, I suggest you respond with the words: *Shiskine, I presume?*

Minutes after storing my clubs in the boot of my car, I returned to the 1st tee and began my delayed course inspection. By this time the wind had raised itself in fury at my low score and the heavy falling rain had given up any hope of maintaining its normal vertical descent. Within the five minutes it took me to reach the 1st green I felt like a man who had inadvertently left his windows open in the local car wash. Shiskine members must forgive any errors I may make in the following description, as my notebook was quickly transformed into a Rorschach inkblot. This simple psychological test supposedly allows therapists to reveal the dark corners of their patients' unconscious by asking for their immediate responses to abstract pictures. (Two weeks after returning from the Isle of Arran my descriptive and dampened jottings of the 2nd hole appeared to represent two well-known politicians in a suspicious act of physical union – though I could have been wrong in this interpretation and have been advised to ring the Rorschach helpline.)

But, however vague my notes or my recollections, I can affirm that Shiskine gradually unfolds into madness, rises into mountainous challenges, descends into hell and finally releases you into a glimpse of paradise, which (unless you're already dead) I guarantee you have yet to experience. And don't be fooled into thinking that a small course (less than 3000 yards in length) leads to small, backwater or Blackwater thinking. By the time you have completed the admirable 2nd hole (bisected by two stunning, free-flowing burns), you will have already realized that you have made one of the best discoveries of your golfing life.

Without exception, the sand-based fairways are tightly cut, the greens run true and the seascape views are unparalleled. From almost every point, the dark waters of Kilbrannan Sound provide a welcome distraction from the frustrations of golfing toil, whilst the granite tongue of the distant Mull of Kintyre seems to ebb and flow in the ever-changing light. An overpoetic description? Perhaps it is. But only by intention. Like good poetry, Shiskine is concise by nature, frugal in detail but powerful in delivery. Every hole is carefully sculpted, every line constructed to make the reader reassess the light and shade of their golfing world.

The line at the par-three 'Crow's Nest' is provided by a black-and-white post and a small pink flag that flutters high on a rocky outcrop, at the north-west corner of the course. The postage-stamp green is completely out of sight and can be hit with only the purest iron shot. This is Shiskine's feature hole, and, in all truth, it is complete madness. But it is delicious madness, which symbolizes the very nature of the golf course. Was golf ever really meant to be a game of earnest faces or brow-beating introspection? Perhaps we have entered a global televisual age, where amateur golfers have begun to mimic their zealous professional heroes and forgotten that the game is there to be enjoyed. If you ever visit Shiskine, let the course wash over you and you'll soon remember why you bought your very first set of second-hand clubs.

The lofty green of the Crow's Nest is followed by two more par threes, which follow the line of the most northerly shoreline, each hole nestling below the dramatic cliffs of the Drumadoon promontory. It was at this point that two walkers briefly stopped me. Their snarling dog obviously saw my rain-soaked body as an opportunity for a nice spot of lunch.

'King's Cave?' asked the husband, as he fought to control his ferocious pet.

'Round the point,' I shouted as I edged further away. 'Tide's in. You'll have to scramble over the rocks. But I think—'

'Thanks.'

If I had been allowed to finish my sentence, I would have informed them that a high tide and a howling gale had probably turned their intended stroll into a highly dangerous activity. As I never saw them again, I can only presume they spent the night in the cave and that their dog ate them both for breakfast.

This brief interlude is only included because, after first discovering the cave's existence some years before, I have always thought of it as Shiskine's 13th hole. Reportedly, this cold, dank residence provided a temporary home for Robert the Bruce who, at the time, was trying to escape from the evil clutches of Edward I. As the local fourteenth-century news-agent refused to deliver papers, the future King of Scotland was forced to spend his time watching a spider persevere with the building of its web. It is said that this creature's resolute philosophy to 'try, try and try again' inspired King Robert to battle on to greater glory. It is a doctrine I have always admired, but have failed to adopt for many years.

The par-four 'Shore Hole' 6th is a real beauty with a deep bowl green, whilst the 'Himalayas' 7th returns you to mountainous madness and (if you've played the 15th at Cruden Bay) a strong whiff of déjà vu. My guess is that both courses would claim that the respective dogleg par threes are unique, yet they are almost identical in construction, both requiring a 'blind wallop' over a gorse-filled hill and then hoping for the best. However, the factor that distinguishes Shiskine's 'Himalayas' from Cruden Bay's 'Blin' Dunt' is the remarkable signalling system invented by a certain A. E. Leslie in the 1920s. Known as Uncle Alec, this clearly formidable man obviously owned a model railway and a mind geared to engineering simplicity. In order to warn people on the 7th tee that players might still be on the green, Uncle Alec introduced Shiskine Golf Club to his two wooden signals, a sturdy tube and an extremely long piece of string.

As you leave the tee, you are required to raise the signal. This in turn lowers the wooden arm of the other signal some 100 yards away, at the side of the unsighted green. Once you have finished putting, you then raise the signal's arm, which, in turn, lowers the signal that can be seen from the tee. I hope that's quite clear and even if you're completely confused, I can assure you that Mr A. E. Leslie's invention is pure Heath Robinson.

The 8th surprisingly turns back to the north as though it is making room for the 'Drumadoon' 9th, the only par five on the course and, despite being tucked away from the shoreline, one of my favourite holes on the course. Given a calm summer's day, you might just reach the green in two but with the slightest breeze you will be faced with two well-hit woods, followed by a glorious pitch over a deep burn and up to a high plateau green. With the surrounding 'whins' and rough, it is a truly links hole which will demand all your imagination.

The final three holes (all par threes) are no less appealing: the 'Paradise' 10th less demanding but breathtaking from the tee; the 11th requiring a blind shot into a deep hollow green; whilst the 12th and final hole ends straight outside the finest 19th hole in Britain.

To give Shiskine its true title, it should really be referred to as The Shiskine Golf and Tennis Club. Adjacent to the clubhouse are not only two fine all-weather tennis courts, but also an equally splendid bowling green. The building itself is even more unusual. Rather than presenting members with giant television sets, gaming machines and velveteen bars (the club does not possess a liquor licence), they are treated to a magnificent tearoom with the best fruit cake and scones I have tasted since bakeries decided to turn themselves into industrial chemical plants. If Shiskine really wanted to promote this wonderful facility they should perhaps call it the 'The Shiskine Golf and Tennis Club and Bowls Club and Tearoom with the Finest Lunches and Afternoon Teas in Britain'. Admittedly, this would incur increased costs in purchasing extremely wide letter-headed office paper, but I think it is worthy of consideration. With raspberry jam and clotted cream still circling my lips, I headed back to my hotel and an unexpected turn of events.

Once in my room, I faced the familiar dilemma of the wet golfer staying in a hotel where the heating doesn't come on for another month. By the time I had bathed and donned a new set of dry kit, every available rail and cupboard door became festooned with dripping clothes, the skirting boards a resting place for sodden shoes, the walls a series of props for wet-grip clubs, the floor a woollen weaved surface for my giant golfing umbrella. Carefully placing a *Do Not Disturb* notice on the door handle (a suspicious act at 7 p.m.), I descended the stairs ready to raise an appetite for yet another solitary supper.

It was the fag end of the season and I made up only the eighth guest in a cavernous dining room. Even worse, we had been distributed as two singles and a table of six and, though I am well travelled, it is virtually impossible for a lone diner to consume food in such a setting, without a constant expression of uneasy apology. On this occasion, the two single tables faced one another at each end of the room, as though forming a lonely parenthesis around the table of six.

Within minutes of receiving the first course, my eyes caught the gaze of the other single diner. If this were a novel, they would have been the eyes of a mysterious brunette tempting me with her sultry glances. I'm sorry to disappoint you. What actually faced me was a tall, lean, bespectacled man who had his own form of attraction. Due to my past and present professions, I can spot a fellow 'social voyeur' from a hundred paces.

Admittedly, his notebook was a bit of a giveaway, as was the frenetic scribbling that punctuated his every mouthful. And it wasn't my own presence that provided his material as, apart from casting me the occasional knowing glance, his gaze was firmly fixed on our other companions.

It soon became apparent that the three husband-and-wife partnerships were on the annual golfing holiday from hell. The conversation, shackled by polite convention, was peppered with barely disguised patronizing barbs. The women tolerated one another. The men fought for supremacy. The women tittered dutifully at their husbands' tired stories through gritted, veneered teeth, their eyes smouldering with resentful boredom. The only reason I ordered a pudding was to prolong the pitiable entertainment. It was worth delaying my exit, as the social vignette that followed proved to be the key to my assessment of The Shiskine Golf and Tennis Club.

Extraordinarily, as the table's conversation began to fill with a series of cringing silences, one of the more vocal wives began to bridge the unnerving gaps by repeatedly humming a barely recognizable tune. Eventually, the most timid of the wives, clearly dying a thousand deaths, tried to save the day.

'*Oklahoma?*' she suggested.

'No idea,' said the hummer tartly.

'*South Pacific?*' offered her embarrassed husband.

'I think you'll find,' interrupted another husband with all the pomposity he could muster, 'that it's from *West Side Story.*'

There was a ruffling of paper at the far end of the room as the other single diner scribbled even more frantically, and I fought hard to prevent my half-consumed, crisp crème brûlée from exploding across the restaurant floor. To avoid any possible embarrassment, I quickly folded my napkin and headed for the bar. Within seconds, I was joined by the lofty frame of Mr Notebook.

'Journalist?' he asked.

'Sort of,' I answered. 'You?'

'Travel magazine,' he replied. 'What was going on in there?'

'The golfers?'

'Yes.'

'There's nothing more entertaining than the British middle classes,' I smiled, 'especially when you stick them round a dining table.'

We had only exchanged a few words yet it was apparent that I was in the company of a gravel-voiced American writer, more familiar with United States meritocracy than the peculiar divisions and protocols of British social behaviour. As 'scribblers' do in Scotland, we began to exchange notes whilst sampling the local whisky. By the third glass we had an intimate knowledge of each other's families, our children, our political leanings and what was drying out in our respective rooms.

'So,' I ventured, 'you're a golfer?'

'I've played every course on Arran,' he smiled, 'except Shiskine.'

'Saving the best till last?' I asked.

'Maybe.'

'Believe me,' I responded, 'you are.'

As we moved on to the earthy Bowmore whisky of the Western Isles, the die was cast. We would meet in combat on Shiskine's 1st tee the following morning, ready to engage in our own international golfing contest. The final round of my trip around the British coastline was to be marked by a private Ryder Cup in which, it was agreed, the ultimate winner would be presented with a symbolic buttered scone in the wondrous Shiskine Tearoom. We were playing for high stakes and no quarter would be given.

Knowing that I would soon be representing my country, I slept fitfully that night but, surprisingly, woke refreshed and ready for the fray. Determined to retain my energy and concentration, I refused all offers of coffee from the breakfast waitress. Instead, I consumed nothing more than weak tea and a gigantic bowl of porridge. I was ready.

Though my opponent's handicap was slightly better than my own, we agreed to play off level. I only engaged in this act of unusual generosity as I had planned to start with a major advantage. As Mr Notebook unloaded his clubs, I slipped quickly into the starter's hut, informed the delightful lady official of our contest and suggested that she might like to see us take our opening drives.

Winning the toss of a coin, and before the starter had a chance to get to the nearby window, I hit my own drive first. As my opponent stepped forward, I glanced back to the hut, delighted to see a face pressed hard against the window. The effect was dramatic. Mr Notebook's drive spun wildly to the right and gave him little chance of reaching the green. As we moved to the 2nd tee, the hole had been secured.

Yet, despite my legal subterfuge, the game was nip and tuck and with three holes to play, I was one down and staring defeat in the face. I beseeched all the Norse gods I had encountered over the last twelve months, invoked the spirit of Old Tom Morris and even promised to pay homage at the cave of Robert the Bruce. But, apart from all these whimpering pleas, I found myself motivated by only one thing: the thought of being unable to raise that buttered scone above my victorious head was simply impossible to contemplate.

We shook hands warmly on the 12th green. My journey was almost over and had ended with one of the tightest matches I had played during the whole of my travels. We sat quietly in the tearoom taking in our last glimpse of Drumadoon Bay and the shaded hills of Kintyre.

'I've played golf all over the world,' said Mr Notebook as he drank in the view.

'And there's nowhere better than this?' I suggested.

'Nowhere,' he answered without a moment's hesitation. 'Nowhere.'

The waiter slid a heavily laden tray onto our table. My opponent reached forward.

'Your buttered scone,' he said simply. 'Well played. Great game.'

✳   ✳   ✳

And so it was, that at seven o'clock on the following morning, I found myself waiting on a rain-soaked slipway, ready to take the ferry back to the mainland and still trying to sum up my reaction to Shiskine. For some reason the word Drumadoon was playing on my lips, teasing me with its cryptic meaning. The harder I tried to break its code the less fathomable it became. As the ship discarded its moorings, I began to pace the deck, wandering back and forth in search of inspiration.

As usual, the mind began to play its tricks, distracting me with thoughts of my 'Ryder Cup' victory, the pleasures of Shiskine's links and my debt to Robert the Bruce. A young woman passed by and as she climbed the steps to the upper deck, I could hear her humming an indistinct tune. And in that moment, I finally had my answer.

I was taken back to the horrors of the hotel dining room and the bitter, humming wife. Closing my eyes, I could recall every note of her tone-deaf delivery. It wasn't *Oklahoma*. It wasn't *South Pacific*. And it certainly wasn't *West Side Story*. Suddenly I knew what it was and why the word Drumadoon had seemed so familiar. The song I had heard was not from Drumadoon, but *Brigadoon*, an American musical first performed in 1947. The fairy-tale plot involves a fictitious, spellbound Scottish village, which disappears into the mists whenever one of its inhabitants dares to leave. Why this information had lodged itself in my memory I shall never know, but I now had that melody in my grasp and was shocked by the irony of its title. The ferocious woman golfer had been humming Alan Jay Lerner's most famous song.

As the Ayrshire coast came into view and the Isle of Arran slipped into the mist, I was certain that I had the solution to my problem. The next time someone asks me whether I enjoyed playing Shiskine, I know how I'll respond.

'Shiskine?' I will say. 'Shiskine? It's unique. And from the way that I feel, I would swear that I'm falling. Yes, I could swear that I'm falling. It's almost like being in love.'

Recommended Alternatives

Machrihanish: I spent months trying to decide between Shiskine and Machrihanish. Shiskine only got the vote because of its pure eccentricity and my love of buttered scones. Machrihanish is a true jewel and definitely worth taking a golfing pilgrimage to the Kintyre Peninsula. (The short ferry crossing from Lochranza is a delight.) The opening hole may well be the finest in world golf but the rest of this magnificent links course gives unending windswept pleasure. Steeped in tradition and simply superb.

Lochranza: Slightly quirky course with double greens but in a beautiful setting. Something of a holiday course but enjoyable to play. If you get cold during your round (as I did), slip into the whisky distillery across the road and beg for a free sample.

Machrie: If you really want to push the boat out (and you'll have to), this stunning links is across the sea, on the Isle of Islay. Don't let the modern hotel complex put you off as the course has retained all its Western Isles charm, challenge and the purity of traditional links golf. This is golfing heaven.

If you don't have time to travel, there's another Machrie on the Isle of Arran. It's only nine holes but is great fun to play and sits close to the finest tearoom in Britain. Like the course, it's pure madness but delicious in every respect.

APPENDIX

Ranking 'On the Edge' Golf Courses

Amongst those friends and golfing partners who monitored my journey around the British coastline, I am constantly challenged with one ubiquitous question.

'Which was your favourite course?'

As my many visits to Scotland confirmed, they might as well have asked me to discriminate between eighteen different single malt whiskies. There simply isn't an answer. Each will have its own flavour, will excite the palate in contrasting ways, will leave a footprint of emotional response, will conjure memories of friendship and context. Golf courses are no different. Each one will have its own unique qualities, delivering varying greens, fairways and scenic ocean views. What they all share, however, is the ability to deliver a sense of untainted pleasure and, like whisky, the occasional, painful headache. Perhaps the only way they can be usefully differentiated is in their delivery of blissful idiosyncrasy, their palpable mark of pure class and their ability to offer a true golfing challenge. In most cases, such manufactured distinctions should be regarded as fully interchangeable.

Pleasure, Pain and Blissful Idiosyncrasy

Ardglass, Brora, Cruden Bay, Nefyn, North Berwick, Seahouses, Shiskine.

Pleasure, Pain and a True Golfing Challenge

Castletown, Dunbar, Pennard, Royal Dornoch, Southerness, Trevose.

Pleasure, Pain and Pure Class

Kingsbarns, Nairn, Royal West Norfolk (Brancaster), St Enodoc, Turnberry, Western Gailes.

'The 19th Hole'
SEAHOUSES
Northumberland, England
April

Do you ever tire of responding to the sanctimonious demands made on your palate? Do you really enjoy your daily five portions of fruit and vegetables or having your stomach bloated by three litres of filtered water? Aren't there just a few moments in life when you would like to smother everything you consume in artery-clogging salt or white refined sugar? Tell me this isn't true, and I'll know that I've been joined by a consummate or consuming liar. The '19th hole' of any golf course is (quite rightly) a place of temptation and hedonistic practices, the tables heaving under the weight of sausages, fried eggs and glistening, golden chips. If it makes it any easier, let me admit my own failings.

I eat well. Invariably, I eat sensibly. But just occasionally, a cholesterol demon invades my rationality and I willingly abandon my judicious lifestyle. And this is never more evident than when I am travelling alone, beating my way along the highways, my eyes peeled for imminent motorway carnage and, more importantly, the tempting glow of a 'greasy spoon' café.

It's sad to report that these culinary treats have become an endangered species and, to such a degree, that they may need explanation. At one time they littered the roads, though far less literally than the litter-inducing modern burger restaurants. Greasy spoon cafés, if you can find one, deliver cheap, wholesome, fried food on piled-high plates with white, heavily buttered bread and pint mugs of tea. To be completely authentic, your meal will be served by an equally wholesome 'maître tea', whose rounded form suggests she has been reared on slabs of beef dripping.

I approached Seahouses in a state of post greasy spoon pleasure, my stomach rumbling its contentment. I had come down from Dunbar like a new Oxbridge graduate with a second-class degree, wary of what the future held in store. I was fully aware that Seahouses Golf Course was not on the tourist 'circuit' and that it was never mentioned in the same breath as the Michelin-starred North Berwick, St Andrews or Kingsbarns. It felt like a gamble I might live to regret.

One piece of advice is worthy of mention. If you decide to visit Seahouses, always approach from the north. If travelling from the south, ignore all the signs, carry on another eight miles or so, and loop back on any road that directs you to Bamburgh. Believe me, it's worth the extra petrol money. Forget the castles at Windsor, Leeds or Edinburgh, the sight that greets you as you enter the picture-postcard village of Bamburgh must be one of the most spectacular in Britain. The thirteenth-century castle stretches high along the skyline, its buttressed walls dominating the panoramic horizon. It'll take your breath away faster than a smoke-filled Arbroath kipper factory. Its origins, I'm told, go back more than a thousand years, though it fell into disrepair after my Danish ancestors decided to turn it into rubble in AD 993. Oddly, as I drove by, I had a sudden desire to jump out of the car and repeat the process. I suppose you can rid yourself of most things – apart from your genes.

Seahouses offers something a little different. On first view, it is little more than a small seaside resort. It probably had some appeal in days of caravan holidays and innocent pleasures, but is now unable to compete with the twenty-first-century obsession with cheap flights and topless Mediterranean beaches. The small harbour has a certain charm, the seafront an old-fashioned appeal, but the centre feels rather cheap and tacky, the proliferation of amusement arcades and fish and chip shops hardly raising the spirits or exciting the gastric juices. I could only hope that the golf course offered a little more.

Pull into the golf club car park, about half a mile outside the town, and I guarantee you will feel there is no end to your growing disappointment. I made an attempt to announce my arrival to the secretary. He was out. I tried to buy a course guide from the professional's shop. No pro's shop. No course guide. I looked for the clubhouse next to a long shack by the final green, only to find that the single-storey building *was* the clubhouse. I was tempted to leave a note, explaining my aborted visit with the excuse that I had just received the terrible news that my tropical fish had drowned or that the neighbour's cat had attacked my guard dog. But, unconvinced by my own convincing excuses, I stepped inside to consider my next move.

As I was to find out later, the 'new' clubhouse at Seahouses is, in fact, an old, wooden cricket pavilion, with long narrow windows looking out towards the waiting course. A small covered veranda stretches along the front of the building though, disappointingly, there was no sign of a scoreboard or scented wives making egg and cress sandwiches for the tea interval. Stepping gingerly through the tight-porched entrance, I found myself transported back to the bankrupt days of post-war Britain. Even the air seemed infused with the melancholic odours of the austere 1950s. Boards creaked and bounced under my feet whilst the shaded windows seemed to dull the sharp sunlight of a perfect day.

In need of caffeine, I ordered a pot of coffee from the small kitchen. An old Wall's ice-cream cabinet purred by the open door, bags of frozen chips clearly visible through its opaque, hinged cover. Taking a seat, I began to absorb my surroundings. The room was laid out simply, the frenzied patterned carpet peppered with Formica tables and plastic chairs, a waist-high partition dividing the bar area from the trestle-tabled dining room. It felt as if I had drawn the shortest straw in the group blind dates of my youth. Yet again, I felt the urge to run away, unwilling to spend any more time with the ugly duckling of my golfing tour.

Perhaps it was a childhood of being imbued with moral responsibility that held me back. Whatever it was, I delayed my exit, slumped into one of the plastic seats and shook my head in despair.

'Ere's ya coffy, pet,' came a voice at my side.

The words were delivered by the waitress, a woman old enough to qualify as my great-grandmother. Yet something happened in that moment, as if this aged sprite had waved her wand and drained me of all my growing cynicism. Though her hands shook with enough tremors to create a tsunami in a bowl of custard, she was an absolute delight, her musical Geordie accent almost bringing a tear to my disparaging eyes.

I had once lived in the north-east of England and, unforgivably, I had forgotten the key to understanding the pleasures of Northumberland. Without doubt, it is the forgotten county, probably offering visitors greater delights than any other part of Britain. Yet it amounts to far more than its stunning beaches, rugged coastline and castle-strewn countryside or simply existing as the gateway to Scotland. Though I risk being accused of overgeneralized romanticism, it is the warmth of its inhabitants that leaves the strongest imprint on my memory. Quite naturally (though I could be wrong), I put this accommodating nature down to the historic forced interbreeding with the Viking gene pool.

Even if this isn't the case, whatever occurred in those few moments made me look out over the course with a completely new perspective. The fairways seemed more lush, the greens fast and true, the pavilion clubhouse strangely attractive. The tattered newspaper's picture of Alan Shearer (pronounced 'Shee-RA'), a now retired football legend (or Hindu god?), smiled at me from the unkempt noticeboard by the entrance. Ripping up my scribbled, vitriolic notes, I quickly finished my now wave-free coffee and headed for my first inspection of the course.

As would become clearer the next day, Seahouses Golf Course is a strange affair, visibly divided into three main sections. Until 1976 it remained a short nine-hole course of little distinction, but was transformed with the help of local businessman and benefactor, George Logan. This wasn't an easy revolution. The extra land needed for this transformation proved to be underwater at high tide. And even after reclamation, it still needs mechanical pumping to save its members from the necessity of wearing wetsuits and flippers. It could so easily have turned into yet another unsatisfactory coastal course, which attempts to mix links and parkland design (the worst of both worlds). Cleverly, and despite crossing main roads and lime quarry lakes to access each of the three sections, the links feel is maintained throughout the eighteen holes.

Measuring only 5,542 yards with a par of 67, it would be easy to think that the course would make few demands on even the least talented of golfers. After a quick inspection, it soon became clear that this would be a false assumption. Without doubt, the strength of Seahouses lies in the six par threes and the vicious wind that often blows directly off the cold, unforgiving North Sea. In addition, fourteen of the eighteen holes are protected by out-of-bounds roads, walls and beaches, whilst lateral water hazards of burns and lakes lie in wait to receive the slightest 'twitchy' shot.

If any conclusion was to be drawn from my initial tour, it was that Seahouses is perhaps a bit of a 'peaks and troughs' golf course, in which flat uninteresting holes are punctuated with high drama. In many ways, the layout allows the links to grow to a crescendo, particularly from the 10th to the 16th holes. It's during this section that the course rises onto the high cliffs above the sea. From this area you will be presented with extraordinary views towards the low-lying Farne Islands and the three nearby castles of Bamburgh, Dunstanburgh and the distant Holy Island. I quickly realized that the following morning would require total concentration and complete trust in my paltry swing.

Satisfied that I now had the measure of the course, I headed back into town, parked the car and wandered down to the harbour. It's said that life is paved with good intentions. Well, I had no intentions worth the sea salt. There was a vague notion that I would have a quick snoop round, return to my hotel for a long soak, slip out for a couple of beers and plan my playing strategy for the morning.

I think it was the strains of 'Rule Britannia' that did it. I'm not sure the eighteenth-century composer Thomas Arne intended the piece to be played on a harmonica, but that's what greeted me as I wandered down to the quayside. As a man with republican leanings, I usually have no truck with such nationalistic propaganda. But on this occasion, I wavered. The music was coming from the lips of a fast food van owner who proved to sell the best cup of tea I'd had since leaving home.

'Going out?' he asked cheerily, wiping the dampened harmonica on his trouser leg.

'Out?' I queried.

'There's one leaving in two minutes.' He smiled. 'You've just got time.'

'For what?' I asked.

I'm not sure if he was on commission, but ten minutes later, I found myself in the middle of the North Sea with ten bird twitchers and a child who was growing paler by the second. I've never really had the bird bug. Like lots of people, I feed them nuts through the winter and love being woken by a trilling blackbird on a dewy May morning. Apart from that, the only thing I've ever pointed a pair of binoculars at is a professional golfer with a 10-foot 'must make' putt.

It may have been the distant sight of Holy Island that began my conversion, or perhaps the prancing dolphins, which seemed to guide us towards the waiting Farne Islands. Whatever the case, I found myself having a serious communication with nature and enjoying every moment of the conversation.

Though I'm not known for my numeric skills, I would guess that during this two-hour trip, I must have seen over 20,000 birds nesting on the small uninhabited islands, everything (as the skipper informed me) from terns, gulls and cormorants to guillemots and red-beaked puffins, flashing across the water. And quietly watching all this squawking mayhem from their private rocky outcrops, colonies of giant lumbering grey seals viewed our ship with dismissive glances, their fish-bloated bodies content to lie back in the evening sun. For one nightmarish moment, I decided to trade in my golf clubs for the best pair of binoculars I could lay my hands on.

It was, of course, a moment of madness. Once we docked, and my feet had regained the comforting sanity of terra firma, rationality returned and I headed for the nearest fish and chip shop. As already noted, Seahouses bristles with these gastronomic delights. Worthy of mention amongst this array of restaurants is one high-street café, which, for some unknown reason, chooses to sells logs and splintered sticks, neatly stacked beside the simmering fish fryer. Wary of battered wood appearing on my plate, I skipped across the road to be served by two Slovak waitresses who had mastered the words 'large cod and chips' but were having terrible trouble with the request for 'a round of brown bread and butter please'. A nightcap of two pints of Guinness in the quaint and highly recommended Olde Ship Hotel soon followed. And though my body was still convinced that it was rising and falling on a North Sea swell, I slept well, ready to take on what Seahouses had to offer.

Despite sleeping alone, I woke up with a stranger in my bed. Whoever looked back at me in the bathroom mirror wasn't the man I had seen the night before. The face was puffier than a puffin, the eyes as narrow as a hunting cormorant. But above all, the skin looked as if it had spent the night on a rotating kebab spit. Who'd expect to get sunburnt on a Northumberland coast in the middle of an English spring?

Though my golfing companions didn't recoil as I glowed my introductions, there was a definite hesitancy in their welcome. Normally, I am red faced after my opening shot, but at Seahouses, and long before we had even stepped onto the tee, I wore a permanent look of blushing humiliation. Fortunately a reasonably hit six iron saw me safely onto the green and I settled quickly into the game. My partner, though playing off a mid handicap and in his seventies, proved to have a swing silkier than a pair of wartime seamed stockings. As I would discover, he was a former county player who had once played with a scratch handicap. It showed.

As I had expected, the opening eight holes proved undramatic but testing, every tee shot demanding total concentration. Unusually the 4th and 7th holes bisect one another, the shared landing areas well guarded by two small lakes. Protecting their adjacent greens from the 5th tee is a line of trees, which, I was informed, were personally planted by Jackie Milburn, a Newcastle footballer whose heroic star still shines brighter than that of Alan Shearer. And it told me a great deal about Seahouses' roots. Its history is not about the course itself but is clearly founded on the hard, post-war working-class culture, which is still embedded in this former mining area. Unlike many other golf clubs, it leaves you with the sensation that rather than being an isolated membership, Seahouses regards itself as no more than a contributor to the Northumbrian community. Pretentiousness and pomposity would feel as out of place at Seahouses as a budgerigar trying to build a nest on Farne Island rock.

We approached the 10th two down with six birdies already recorded on our cards. It had become an enjoyable, relaxed, social game, with a soft coating and a hard nut interior. 'Logan's Loch' (the gateway to the wonderful back nine) lay before us. In many ways it is uncharacteristic of links golf, yet, because of the nearby sea and the wind whistling through the gully of rocks, this short par-three hole maintains its authentic nature. The landing area is narrow and treacherous. Under-club and you will see your ball roll back into the water. Over-club and you will be faced with an almost impossible chip back onto a sloping green. There is simply no room for error and it is a hole that must have ruined many promising cards. Though only 165 yards, the walk to the green (unless you like swimming with a bag on your back) is probably twice that length. My paltry four felt like a good result, but my partner's skilful three saw us safely home and within one hole of the opposition.

The remaining holes take you along the shoreline, the ocean views crumbling your concentration with the castled panorama and island silhouettes. And there's a constant sense of anticipation as you make your way around the headland and approach the 15th. 'The Cove' is no more than 124 yards from the back tee. The minor difficulty is that you have to carry your ball over crashing waves onto a postage-stamp green that is even less forgiving than Logan's Loch. It was my turn to play the hero.

Possibly the sweetest nine iron I have ever hit rolled to a halt no more than 6 feet from the pin and I strode round the cove with more nonchalance than an overpaid footballer. Unfortunately, one member of the opposition had not read the script, and holed an audacious breaking putt from 15 feet for yet another birdie. Luckily, I settled over my own putt with complete confidence and watched it roll comfortably towards the gaping hole. It hit the target with just the right pace but with enough speed to see it hit the back rim, pirouette 180 degrees and hang tantalizingly on the edge. I cursed, I blew, I stamped my foot, but nothing would convince that ball to take the final plunge. Two down and three to play. Golf can be cruel at times.

Looking back, I think the missed putt can be attributed to my desperation to relieve myself of the politically and medically correct two litres of water I had drunk before breakfast. As links courses tend to be of an open nature, I was delighted to see the bird hide situated close to the 15th tee. Stepping briefly away, I sidled round the corner only to be met with a large sign stating *Please do not use this wall as a urinal.*

Given the bare state of the ground, this notice had clearly been ignored by the majority of players. But, as a guest, and in the company of three senior members, I resisted treating my own member to a little fresh air and played my tee shot in a state of commendable restraint. By the time I reached the green, my bladder-enhanced adrenalin obviously resulted in giving that missed putt just an extra ounce of pace. It's on small matters such as this that a game can soon turn.

The 16th brings you back to the edge of 'Logan's Loch', a tricky and favourite hole with a sunken-bowled green that requires the most delicate of second shots to give you any chance of hitting the green. The final two holes return you to the rather mundane area around the pavilion clubhouse but, yet again, they demand both skill and accuracy to keep your card intact.

By now we had shaken hands in defeat and a 25-pence birdie down. Sadly, my tee shot from the 18th splayed horribly to the right and demanded a well-hit three wood to get me to the distant green. As I approached, the secretary came out to meet us, just in time to witness my 30-yard chip, which disappeared into the hole on the first bounce.

'Played like that all the way round?' he shouted.

'Eight birdies,' I answered simply, carefully omitting the fact that I could only lay claim to that final hole.

'Well done, well done,' he enthused.

It seemed a shame to ruin my reputation with a truthful admission and I disappeared quickly to pack my car and prepare for the long journey home.

Thirty miles south of Newcastle, I spotted the object of my desire. Following an articulated lorry off the main road, I pulled into the potholed car park of the transport café and prepared to dine in style. Ten minutes later, the bacon, eggs, sausage and beans dripped over the edges of a chipped white plate, whilst a pint of steaming tea nestled on the plastic table. And at that moment, I knew why I had enjoyed Seahouses so much.

The following night, I was booked into an expensive restaurant to celebrate a friend's birthday. I would be trussed up in a suit and tie and fussed over by over-attentive waiters. I knew the food and the company would be good but I would certainly be starched into discomfort. Sometimes you need an honest greasy spoon café where you can relax and indulge yourself in simple budget pleasures, free of stiff-collared humbug.

If you take this as a criticism of Seahouses golf course, then you misunderstand my intent. It's a place that can only be understood within its unique context and, to employ the terminology of a fast food world, if you go to Seahouses, go large. Play the course but give yourself time to sail with the dolphins and seals; to cruise around the bird-laden Farne Islands; to gasp at the architectural genius of a thirteenth-century world; to saunter along the wide-open beaches and suck salted air into your city lungs. Then you'll understand the appeal of Seahouses. It might be my '19th hole', but you'll want to return.

Recommended Alternatives

Bamburgh Castle: One of the most scenic, heathland courses in Britain, bristling with heathers and gorse. Stunning, beautiful and an absolute delight.

Berwick upon Tweed: A true links with superb views along the North Sea coast. Tricky fairways and fast greens provide a real challenge.

Dunstanburgh Castle: Underrated links course, which (like many similar courses) plays far better than it looks. Tough narrow fairways, sea vistas, castle ruins and good value make this worth a visit.

The 'Golf on the Edge' Fantasy Golf Course

If I could build my own links golf course, this would be it. Admittedly, it's a highly subjective selection and, on only a few occasions, contains the recognized 'feature hole' of the separate, listed courses. As a collection of eighteen holes, it would, however, provide a perfectly balanced challenge. It is guaranteed to give immense pleasure and obligatory pain to anyone, like myself, whose golfing heart is in traditional links courses.

OUT

Hole 1. North Berwick 17th, 'Point Garry'; 425 yds, par 4

The perfect wake-up call on a cold morning. Even if you hit the ideal drive, the second shot is to a blind, high green, completely exposed to the elements but with wonderful coastal views across to Bass Rock.

Hole 2. Castletown 17th, 'Gully'; 399 yds, par 4

Possibly one of the most intimidating but scenic driving holes in British golf. Fail to carry the deep ravine over the sea and it's time to 'reload'. If you get a chance, play off the championship tee. The view from here is truly magnificent.

Hole 3. Royal Dornoch 6th, 'Whinny Brae'; 163 yds, par 3

A beautiful, but daunting, par three. The tee shot is to a heavily sloping green on the side of a hill, naturally guarded by thick gorse, and five deep bunkers. You wouldn't complain about making a four.

Hole 4. Kingsbarns 12th, unnamed; 566 yds, par 5

An outstanding par five, which fulfils the dreams of every links golfer. The horseshoe fairway winds around the rocky shoreline. Unless you're a scratch golfer, it's a full three shots to the cleverly contoured green. It's a hole with no name. They should call it 'Heaven'.

Hole 5. Dunbar 12th, 'The Point'; 457 yds, par 4

A hole that had me scribbling the word 'Superb' the first moment I saw it. A 'simple' dogleg par four running along the edge of the Firth of Forth. The bunker-guarded green sits on a sea-washed promontory. Make the putting surface with your second and you've just hit a 'career shot'.

Hole 6. Trevose 17th, unnamed; 375 yds, par 4

Short in yardage but long in pleasure. The drive needs to carry or land on a narrow strip of fairway whilst the second demands a precise shot over a deep-flowing burn. The small, tight, sloping green has no bunkers. It doesn't need them. The burn and surrounding deep rough provide enough hazards for any links golfer.

Hole 7. Shiskine 9th, 'Drumadoon'; 506 yds, par 5

Perhaps a strange choice for Shiskine, as it's the only par five on the course and well away from the dramatic coastline. But it is beautifully designed and, if you can get a good drive away, you might be tempted into making the green in two. Don't be put off by the fact that you have to carry a deep gully and burn before landing on a high contoured green. It might just be your lucky day.

Hole 8. Cruden Bay 4th, 'Port Erroll'; 183 yds, par 3

With a river to the left, deep rough to the right and a valley between tee and green, this is a glorious brute. If the wind's in the west you might get there with a five iron. If it's in the east, you may well be reaching for your driver. Though it tore me to shreds, it's a divine golfing hole.

Hole 9. Nairn 5th, 'Nets'; 377 yds, par 4

This has to be one of the finest 'short' par fours in links golf. The tee sits on the very edge of the Moray Firth, your drive needs pinpoint accuracy and the raised green is heavily guarded by deep bunkers, heavy rough and gorse. If you're playing into a north-east wind, you may walk off the green with a five. It will feel like a birdie.

IN

Hole 10. Ardglass 11th, 'St Johns'; 488 yds, par 5

'Diabolical', 'terrifying', 'a card wrecker'. These are a few of the descriptions I heard from club members. I played it badly, lost two balls in the sea and yet still think it's a fine hole. If you can hold your drive whilst those around you are losing theirs, you will be a fan and not undone. A stunning coastal nightmare – and all the better for it.

Hole 11. Western Gailes 7th, 'Sea'; 171 yds, par 3

An extraordinary par three that seems to play far longer than its yardage. Played from a high tee, close to the beach, the green nestles in an amphitheatre of humps, hollows, bunkers and gorse-filled banks. Stunning.

Hole 12. Brora 17th, 'Tarbatness'; 438 yds, par 4

A classic James Braid designed par four. The narrow neck of the undulating fairway demands total accuracy, whilst you can only hold the green if your ball is fired into the right-hand side. Even if you play it badly, the sea views are truly stunning.

Hole 13. Pennard 7th, 'Castle'; 351 yds, par 4

A short but fierce par four that demands a long carry across dipping ground from an elevated tee. The eerie ruins of Pennard Castle nestle on the right against a dramatic backdrop of Three Cliff Bay. With a green defended by threatening sand dunes, it presents a real but beautiful challenge.

Hole 14. St Enodoc 10th, unnamed; 457 yds, par 4

A very tough, dogleg par four, with a lateral water hazard to the left, and high-banked ground to the right. What makes it so unique is the eleventh-century church, which glowers down onto the waiting green. The poet John Betjeman is buried in the graveyard and seems to have bequeathed his chuckling charm to this quiet corner of the course.

Hole 15. Nefyn 14th, unnamed; 165 yds, par 3

A gentle par three on the glorious madness of the peninsula. Stand on this tee, with the coastguard tower looming above you and the sea crashing onto the distant rocks, and you'll know exactly why you have such a passion for links golf.

Hole 16. Southerness 12th, unnamed; 421 yds, par 4

A minefield of a dogleg hole that will test all your golfing skills. A heavily bunkered fairway is followed by a green defended by grass banks, bunkers, a pond to the left and, just to make it more interesting, the Solway Firth waiting to swallow your ball, only 10 yards behind the green.

Hole 17. Brancaster (Royal West Norfolk) 8th, unnamed; 494 yds, par 5

The club describes this hole as '100 years of unchanging brilliance'. In many ways this claim sums up 'RWN'. The hole makes simple demands. Two shots over tidal 'lagoons' to island fairways are followed by a 'hands and arms' chip onto an unguarded green. Sound easy? Don't be fooled. It's as tough as old boots and, like my ageing golf shoes, totally absorbing.

Hole 18. Turnberry 16th, 'Wee Burn'; 380 yds, par 4

What a finish this would make to any round of golf. It's spectacular in every respect and a particular favourite. Whilst the drive is not one of the most demanding, the right club selection for your second is crucial. The green sits high to the left, guarded by a cavernous natural burn. As a final links hole, this would test the character, nerve and skill of any golfer. Sensible course management will be rewarded. Timidity or overconfidence could wreck your card. Wonderful.

Yardage

OUT	3451	Par 36
IN	3365	Par 36
Total	6816	Total 72

SCORE CARD

THE *GOLF ON THE EDGE* FANTASY LINKS GOLF COURSE

	Course	Yards	Par			Course	Yards	Par	
1	North Berwick 17th	425	4		10	Ardglass 11th	488	5	
2	Castletown 17th	399	4		11	Western Gailes 7th	171	3	
3	Royal Dornoch 6th	163	3		12	Brora 17th	438	4	
4	Kingsbarns 12th	566	5		13	Pennard 7th	351	4	
5	Dunbar 12th	457	4		14	St. Enodoc 10th	457	4	
6	Trevose 17th	375	4		15	Nefyn 14th	165	3	
7	Shiskine 9th	506	5		16	Southerness 12th	421	4	
8	Cruden Bay 4th	183	3		17	Brancaster 8th	494	5	
9	Nairn 5th	377	4		18	Turnberry 16th	380	4	
	OUT	3451	36			IN	3365	36	
						OUT	3451	36	
						TOTAL	6816	72	

The British shoreline enjoys more traditional coastal golf courses than anywhere in the world. Brutal yet blissful, fearsome yet fulfilling, these seaside links courses present players of every standard with an intoxicating mix of undiluted pain and pure enjoyment.

When Stephen Cartmell set himself the challenge of finding and testing eighteen of the most outstanding links courses in Britain, he decided that they had to meet a number of criteria, the most important of which was that the sea had to be visible from the course. There's nothing like salt in the air, or the sound of crashing waves breaking on the shore, to make a golfer quiver with delight or fear. Committed links players prefer their golf to be tough and unpretentious. Stepping onto the first tee, they are prepared to do more than test their golfing skills. They will be ready to do battle with nature.

Packed with fascinating detail, and often hilarious anecdotes, this is the perfect guide to some of the most beautiful sea-flanked courses in Britain. It also whets the appetite for the sublime pleasures that lie in store for anyone tempted to play golf on the edge.

ISBN 978-0-553818-08-6

£7.99
Can $21.95

9 780553 818086

www.rbooks.co.uk

Illustration by Peter Greenwood